MINDS, FREEDOMS AND RIGHTS

Recent developments in the cognitive sciences, particularly the emergence of neurotechnologies and their potential applications in a variety of contexts, have prompted a debate on what freedoms and rights people have in relation to their brains and minds. Lawyers and philosophers are especially interested in the possibilities offered by the neurosciences in conducting risk assessments and risk management. *Minds, Freedoms and Rights* deepens our understanding of these legal issues by investigating the human rights that relate to the mind and by exploring their implications for possible uses for neurotechnology for criminal rehabilitation or "neurorehabilitation". By harnessing and integrating both legal and ethical perspectives, the authors investigate possible uses of neurorehabilitation that are cutting-edge yet simultaneously protect and respect human rights and freedoms. This title is also available as open access on Cambridge Core.

Dr. Sjors Ligthart is an associate professor of criminal law at Tilburg University, the Netherlands, and the principal investigator of the project Mental Liberty in the Age of Modern Technology: Towards Absolute Protection of the Mind? (VI.Veni.231 R.022). He is a postdoctoral researcher at the Willem Pompe Institute for Criminal Law and Criminology, Utrecht University, the Netherlands, on the research project Law and Ethics of Neurotechnology in Criminal Justice (VI.C.201.067). Ligthart is the author of *Coercive Brain-Reading in Criminal Justice: An Analysis of European Human Rights Law* (Cambridge University Press 2022) and co-editor of *Neurolaw: Advances in Neuroscience, Justice and Security* (Palgrave Macmillan 2021).

Dr. Emma Dore-Horgan is a Government of Ireland postdoctoral research fellow at the Department of Philosophy, University College Cork, previously working on the research project Law and Ethics of Neurotechnology in Criminal Justice (VI.C.201.067). She is an honorary research associate of the Uehiro Oxford Institute for Practical Ethics. She has published in *Ethical Theory and Moral Practice, Criminal Law and Philosophy, Bioethics, AJOB Neuroscience and the Journal of Law and the Biosciences.*

Prof. dr. Gerben Meynen is full professor of ethics, in particular bioethics, Department of Philosophy, VU University Amsterdam, and full professor of forensic psychiatry, Willem Pompe Institute for Criminal Law and Criminology of Utrecht University. He is the author of Legal Insanity. Explorations in Psychiatry, Law, and Ethics (Springer 2016) and he co-edited *Neurolaw: Advances in Neuroscience, Justice and Security* (Palgrave Macmillan 2021). In addition, he is one of the editors of *Brain and Crime*, Volume 197 in the Elsevier series Handbook of Clinical Neurology (2023). In 2021, he received a Vici grant from the Dutch Research Council (NWO) for the project Law and Ethics of Neurotechnology in Criminal Justice (VI.C.201.067). He also works as a psychiatrist.

LAW AND THE COGNITIVE SCIENCES

Law and the Cognitive Sciences publishes book monographs exploring connections between law and the cognitive sciences. The books will be of interest to academics, students, and practitioners, and in particular to the scholars in the fields of legal theory, philosophy of law, psychology of law, the theory of law and artificial intelligence, general theory of private and criminal law, and evidence.

Minds, Freedoms and Rights

ON NEUROREHABILITATION IN CRIMINAL JUSTICE

SJORS LIGTHART
Tilburg University and Utrecht University
EMMA DORE-HORGAN
VU University Amsterdam
GERBEN MEYNEN
Utrecht University and VU University Amsterdam

CAMBRIDGE
UNIVERSITY PRESS

CAMBRIDGE
UNIVERSITY PRESS

Shaftesbury Road, Cambridge CB2 8EA, United Kingdom

One Liberty Plaza, 20th Floor, New York, NY 10006, USA

477 Williamstown Road, Port Melbourne, VIC 3207, Australia

314–321, 3rd Floor, Plot 3, Splendor Forum, Jasola District Centre, New Delhi – 110025, India

103 Penang Road, #05–06/07, Visioncrest Commercial, Singapore 238467

Cambridge University Press is part of Cambridge University Press & Assessment, a department of the University of Cambridge.

We share the University's mission to contribute to society through the pursuit of education, learning and research at the highest international levels of excellence.

www.cambridge.org
Information on this title: www.cambridge.org/9781009486330

DOI: 10.1017/9781009486309

When citing this work, please include a reference to the DOI 10.1017/9781009486309

First published 2026

A catalogue record for this publication is available from the British Library

A Cataloging-in-Publication data record for this book is available from the Library of Congress

ISBN 978-1-009-48633-0 Hardback

Contents

Acknowledgements

We would like to express our gratitude to all those who have inspired us and provided the necessary conditions to explore and develop our thoughts captured in this book. In particular, we wish to thank Vera Tesink, Naomi van de Pol, Melina Mouris, Timo Istace, Tom Douglas, Jesper Ryberg and Antoine Buyse for their valuable comments on earlier versions of different parts of the book. We are also grateful to Marline Wijsman for her editorial assistance. Moreover, we warmly thank the Dutch Research Council (NWO) for their generous funding (VI.C.201.067 and VI.Veni.231 R.022).

Sjors Ligthart
Emma Dore-Horgan
Gerben Meynen

1

Neurorehabilitation in Criminal Justice

Scientific Developments and Normative Concerns

1.1 INTRODUCTION

Until recently, our inner mental lives have enjoyed a considerable degree of natural protection from others' gaze and influence. Third parties are sometimes able to attribute particular mental states to us on the basis of our behaviour, particularly if they know us well. These parties are also often able to influence our mental states by means of rational persuasion or manipulation. But our thoughts, desires and emotions have typically had some defence against others' access and influence by virtue of the fact that these mental phenomena play out in our brains, shielded by a solid skull.

Advances in science and technology are, however, beginning to change things. Today, a range of technologies and techniques are being developed, used and introduced that enable others to access, monitor, and influence mental states in novel ways. Examples include nudging interventions that influence our choices by harnessing our cognitive biases or judgement-making mental shortcuts,[1] AI-based emotion recognition through facial analysis[2] and the use of microtargeting.[3]

Specific attention has been devoted, furthermore, to *neurotechnologies* – that is, technologies that, in one way or another, interact directly with the brain, either to *obtain information* about a person's mental phenomena or to *modify* such phenomena and hence, ultimately, the person's behaviour. Examples are neuroimaging,[4]

[1] Thaler & Sunstein 2009; Douglas 2022. See Tversky & Kahneman 1974 for early discussion of the concept of cognitive biases.

[2] Something that could enable intelligent machines to make inferences about our emotional states: Ballesteros et al. 2024.

[3] Microtargeting is a marketing strategy that involves analysing people's personal data to identify their interests and preferences and steer them towards a specific direction. It has become a feature of contemporary political campaigning; see Witzleb & Paterson 2021.

[4] Where computational techniques are used to visualise brain structure or activity: Sharma & Weintraub 2016.

brain-computer interfaces[5] and brain stimulation.[6] And while not strictly speaking a technology, neuropharmaceuticals similarly work by interacting directly with the brain to modify a person's mental states.

Neurotechnologies are currently used in healthcare contexts, for example, for the diagnosis or treatment of Parkinson's disease.[7] Yet, they could also be employed for a variety of purposes within other societal domains in the future, including the military,[8] education[9] and direct-to-consumer applications such as for meditation.[10] Another area to which neurotechnology could possibly be applied is criminal justice – a domain concerned, at least in part, with the mental states and behaviours of those who offend.[11] Neurotechnology might, for instance, be harnessed to assess whether a person is likely to reoffend based on information about their brain states.[12] It might also be capable of modifying certain crime-relevant mental states and hence may help to reduce the risk of a person reoffending.[13]

The emergence of neurotechnologies and their potential applications in a variety of contexts has prompted a debate on the freedoms and rights people have in relation to their brains and minds, and what these freedoms and rights could mean for the use of neurotechnologies. Some scholars have considered these questions at the level of fundamental morality, asking for instance whether we have a moral right against (non-trivial) mental interference,[14] what the concept of mental integrity implies for the regulation of neurotechnologies,[15] and whether we have a moral right to seek to control our own consciousness free from third-party interference.[16] These questions have also been considered through the lens of the law, in particular human rights law. Scholars have interrogated whether, and to what extent, established human rights protect against unsolicited interference with our brains and minds.[17] They have also considered whether established human rights entail entitlements for rights holders to make use of self-enhancing neurotechnologies.[18]

At the time of writing, these issues regarding human rights vis-à-vis emerging neurotechnology are receiving attention of policy makers and human rights bodies,

5 Where a direct communication pathway is created between the brain's electrical activity and an external device such as a computer or a robotic limb: Shih, Krusienski & Wolpaw 2012.

6 Where magnetic fields or electricity are applied to particular areas of the brain in order to modulate the activity of these brain areas: Reti & Chang 2015.

7 Foltynie 2024.

8 Rickli & Ienca 2021.

9 Privitera & Du 2022.

10 Tarrant 2020.

11 Pardo & Patterson 2015; Vincent, Nadelhoffer & McCay 2020.

12 Nadelhoffer et al. 2012.

13 Birks & Douglas 2018; Ryberg 2020; Knehans et al. 2022.

14 Douglas 2024.

15 Craig 2016; Lavazza 2018; Zohny et al. 2023.

16 Boire 2000; Sententia 2004; Dore-Horgan & Douglas 2025.

17 Bublitz & Merkel 2014; Ienca and Andorno 2017; Bublitz 2022; Ligthart et al. 2023a; Farahany 2023.

18 Bublitz & Merkel 2014; Ienca and Andorno 2017; Ligthart et al. 2023a; Farahany 2023.

including the United Nations Human Rights Council,[19] the Council of Europe,[20] the United Nations Educational, Scientific and Cultural Organization (UNESCO)[21] and the Organisation for Economic Cooperation and Development (OECD).[22]

This book aims to contribute to the shaping of our understanding of freedoms and rights that relate to the mind and to explore their implications for the possible use of neurotechnology in criminal justice. We focus on criminal justice as this context is one where *non-consensual* use of neurotechnology might be considered – which would raise a variety of questions regarding fundamental rights and freedoms. Pressure or even full-blown coercion is already often used within criminal justice contexts to effect changes to an individual's mental states and behaviour, for example, by requiring participation in a treatment programme as part of a criminal sentence or when a person is committed to a forensic mental institution.[23]

Therefore, the question arises: how could neurotechnologies be used responsibly – respecting people's freedoms and rights – in criminal justice, given that (i) neurotechnologies might interfere with people's mental states and resultant behaviours, and (ii) criminal justice contexts allow for a broad range of measures to be imposed on those who offend against their will?[24] Notably, because of the coercive context of criminal justice, even *offering* a certain intervention may still raise concerns about the actual voluntariness of a convicted person's consent – something frequently discussed in both ethical and legal scholarship.[25]

Relatedly, focusing on neurotechnology in criminal justice is also productive because criminal justice is a context where some *limitations* of freedoms and rights are legally permissible, insofar as they serve important objectives such as crime prevention, or insofar as they constitute permissible punishment.[26] For example, coercively taking and examining a person's DNA infringes the right to privacy and bodily integrity but can be permissible when used for the prosecution and prevention of crime. In such cases,

19 UNHRC, Neurotechnology and Human Rights, A/HRC/51/L.3 (29 September 2022).

20 Ienca, Common human rights challenges raised by different applications of neurotechnologies in the biomedical field, Report commissioned by the Committee on Bioethics of the Council of Europe (2021).

21 UNESCO, First draft of a Recommendation on the Ethics of Neurotechnology, SHS/BIO/AHEG-Neuro/2024/29 (27 August 2024).

22 OECD, Recommendation of the Council on Responsible Innovation in Neurotechnology, 11 November 2019.

23 Certain subpopulations of those who offend are, for instance, sometimes required to submit to substance abuse treatment, anger management treatment or treatment for sexual offending in various jurisdictions; see Werb et al. 2016; Forsberg 2021; Wilson, Feder & Olaghere 2021; Levenson et al.2023.

24 Several scholars have interrogated this question, in relation to both neurotechnologies and neuropharmaceuticals. See, for example, Ryberg 2020; Vincent, Nadelhoffer & McCay 2020; Tortora et al. 2020; Meynen et al. 2023; Bublitz 2018; Ligthart 2022; Tesink et al. 2023.

25 Green 1986; Farah 2002; McMillan 2014. Though see Pugh 2018 and Bomann-Larsen 2013 for doubts that the criminal justice context necessarily undermines voluntariness of consent to treatment.

26 Restricting the rights and freedoms of those who offend in some way is also typically thought to be *morally* permissible, though see Golash 2005; Boonin 2008; Caruso 2021 for alternative views. See also the literature that challenges the moral permissibility of incarceration as a form of punishment, for example, Davis 2003.

although infringed, the rights at stake are not violated. Similarly, although imprisonment seriously and constantly infringes the incarcerated person's freedom of movement, detaining convicted persons is broadly accepted as lawful in at least some cases. The context of criminal justice thus requires us not only to look at the scope of freedoms and rights that protect the mind but also to consider their permissible limitations.

Put differently, criminal justice is a domain where the *stakes are high*, not just for society but also for convicted persons. Introducing neurotechnology into this domain would be a high-stake issue for those who offend, given the mental and behavioural effects these technologies might have on them and the coercive context in which the technology would be delivered. Clearly, insofar as it might help to mitigate risk factors for dangerous and offending behaviour, neurotechnology is something that society in general would have a stake in, as this outcome might help to make society safer. Furthermore, convicted persons themselves may also have a stake in having access to safe and effective neurotechnologies, as and when neurotechnological intervention promises to help them live more fulfilling and crime-free lives.[27]

For these reasons, we take criminal justice as the focus in this book. In particular, we focus on the use of neurotechnology as an aid to social rehabilitation, henceforth just "rehabilitation". We use the term "rehabilitation" to refer both to the psychological and social process, whereby those who offend become no longer disposed to engage in crime, and to the provision of interventions that better enable this process. We understand rehabilitative interventions as those interventions that help persons to desist from future offending, to (re)integrate into the community and to lead fulfilling lives going forward, but which do not produce these effects by making crime physically impossible or by merely disincentivising persons from offending.[28] We also continue to use the term "rehabilitation" rather than the alternatives of "resocialisation" or "resettlement" often favoured in the European legal context. We recognise that there have been reservations about using the former term, at least historically, owing to its past association with coercive and oft-inappropriate and abusive "therapeutic" interventions. However, we think the term has divested itself of these negative associations in recent times and is a more apt and broader descriptor than the aforementioned alternatives.[29] Consequently, it is our term of choice here, and when referring to the use of *neurotechnology* or *neuropharmaceuticals* as an aid to rehabilitation,[30] we invoke the term "neurorehabilitation".[31]

[27] Remaining crime-free might be one way of leading a more flourishing life, but neurotechnological intervention might also help enable flourishing in other ways – for example, if the intervention helped the relevant parties better forge and maintain social connections, or if it led to them feeling more at peace with themselves or better enable to satisfy their desires.

[28] See Douglas & Forsberg 2021, p. 105, for a similarly broad understanding of rehabilitation.

[29] It is also the term used in the human rights discourse, such as by the UN Human Rights Committee and the European Court of Human Rights: CCPR General Comment No. 21: Article 10; ECtHR (GC) 26 April 2016, 10511/10 (*Murray/the Netherlands*).

[30] I.e., as a means toward facilitating the psychological process of rehabilitation.

[31] See also Dore-Horgan 2023.

We adopt this focus on neurorehabilitation as against a focus on neuro*punishment*. We do not explore the possibility that neurotechnologies could be utilised as a form of punishment in this book – that is, that they could be imposed as a burden on those who offend and with the aim of communicating societal disapproval of their offence(s)[32] – though we acknowledge that other scholarship has reflected on this possibility.[33]

1.2 SETTING THE STAGE: CRIMINAL JUSTICE, CRIME PREVENTION, AND REHABILITATION

In legal systems all over the world, traditionally, criminal justice is foremost grounded in ideas of retribution and basic desert. From that perspective, punishing those who have offended is a key goal of criminal justice, and punishment is justified (when it is) because the relevant parties have committed a crime and thus *deserve* to be punished. Whereas retributivism, on the one hand, provides a moral justification for punishment, it also produces rules and principles that delimit individual criminal sentencing. For example, those who offend are only legitimate targets for punishment, according to retributivism, when it has been proven that they have indeed committed a criminal offence. The imposed punishment should also, somehow, be proportionate to the severity of the crime committed.[34]

This dominant, backward-looking retributivist justification of punishment is increasingly complemented by a forward-looking approach toward corrections more generally. By this, we mean, that while retribution is often deemed to be the primary goal of *punishment* in contemporary justice systems, these systems are increasingly seeing the *prevention of harm to others* as an important criminal justice goal. This goal may be furthered by punishment, but can also be pursued via non-punitive interventions, and perhaps even after a person has undergone punishment.[35] By non-punitive interventions, we mean interventions that are *not intended as* punishment and which, therefore, have no reprobative element. So,

32 Many theorists accept and understand punishment as burdensome and as having a reprobative aspect; see Feinberg 1970; Duff 2001, pp. xiv–xv; Boonin 2008, pp. 21–23. Though see Lee 2019 for an argument against punishment's expressive function.

33 See, for example, Ryberg 2020, 2018, 2012, for discussion of this possibility. See Birks 2018 for an argument against the use of neuropharmaceuticals and neurotechnologies as punishment.

34 Frase et al. 2020; Ryberg 2021.

35 To be clear, forward-looking considerations are not a new feature in criminal justice. The imposition of punishment is also often thought to be partly justified by forward-looking considerations. Some theories see punishment as justified by its potential power to deter or disincentivise crime, see Bentham 1988 [1780]; Kelly 2018; Ellis 2003. Other theories (now less prominent in contemporary discussion) see punishment's justifying goal as the moral education or reform of those who offend, see Morris 1981; Hampton 1984. Forward-looking considerations have also been a component of modern criminal justice systems, for instance regarding treatment of mentally ill offenders in order to reduce their future dangerousness.

the prevention of harm to others might be achieved by a traditional (reprobative) punishment such as imprisonment that disincentivised a person from reoffending, and/or caused them to reflect on their crimes and rehabilitate themselves. It might also be achieved by non-punitive measures such as rehabilitation or mere incapacitation. By incapacitation, we mean, making it physically impossible for a person to commit crimes while not intending to censure them – for example, by detaining a person beyond (or before or instead of) a term of punishment. This is sometimes termed "preventive detention"[36] and is a contested practice, given that it may involve detaining a person beyond that which is proportionate to their crime's severity, on the basis of their presumed dangerousness and consequent risk to the community.[37]

The increased focus on crime prevention has been described as the "preventive turn" in criminal justice.[38] On the one hand, the focus on prevention is a good thing. Successful prevention is not only advantageous for society but often also for the person who has offended, at least in the case of prevention by means of rehabilitation. Consider how it may be particularly valuable for a person to have their "criminal cycle" broken following their successful rehabilitation, such that they may fully participate in society again. On the other hand, this preventive turn gives rise to new normative challenges. There are normative questions about the justifiability of, and the justifiable limits on, imposing extended or indefinite prison sentences on people – and hence depriving them of their liberty – on the basis of their predicted future conduct.[39] There are also normative questions about the state's use of rehabilitation as a means to crime prevention: for instance, questions about the limits that should be applied to the state's pursuit of rehabilitation.[40]

This book is firmly anchored within the legal and ethical scholarship dedicated to discerning what responsible crime prevention looks like – though, as said, our analysis is on the specific issue of responsible neurorehabilitation in view of human rights, particularly human rights for the mind. Before moving to discuss neurorehabilitation vis-à-vis human rights, however, we must first say more about the role that neurotechnology might play in the service of rehabilitation and crime prevention.

36 It is also sometimes referred to as risk-based sentencing; see Lewis 2022.

37 Clearly, punitive imprisonment also incapacitates. Incapacitation is also likely to be experienced as burdensome, even if the intention is non-punitive. This has led many to claim that "preventive detention" is just punishment by another name, and there may be some truth to this. Nonetheless, a difference exists at the level of the supposed justification and goals of each practice. Punishment burdens and censures, possibly also in the service of some future goals such as crime prevention. Preventive detention has crime prevention as its sole aim.

38 See Carvalho 2017.

39 Harcourt 2007; Ashworth & Zedner 2014; Tonry 2019; Lewis 2022.

40 Day, Tucker & Howells 2004; Ward 2011, 2017.

1.3 NEUROPREDICTION AND NEUROINTERVENTION

Two activities are becoming increasingly important with the preventive turn in criminal justice: (1) *risk assessment*, that is, estimating how "dangerous" a person is, and (2) *risk management*, that is, making efforts to reduce the person's risk to the community. The dominant model of rehabilitation, known as the Risk-Need-Responsivity model, centres exclusively on risk assessment and the subsequent management of identified risks.[41] This model operates on three primary principles: (a) that rehabilitative interventions should be delivered at an intensity that matches the offending person's risk level; (b) that rehabilitative interventions should target a person's dynamic risk factors – that is, those factors that are changeable; and (c) that the interventions utilised should take into account, and be tailored to, those characteristics that may influence the person's responsivity to treatment.[42] An alternative, also prominent, model of rehabilitation, the Good Lives Model, focuses primarily on enabling convicted persons to live "good" – or meaningful and fulfilling – lives.[43] However, this model too is concerned with risk reduction, integrating principles of risk management into its overall strengths-based approach.[44]

Both *assessing* a person's future dangerousness and *reducing* risks of recidivism to an acceptable level are confronted with serious challenges. The predictive accuracy of current risk assessment tools is, in general, low to moderate,[45] which raises ethical concerns about the increasing use of risk assessment within criminal justice.[46] Furthermore, the efficacy of existing rehabilitative interventions varies,[47] with some offending subpopulations proving particularly refractory to treatment.[48] In addition, evidence suggests that carceral incapacitation (whether punitive or non-punitive) can be counterproductive to the reduction of a person's risk after release.[49]

41 Andrews, Bonta & Hoge 1990; Andrews & Bonta 2006.

42 Willis & Ward 2010; Bonta 2023.

43 Birgden 2002; Ward 2002; Ward & Brown 2004.

44 Fortune & Ward 2013.

45 Fazel et al. 2012. Current risk assessments tools include clinical assessments and actuarial assessments.

46 Douglas et al. 2017.

47 See Larden et al. 2018 and Mews, Di Bella & Purver 2017 for studies that seem to support the inadequate efficacy of some rehabilitation programmes – though see Lösel et al. 2020 for discussion of the controversial methodological design of the Mews, Di Bella & Purver study. See Hoogsteder et al. 2018 and Travers et al. 2013 for studies that document significant reductions in recidivism following the delivery of particular rehabilitation programmes.

48 For example, some persons scoring highly on measures of psychopathy may fail to desist from crime despite extensive rehabilitative interventions. Indeed, no specific conventional rehabilitative intervention is consistently efficacious in this population; see Rice & Harris 2013; and Hecht 2018.

49 Cid 2009; Wermink et al. 2018. Recidivism rates after incarceration generally remain high, see Alper 2018; Yukhnenko, Sridhar & Fazel 2020. This could indicate one or more of three things: (a) rehabilitation is often not adequately provided to those who offend, (b) provided rehabilitative interventions often have inadequate efficacy, or (c) the prison environment counteracts the effect of provided rehabilitative interventions.

Carceral incapacitation also does not preclude the possibility of a person committing crime within the prison walls.

To strengthen both risk assessment and risk management, neuroscientists, lawyers and philosophers are increasingly looking to the possibilities offered by neurotechnology.[50] Regarding *risk assessment* with the help of neurotechnology, also referred to as "neuroprediction",[51] various forms of neuroimaging that could obtain relevant information about a person's brain and behavioural dispositions have been considered.[52] Regarding *risk management*, the emphasis in the literature is on the potential of psychotropic medication and different forms of brain stimulation to change brain states and influence behaviour in a way that contributes to mitigating recidivism risk – also referred to as "neurointervention".[53]

Neuroprediction seeks to predict a person's risk of future offending by looking to whether they exhibit neurobiological features that correlate with recidivism. Several types of neurobiological features have been studied for their relevance for offending, including various hormones, neurotransmitters, brain structures and activity levels in particular brain regions.[54] One example is the oft-reported correlation between reduced activity in the brain's frontal lobe and impulsivity and poor behavioural control[55] – characteristics that appear to be positively associated with criminal behaviour.[56] In a prominent study conducted by Aharoni et al., researchers used functional magnetic resonance imaging (fMRI) to measure brain activity in a population of ninety-six convicted males.[57] The brain activity was measured while participants performed an impulse-control task, and the researchers subsequently related this neuroimaging data to participants' re-arrest rates four years after release. They observed that those participants with relatively low activity in the anterior cingulate context had roughly doubled the likelihood of re-arrest over this time period when compared to those exhibiting high activity in this region. This same research group recently documented a relationship between low dorsal anterior cingulate cortex activity while

50 See, for example, Nadelhoffer et al. 2012; Witzel 2012; Delfin et al. 2019; Birks & Douglas 2018; Choy, Focquaert & Raine 2020; Ryberg 2020; Vincent, Nadelhoffer & McCay 2020; Ligthart 2022; Sergiou et al. 2022; Meynen et al. 2023.

51 Nadelhoffer et al. 2012.

52 Glenn & Raine 2014; Bedard 2017.

53 Vincent, Nadelhoffer & McCay 2020.

54 Glenn & Raine 2014; Rosell & Siever 2015; Poldrack et al. 2018. See also Nadelhoffer et al. 2012; Bedard 2017.

55 Glenn & Raine 2014; Rosell & Siever 2015; Poldrack et al. 2018. See also Nadelhoffer et al. 2012; Bedard 2017. Glen & Raine 2014, p. 56 claim that "[r]educed functioning in the frontal lobe of the brain is to date the best-replicated brain imaging correlate of antisocial and violent behavior".

56 Gottfredson & Hirschi 1990; Wang & Diamond 1999; Pratt & Cullen 2000; Griffin, Lynam & Samuel 2018. Though see Wendel, Rocque & Posick 2022 for a more nuanced discussion of the relationship between impulsivity and crime.

57 Aharoni et al. 2013. See also Aharoni et al. 2014.

performing an impulse-control task and the re-arrest rate in a female offending population.[58]

Neuroprediction need not replace existing tools of risk assessment. Instead, it could be integrated into – or combined with – existing types of risk assessment, aiming to better inform this assessment.[59] Delfin and colleagues have provided evidence of the potential of neuropredictive tools to enhance the efficacy of risk assessment.[60] They investigated whether adding neuroimaging data to traditional risk factors served to increase predictive success over the use of traditional risk factors alone, and they concluded in the affirmative. Comparable findings were reported by Zijlmans and colleagues, who concluded that incorporating neurobiological data had "incremental predictive value above traditional risk factors" in delinquent young adults (they used, among other measurements, data obtained from EEG).[61] This research is, of course, still in its infancy, and no strong conclusions for potential criminal justice application of these technologies can be drawn at this moment. However, the above findings are suggestive of a new type of risk assessment that might become possible in the near future and which could add valuable data to existing forms of risk assessment. It thus behoves us to ask how these kinds of technologies should be used.

Whereas neuroprediction involves monitoring brain activity, *neurointervention* involves modifying a person's brain and mental processes. This is done via direct physical, chemical or biological influence, aiming to ultimately change the person's behaviour. In the criminal justice context, such change would mean reducing a person's likelihood of reoffending and promoting their rehabilitation more generally.[62] Roughly, two broad types of neurointervention can be distinguished: (1) psychoactive drugs or neuropharmaceuticals and (2) technological neuromodulation (whereby a stimulus is delivered to alter activity in the nervous system).

Candidate psychoactive drugs that have or might be used in the service of rehabilitation include drugs to reduce the libido of those who have committed sexual offences, and the use of selective serotonin reuptake inhibitors as a means of reducing impulsive aggression in those convicted of violent offences.[63] Candidate neuromodulatory technologies include transcranial direct current stimulation (tDCS), transcranial magnetic stimulation (TMS) and deep brain stimulation

58 Allen et al. 2022. This study involved 248 participants and re-arrest rates were observed over an eleven-year period.

59 Witzel has gone so far as to suggest that it is only through "the integration of both sides of the coin (psychological and biological)" that we will be able to "formulate a higher quality risk assessment", see Witzel 2012, p. 195.

60 Delfin et al. 2019. Cf. Kiehl et al. 2018.

61 Zijlmans et al. 2021.

62 For this definition, see Birks & Douglas 2018, p. 2.

63 See Chew et al. 2018 for review. Note, too, that there have been concerns that selective serotonin inhibitors might actually increase rather than reduce the risk of violent crime; see, for example, Molero et al. 2015. Further studies on this purported relationship are therefore needed.

(DBS).[64] The first two of these techniques require neither surgery nor even intense physical contact and typically operate without inflicting pain or serious discomfort on the recipient.[65] These techniques involve placing electrodes or magnets on the scalp respectively aiming to alter activity in the targeted brain regions.[66] This is different from the third technique mentioned above, DBS, which is an invasive type of neurointervention, involving the surgical implanting of electrodes into the brain.[67]

Some psychoactive drugs, like antilibidinal drugs, are already used for rehabilitative purposes in different criminal justice systems.[68] Other psychoactive drugs are being studied for the effects they might have on crime-relevant behaviours and recidivism.[69] The use of neurotechnologies as an aid to rehabilitation is still very much in the early research stage. Some experimental research has, however, been performed.

A number of studies have documented that targeting the prefrontal cortex with tDCS reduced self-reported aggression in recipients.[70] A Dutch double-blind, placebo-controlled, randomised trial found that tDCS targeting the ventromedial prefrontal cortex reduced self-reported aggression in a forensic population.[71] Another study found reduced self-reported aggressiveness after three sessions of bilateral prefrontal cortex tDCS in a population imprisoned for violent offences.[72] Targeting the prefrontal cortex with tDCS has also been shown to have positive effects on decision-making in certain populations. A German research group reported that tDCS increased prefrontal activity and improved decision-making in a population convicted of violent offences, such that these individuals made less risky decisions.[73] This preliminary finding makes space for the possibility that tDCS may have potential to improve decision-making in violent populations. Meanwhile, the samples of these studies were relatively small and further research is needed to learn more about the effectiveness of tDCS to reduce agression.[74]

Further research has explored the potential effects of DBS on crime-relevant behaviours. Several studies have found that DBS in specific brain regions reduced aggressive behaviour in clinical populations.[75] Franzini et al. describe the results of

64 Molero et al. 2015.

65 A review by Knehans et al. 2022 indicates that the side effects of non-invasive neuromodulation are generally mild, with itchiness and a tingling being the most common side effects.

66 Chail 2018; Chase et al. 2020.

67 Meanwhile, brain tissue remains intact. This is different from neurosurgery that destroys brain tissue, which may be used in the treatment of epilepsy, Chang, Englot & Vadera, 2015. However, to our knowledge, this latter type of intervention is not currently under consideration for rehabilitative purposes.

68 For an overview of the antilibidinal agents that have or are being used in some jurisdictions see Thibaut et al. 2010; Forsberg 2021.

69 See, for example, Chang et al. 2016; Felthous et al. 2021.

70 An association between aggression and specific regions within the prefrontal cortex has long been reported, see Knehans et al. 2022.

71 Sergiou et al. 2022.

72 Molero-Chamizo et al. 2019.

73 Kuhn et al. 2024.

74 Denson et al. 2025.

75 Torres et al. 2013; Harat et al. 2021; Benedetti-Isaac et al. 2021; Escobar Vidarte et al. 2022.

DBS targeting the posterior hypothalamic region in seven cases of patients with mental retardation and aggressive and disruptive behaviour.[76] Six of these patients showed "a clear reduction in the aggression and disruptive bouts, with subsequent simplification of familiar management".[77] The authors thus concluded that DBS in this brain region could be an effective treatment for a subgroup of patients with intellectual disability who show aggressive behaviour.[78] Additionally, Fuss and collaborators have discussed the possible future use of DBS as an intervention for those convicted of sexual offences.[79] The researchers identify a candidate brain region for DBS – namely the ventromedial hypothalamus – claiming that this region is "so far the best investigated target to reduce sexual drive".[80]

As said, investigations into the potential of these neurotechnologies for facilitating rehabilitation are still at an early stage. Yet, assuming that some rehabilitative applications of these technologies will be available in the future – and assuming also that the range of neuropharmaceuticals at our disposal for facilitating rehabilitation broadens – we must ask whether, and if so how, neurointerventions could be deployed in criminal justice while protecting and respecting human rights and freedoms. For instance, we must ask: Which human rights would be infringed, or even violated, if brain stimulation were employed without valid informed consent? And would human rights produce compelling arguments in favour of offering such interventions to convicted persons, to foster their rehabilitation?

1.4 FREEDOMS AND RIGHTS

In this book, as said, we consider neurorehabilitation in view of human rights, with a special interest in human rights for the mind. More precisely, the book considers the question of responsible use of neurorehabilitation through the lens of convicted persons' freedoms and rights – something which necessarily involves interrogating the interpretation and construction of human rights for the mind. Hitherto, much valuable scholarship has explored the legal and moral questions that arise regarding the neurorehabilitation of convicted persons.[81] Several scholars have also considered how we should use and delimit neurointervention and neuroprediction in criminal justice,[82] with some specifically asking whether the use of these techniques invokes – and is delimited by – certain human rights.[83]

76 Franzini et al. 2013, p. 11.

77 Franzini et al. 2013, p. 11.

78 Franzini et al. 2013, p. 11.

79 Fuss et al. 2015.

80 Fuss et al. 2015, p. 429. They refer to reports of how brain surgery of this region in a population of patients with paraphilic sexual desires reduced their sexual drive (these procedures took place from 1962 to the late 1970s).

81 Nadelhoffer et al. 2012; Birks & Douglas 2018; Vincent, Nadelhoffer & McCay 2020.

82 Ryberg 2020; Tortora et al. 2020; Vincent, Nadelhoffer & McCay 2020; Forsberg 2021; Ligthart 2022; Meynen et al. 2023; Dore-Horgan 2023.

83 Bublitz 2018; Ligthart 2022.

This book's distinct contribution to this burgeoning literature lies in its comprehensive and holistic approach. Though our analysis here is primarily legal, we harness and integrate both *legal* and *ethical* perspectives when considering whether and how neurorehabilitation might be deployed while protecting and respecting human rights and freedoms. Our analysis also pertains to *both* neuroprediction and neurointervention.[84] And we consider both *negative* and *positive* rights and freedoms in our analysis.

Our reasons for adopting this integrative, legal-ethical approach are twofold. First, human rights are typically taken to be both moral and legal concepts. Human rights are understood as those moral rights that apply universally, to all human beings, and which have a high priority.[85] By moral rights, we mean, rights that exist independently of whether they are protected in law, and which are justified and motivated by moral considerations and arguments. The term "human rights" also describes, and indeed emerged with, the set of established legal human rights that are enshrined in various human rights instruments, such as the International Covenant on Civil and Political Rights. Any fundamental discussion of human rights thus typically invokes both legal and moral issues.[86] It consequently makes sense to strive for an integrative approach when addressing profound questions about human rights protection of the mind and the human rights issues raised by neurorehabilitation.

Second, this integrative approach is likely to be the most productive. On the one hand, the conceptual analysis that is central to moral philosophy will provide valuable insights for the law, particularly when it comes to understanding the contours of concepts such as identity, privacy, health and mental integrity. Moral arguments may also strengthen the case for embracing the protection of particular rights at various levels of legal implementation.

While we adopt this integrative approach, our ultimate interest is in discerning to what extent the discussed freedoms and rights exist or ought to be embraced in law and, if so, what this might mean for neurorehabilitation in criminal justice. We are thus examining whether there are *legal* rights that could impact the permissible delivery of neurorehabilitation. Consequently, when speaking of "rights" throughout, we mean legal rights unless specified differently. This ultimate legal focus means that analysing and interpreting literature, treaties, comments and case law on human rights and freedoms is central to this book. We focus on the International Covenant on Civil and Political Rights (ICCPR), which is the binding international legal instrument for the protection of human rights, and on the European Convention on Human Rights (ECHR), on which the European Court of Human Rights (ECtHR) has produced much and detailed case law.

84 A greater portion of the book is devoted to the rights and freedoms that have relevance for neurointervention, as these are greater in number.

85 Campbell 2004; Nickel 2007; Griffin 2008.

86 Though some theorists have claimed that legal human rights can be justified without any appeal to moral rights, see Buchanan 2013.

We consider both neurointervention and neuroprediction because each kind of technique has the potential to raise human rights questions. Neuroprediction brings issues of mental privacy to the fore, particularly if deployed in non-consensual or dubiously consensual circumstances. The delivery of neurointervention, on the other hand, raises concerns about persons' identity, personal integrity, mental self-determination and health, while also prompting us to question whether and when convicted persons may have a right to avail of this kind of rehabilitative option.

Our holistic approach is also evident in our consideration of both negative and positive rights throughout this book. Though the boundaries between negative and positive rights are not clear-cut, with many rights having both negative and positive dimensions, we understand the distinction between negative and positive roughly as follows. By negative rights, we mean protective rights *against* actions by the state – for example, rights against unwanted state interference in particular domains. By positive rights, we mean rights *to* a certain action from the state – for instance, in the service of providing certain resources (e.g., educational or healthcare resources) that may be conducive to human interests or flourishing. In order to delimit the scope of the book, our analysis will focus on:

- Negative dimension: (i) personal identity, (ii) personal integrity and (iii) mental privacy.
- Positive dimension: (i) mental self-determination, (ii) mental health and (iii) rehabilitation.

Our analysis is organised as follows.

Part I: The Negative Dimension: Protection against Neurorehabilitation

Chapter 2 Personal Identity

First, we consider the neurorehabilitation of convicted persons through the lens of a right to personal identity. It has been argued that modifying brains and mental states through neurotechnology and pharmaceuticals could affect different conceptions of personal identity, including psychological continuity and narrative identity. Until now, this debate has focused strongly on the (side) effects of brain stimulation for therapeutic purposes, such as DBS in the treatment of Parkinson's disease. We extrapolate this discussion to the context of criminal justice. In addition to earlier ethical evaluations of brain stimulation vis-à-vis personal identity, scholars are now also considering the legal protection that should be offered to personal identity in this context, particularly through human rights – and some have argued for the introduction of a specific human right for this purpose, that is, a right to psychological continuity. The relevance and implications of a right to personal identity for neurorehabilitation plausibly depends on how one understands personal identity, something this chapter will also consider.

Chapter 3 Personal Integrity

Next, we investigate the relevance and implications of the right to personal integrity – that is, the right to bodily and mental integrity – for the neurorehabilitation of convicted persons. How could neurotechnology in this context infringe this right? And could such infringements be permissible in some cases? Regarding the right to bodily integrity, we closely stick to the interpretation of the right as follows from established human rights law, particularly the ICCPR and ECHR. Under both treaties, a right to bodily integrity is clearly defined and developed. For our analysis of the right to mental integrity – which is less developed in human rights law yet – we will also rely on the philosophical literature aiming to define a moral right to mental integrity. Informed by philosophy, we explore some possible understandings of the human right to mental integrity. Along the way, we consider the implications of (different interpretations of) the right to bodily and mental integrity for the neurorehabilaition of convicted persons.

Chapter 4 Mental Privacy

Whereas personal identity and personal integrity are mainly relevant in relation to neuro*interventions*, we consider the implications of a right to mental privacy for the use of neuro*prediction* in criminal justice. We offer a preliminary analysis of the human rights protection of mental privacy by three established human rights: (1) the right to privacy, (2) the right to freedom of expression and (3) the right to freedom of thought. We consider the interplay between these different rights and explore a threshold criterion for engaging absolute protection by the oft-assumed "absolute" right to freedom of thought, over and above the qualified protection provided by the right to privacy and the freedom of expression.

Part II: The Positive Dimension: Arguments for Offering Neurorehabilitation

Chapter 5 Mental Self-Determination

This chapter examines the case for a legal right to mental self-determination, understood as the right to voluntarily alter and exercise control over our mental states (including with the help of neurotechnologies and other techniques) without being thwarted in these efforts by third parties. We examine three legal rationales and one moral rationale that lend support to this right, including the rationale that a right to mental self-determination derives from the more general right to self-determination. We then interrogate whether and when the putative right to mental self-determination might imply a state duty to *offer* or *provide* neurorehabilitation.

Chapter 6 Mental Health

Next, we explore whether – and if so, how – a right to mental health could produce an argument in favour of offering neurorehabilitation to some populations of convicted persons. As outlined in this introductory chapter, the primary focus of this book is on the potential of neurotechnology to support risk assessment and risk management – rather than the use of neurotechnology to diagnose and treat mental or brain disorders. Still, there are different conceptualisations of (mental) health that may or may not include such broader applications of neurotechnology. In general, health can be conceived of as "absence of disease" but it can also be approached in terms of functioning well or flourishing. We will analyse these approaches and determine the conceptualisation that is used in human rights law. Next, we explore the meaning and implications of the right to (mental) health regarding the possibility of offering neurorehabilitation to convicted persons.

Chapter 7 Rehabilitation

In this chapter, we interrogate whether and when states have a duty to provide convicted persons with neurorehabilitation as part of a right to rehabilitation. We examine the existing law and jurisprudence surrounding rehabilitation, present the rationales that have been (or may be) advanced in support of a right to rehabilitation and analyse what these judgements and arguments imply for the specific case of neurorehabilitation. More precisely, we explore whether – and if so, how – persons' moral and legal right against cruel, inhuman or degrading punishment, and persons' putative moral right to socially contribute, implies a right to have access to rehabilitative interventions under certain conditions. We then consider whether and when these rights also imply a right to have access to neurorehabilitative interventions.

Chapter 8 Synthesis and Discussion

Finally, based on the analyses in the preceding chapters, we tentatively identify some types and forms of neurotechnological applications, the use of which in criminal justice appears either plausibly permissible or plausibly impermissible, in view of the considered rights and freedoms.

Before proceeding, three final points are in order.

First, as the *mind*, in relation to neurotechnology and the law, is central in this book, it may be helpful to clarify our position on the mind-and-brain relationship. In our analyses throughout, we do not commit to any specific theory of the mind-brain relationship. Still, given that we consider the impact of *neuro*technologies on the mind, we assume that brain changes can influence the mind and (relatedly) that information about the brain can provide information about the mind. This approach is in line with much recent theorising on mind and brain.

Second, we acknowledge that, in addition to present-day concerns about the neurorehabilitation of convicted persons and their human rights, there is a long and problematic history of "brain and crime" more broadly.[87] At one level, past attempts to explore the relationship between criminal behaviour and the brain were marked by a form of biological determinism and reductionism – that is, by the idea that criminal behaviour is wholly the product of a person's physiology.[88] At another level, twentieth-century usage of neurotechnologies to change a person's mind and/or behaviour has led to several inhumane treatment practices: most prominently, the use of lobotomy (which involved a type of surgery in which connections between the frontal lobe and the rest of the brain were severed) and the problematic use of electroconvulsive therapy (which involves eliciting an epileptic seizure).[89]

This history may give rise to concerns that recent neuro-approaches to criminal offending are also deterministic and reductionist,[90] and that pursuing these neuro-approaches will once again lead to abusive practice. While we will not consider the issue of determinism or reductionism in relation to contemporary neuro-approaches to crime in this book, we wish to highlight that our particular perspective is neither brain-deterministic nor reductionist. Rather than conceiving of the brain as determining persons' behaviour without any possibilities for change, our approach sees the brain as both vulnerable and plastic. We see the brain, mainly, as an organ that makes it possible to respond and adapt to different environments and their challenges, and to learn to regulate behaviour and emotions.[91] We also do not propose to *reduce* rehabilitation to neuro-approaches. We focus on neurotechnology in criminal justice, not because we believe it is the only or preferable approach to rehabilitation (certainly not) but because it is an emerging field that evokes fundamental questions about people's rights and freedoms which require a thorough analysis.

Moreover, the fact that neurotechnologies have been applied inhumanely in the past need not necessarily imply that their use will always lead to unethical practices, as Ryberg emphasises.[92] Indeed, electroconvulsive therapy is now, after crucial modifications, an important – and humane – treatment option in severe mental illness, in particular depression.[93] There is also evidence to suggest that the general public considers some candidate contemporary neurotechnological approaches to

87 McTernan 2018; Ryberg 2020.

88 Cesare Lombroso, for example, believed that some people were "born criminal" and that this could be identified by certain physical markers, among which the shape of one's skull, and, more precisely, one's forehead; see Delisi 2015.

89 Faria 2013. The use of electroconvulsive therapy and lobotomy was forcefully depicted in the movie *One Flew over the Cuckoo's Nest*.

90 Fallin et al. 2019.

91 See the Preface of Swaab & Meynen 2023 for a similar approach.

92 Ryberg 2020.

93 Chatham, Shafi & Hermida 2022.

rehabilitation to be acceptable, so long as those who offend are allowed to freely choose whether or not to submit to them.[94] Still, history highlights how careful consideration and implementation of neurotechnological applications to modify brain and/or behaviour is necessary if we are to avoid abusive practice. This involves protecting and respecting the human rights of all persons, including those who offend – a task to which the analysis in this book aims to contribute.

Lastly, though the focus of the book is on neurorehabilitation in criminal justice, given the nature of our arguments – considering the relevant freedoms and rights more broadly – the analysis is likely to have implications for neurotechnological applications in other societal domains too, such as in health care, education and the military. Additionally, given the scope of the freedoms and rights discussed, the analysis in this book may also have implications for other emerging technologies that have impact on our minds and brains.

[94] Denson, Griffiths &Smith 2024. The authors describe "neuronormalization" as "brain-based treatments" for rehabilitation – something akin to neurointervention or neurorehabilitation as we have defined it. They report that participants in their study considered neuronormalisation and psychological therapies to be a more ethical response to violent offending than incarceration, while also endorsing the idea that relevant parties should be given a choice as to whether they avail of these interventions (p. 15).

PART I

The Negative Dimension

Protection against Neurorehabilitation

2

The Right to Personal Identity

On Psychological Continuity and Narrative Identity

2.1 INTRODUCTION

This chapter considers the potential of neurorehabilitation to interfere with a person's identity, and hence its potential to infringe human rights that protect (different aspects of) personal identity.[1] It builds upon previous arguments and suggestions in the literature that some forms of interference with the brain, such as the use of brain stimulation techniques, can cause psychological changes that disrupt a person's identity.[2] Until now, this debate has focused strongly on the side effects of brain stimulation for therapeutic purposes, such as DBS in the treatment of Parkinson's disease.[3] We extrapolate this discussion to the context of criminal justice.[4] In addition to earlier *ethical* evaluations of brain stimulation vis-à-vis personal identity, scholars are now considering the *legal* protection that should be offered to personal identity in this context, particularly through human rights. Some have argued for the introduction of a specific human right for this purpose: a right to psychological continuity.[5]

The primary aim of this chapter is to investigate the relevance and implications of a right to personal identity for neurorehabilitation. How could neurointerventions, deployed in this context, affect personal identity? To what extent does human rights law protect against such effects? And what does this mean for neurorehabilitation in criminal justice? The answers to these questions plausibly depend on how one understands personal identity, something this chapter will discuss.

Much of the concerns about identity and brain stimulation voiced in the neuroethical literature appeal to a *psychological-continuity* account of identity.[6] We

1 Some parts of the analysis in this chapter borrow from Ligthart 2024.

2 DeGrazia 2005b; Schechtman 2010; Jotterand & Giordano 2011; Klaming & Haselager 2013; Lipsman & Glannon 2013; Cabrera, Evans & Hamilton 2014.

3 DeGrazia 2005b; Schechtman 2010; Jotterand & Giordano 2011; Klaming & Haselager 2013; Lipsman & Glannon 2013; Cabrera, Evans & Hamilton 2014.

4 See also Ryberg 2020.

5 Ienca & Andorno 2017. Cf Ligthart 2024.

6 See section 2.2.1.

challenge, however, the idea that present forms of brain stimulation are likely to disrupt personal identity in this sense – at least as far as their potential use in criminal justice is concerned. Another influential account of identity in contemporary philosophy is the narrative self-constituting view, also referred to as *narrative identity*, which has been suggested to be more appropriate for capturing the moral concerns about brain stimulation and identity.[7] We consider this line of thought with a focus on brain stimulation in criminal justice. Furthermore, we consider whether and, if so, to what extent psychological continuity and narrative identity receive protection from established human rights and explore the implications for the neurorehabilitation of convicted persons.

This chapter proceeds as follows. Section 2 discusses the central concerns voiced in the literature about brain stimulation and personal identity and considers neurorehabilitation in that regard. We focus on the two (abovementioned) dominant accounts of personal identity that are central to the debate over neurotechnological brain stimulation: the (1) psychological-continuity and (2) narrative identity account. Section 3 investigates the human rights protection of personal identity and explores the implications for neurorehabilitation. Section 4 draws conclusions.

2.2 NORMATIVE CONCERNS ABOUT BRAIN STIMULATION AND PERSONAL IDENTITY

2.2.1 *Psychological Continuity*

In an influential contribution to the contemporary debate on the adequacy of human rights protection of our brains and minds, Ienca and Andorno make a case for reinforcing this protection, through the creation of specific "neurorights".[8] Among other things, they argue for recognising a right to psychological continuity, as "a special neuro-focused instance of the right to identity".[9] Part of their motivation for arguing this is that emerging neurotechnologies that stimulate and modulate human brain functions – such as tDCS, TMS and DBS – have the potential, in their words, to "cause alterations in mental states critical to personality (...) thereby affecting an individual's personal identity".[10] Some of these brain stimulation techniques are currently used in day-to-day clinical practice, for example, to treat neurological disorders such as Parkinson's disease and epilepsy.[11] Moreover, as mentioned in the introductory chapter, researchers are increasingly examining the

7 DeGrazia 2005b; Schechtman 2010; Pugh 2020.

8 Ienca & Andorno 2017.

9 Ienca & Andorno 2017, p. 21.

10 Ienca & Andorno 2017, p. 20. See also UNESCO, Executive Board, Preliminary study on the technical and legal aspects relating to the desirability of a standard-setting instrument on the ethics of neurotechnology (6 April 2023), par. 7.

11 Foltynie et al. 2024; Salama et al. 2024.

potentials of brain stimulation beyond the context of standard medical care, including their use to reduce aggressiveness in forensic populations.[12]

Ienca and Andorno highlight that changing a person's brain functioning through brain stimulation "may have an impact on the psychological continuity of the person, i.e. the crucial requirement of personal identity consisting in experiencing oneself as persisting through time as the same person".[13] They substantiate this claim by referring to reports of the experience of different kinds of self-estrangement after or during treatment with DBS or following implantation of a BCI.[14] Some patients reported, for instance, that BCI implantation "made me a different person",[15] or that DBS treatment (in this case, for Parkinson's disease) made them "feel like a machine", reporting that "I've lost my passion. I don't recognize myself anymore".[16] Ienca and Andorno also cite studies that demonstrate that some individuals experience significant mental and behavioural changes as side effects following DBS – for example, increases in impulsivity and aggression, or changes in sexual behaviour – that may, in turn, and depending on the individual, cause them to experience self-estrangement and feel disassociated from themselves.[17]

Ienca and Andorno's claim that we ought to recognise a right to psychological continuity is also motivated by the expectation that the advent of brain stimulation techniques may open up possibilities for third parties to induce *non-consensual* personality changes. Brain implants like DBS bear the risk of being hacked by third parties aiming to exert malicious control over the user's brain activity.[18] Furthermore, in some contexts (e.g., the military and criminal justice), we can anticipate that brain stimulation might be administered on a mandatory basis, given that mandated undertakings are a frequent feature of these contexts. Ienca and Andorno thus argue for the recognition of a right to psychological continuity in order to protect persons against the potentially adverse effects non-consensual brain stimulation might have on their identity. They understand this right as "ultimately tend[ing] to preserve personal identity and the coherence of the individual's behaviour from non-consensual modification by third parties. It protects the continuity

[12] E.g., Sergiou et al. 2022; Knehans et al. 2022. Furthermore, Ienca & Andorno 2017 point to the context of the military and intelligence agencies, where (potential) human rights violations have been reported in relation to experiments involving brain electrodes, psychoactive drugs, hypnosis and brainwashing. See, for example, Ross 2007; Rickli & Ienca 2021.

[13] Ienca & Andorno 2017, p. 20. Note that when talking about the crucial requirement of personal identity consisting in *experiencing oneself* as persisting the same person over time, their concerns seem more related to narrative identity, rather than to psychological continuity (see section 2.2.2).

[14] See, for example, Gilbert et al. 2017.

[15] Gilbert, Ienca & Cook 2023, p. 786.

[16] Schüpbach et al. 2006, p. 1812. See also Kraemer 2013.

[17] Ienca and Andorno 2017 cite Frank et. 2007; Sensi et al. 200; and Houeto et al. 2002 – though these particular studies did not investigate whether those affected by the relevant side effects experienced self-estrangement.

[18] Ienca & Androno 2017, p. 21; Farahany 2023, p. 109 et seq; Pycroft et al. 2016; Ienca & Haselager 2016; Pugh et al. 2018. See also UN Special Rapporteur on Torture and other cruel, inhuman or degrading treatment or punishment, 20 March 2020, A/HRC/43/49, par. 31–32.

across a person's habitual thoughts, preferences, and choices by protecting the underlying neural functioning".[19]

The idea of developing a right to psychological continuity to protect personal identity from unsolicited (neurotechnological) interferences by others has been picked up on by human rights treaty bodies, both in Europe and internationally. For example, in November 2019, the Council of Europe launched a Strategic Action Plan on Human Rights and Technologies in Biomedicine (2020–2025). One of the plan's concrete action points is to assess the relevance and sufficiency of existing human rights in view of emerging threats posed by neurotechnology, including threats to personhood and psychological continuity. This plan noted the need to assess "whether new human rights pertaining to cognitive liberty, mental privacy, and mental integrity and *psychological continuity*, need to be entertained in order to govern neurotechnologies".[20]A report commissioned by the Committee on Bioethics of the Council of Europe furthermore claims that a human right to psychological continuity would "offer solid normative ground to (...) preserve a person's self-determination and sense of personal identity from subconscious manipulation".[21] This report further adds that a right to psychological continuity "may become particularly important in the context of national security and military research, where neurotechnology applications that modulate personality traits (e.g., neurostimulation techniques) are currently being tested for combatant enhancement".[22] Other human rights bodies have noted the nature of the concern that some neurotechnologies might pose to psychological continuity, as it is characterised by Ienca and Andorno. In their 2024 report on neurotechnology and human rights, the Advisory Committee of the UN Human Rights Council highlights that "[p]atients having undergone deep brain stimulation have reported feeling a changed sense of agency and identity; thus, ensuring 'psychological continuity' may be important".[23]

We have been referring to "psychological continuity" as though the concept is widely known and understood. But while the concept of "psychological continuity" is familiar to ethicists and philosophers, it is not commonly invoked in human rights

[19] Ienca & Andorno 2017, p. 21.

[20] Committee on Bioethics of the Council of Europe, *Strategic Action Plan on Human Rights and Technologies in Biomedicine (2020–2025)*, Adopted by DH-BIO, 16th meeting (19–21 November 2019), p. 7 (emphasis added).

[21] Ienca, M., *Common human rights challenges raised by different applications of neurotechnologies in the biomedical field*, Council of Europe, October 2021, p. 61.

[22] Ienca, M., *Common human rights challenges raised by different applications of neurotechnologies in the biomedical field*, Council of Europe, October 2021, pp. 61, 62. This report mentions that neurostimulation techniques are being tested to see if they can "increase the ability of soldiers and other military personnel to perform with motivation and determination even under stress or in the absence of sleep".

[23] Advisory Committee, UNHRC, Impact, opportunities and challenges of neurotechnology with regard to the promotion and protection of all human rights, A/HRC/AC/31/CRP.1 (8 August 2024), par 27, footnote 36.

law. As Ienca explains, the concept is borrowed from a specific philosophical understanding of personal identity found in psychological-continuity views.[24] One such view has been developed by John Locke. In developing his view, Locke's focus is on accounting for what preserves *numerical identity*,[25] or the persistence of a single entity over time.[26] Numerical identity concerns whether, for instance, Norah at the age of forty (time t_2) is the same person as Norah at the age of twenty (time t_1). Scholars often address this question by referring to the physical or psychological relations that obtain between the relevant entities at t_1 and t_2. Locke's account of personal identity appeals to a specific *psychological* relation. It appeals to the idea of "sameness of consciousness" – that is, that a person at time t_1 remains the same person at time t_2 if and only if they *share the same consciousness* at these two times.[27] Locke is admittedly unclear about what sharing the same consciousness means. But his remark that "for as far as any intelligent Being can *repeat* the Idea of any past Action with the same consciousness it had of it at first (...) so far it is the same personal self"[28] has led some to conclude that, by sharing the same consciousness, Locke means *remembering*.[29] As Shoemaker phrases it, on one interpretation of Locke, "a person – a moral agent – Y at t_2 is identical to a person X at t_1 when Y's consciousness 'can be extended backwards' to X, and this is typically taken to mean that Y *remembers* X's thoughts and experiences".[30]

The idea that a person remains the same person if and only if they remember their earlier thoughts and experiences has faced various objections. One objection is that it produces some logically impossible results. To illustrate, take the case of an elderly man who remembers the events of his middle years while forgetting the events his physical self experienced in its youth, and suppose that, *when* in his middle years, the middle-aged man remembered the events of his youth. Here, we have a situation where – if persistence of the self consists in remembering or sameness of consciousness – the youth is the same person as the middle-aged man, the middle-aged man the same as the elderly man, but the youth is *not* the same person as the elderly man, and this cannot possibly obtain. Assuming that identity is transitive, we cannot logically have A being equal to B, and B being equal to C, without A *also* being equal to C.

A prominent contemporary approach to avoiding this objection involves amending Locke's account such that memory plays a less central role in the preservation of

24 Ienca, M., *Common human rights challenges raised by different applications of neurotechnologies in the biomedical field*, Council of Europe, October 2021, p. 61, referring to Van Inwagen 1997. See also Gilbert, Ienca & Cook 2023, p. 87; Report of the International Bioethics Committee of UNESCO, *Ethical Issues of Neurotechnology*, SHS/BIO/IBC28/2021/3Rev., 15 December 2021, par. III.1.2.

25 Locke/Nidditch 1975. See also Perry 2008.

26 DeGrazia 2005a, Ch. 2.

27 DeGrazia 2005a, pp. 13–14.

28 Locke/Nidditch 1975, Book II, Ch. XXVII, par. 10 (emphasis added).

29 Note that some dispute that Locke considered the sharing of the same consciousness to equate to remembering, see, for example, Behan 1979; Atherton 1983 and Winkler 1991.

30 Shoemaker 2021, par. 1 (original emphasis).

identity across time, and other mental features such as intentions, goals, beliefs, desires and similarity of character also assume significance.[31] Arguably, the most influential psychological-continuity account that so amends the Lockean view has been developed by Derek Parfit.

Parfit argues that for X and Y to be the same person at different times, there must be an overlapping chain of enough – that is, *strong* – psychological connectedness between X today and Y sometime in the past or future.[32] So, for Norah to be the same person as the Norah that inhabited her body twenty years ago, she must have a sufficient number of overlapping psychological features like desires, beliefs and intentions that persisted from each day to the next over these twenty years. Such an overlapping chain of strong psychological connectedness across time is what Parfit calls *psychological continuity*; and for Parfit, such strong connectedness exists "if the number of connections, over any day, is *at least half* the number of direct connections that hold, over every day, in the lives of nearly every actual person".[33] Hence, if a person loses *over* half the psychological connections one has to themselves – when compared to the connections that obtain within other persons – psychological continuity, and hence numerical identity, will be disrupted, and a different person will come to exist. Note that numerical identity is binary: either the person continues or ceases to exist; either the person keeps or loses their identity.

A psychological-continuity account of identity has enjoyed majority support in philosophy.[34] It has also been widely invoked in the ethical literature on brain stimulation techniques.[35] Scholars in this literature raise the same concern as Ienca and Andorno about these techniques, again drawing on empirical data to motivate the idea that brain stimulation has the potential to disrupt psychological continuity. For example, Holmen argues that some mental features central to psychological continuity – desires, beliefs and memories – seem already malleable through both pharmaceutical and neurotechnological means, and if changes to these features were effected in a "sweeping" or sudden and widespread manner, then we would have a disruption of numerical identity.[36] In the same vein, Vincent claims that there are "non-insignificant grounds to worry that direct brain interventions which implement large-scale changes in one fell swoop could sever

31 See, for example, Shoemaker 1970; Lewis 1976; Parfit 1984.

32 Parfit 1984, p. 206. See also Parfit 1971.

33 Parfit 1984, p. 206 (original emphasis), adding in footnote 6: "This suggestion would need expanding, since there are many ways to count the number of direct connections. And some kinds of connection should be given more importance than others. (. . .) more weight should be given to those connections which are distinctive, or different in people (All English-speakers, for example, share many undistinctive memories of how to speak English)."

34 DeGrazia 2005b, p. 265. But this account also received fundamental objections, e.g., from Schechtman 1996 (see below).

35 Pugh 2020, p. 1659.

36 Holmen 2022, pp. 743–744. Holmen refers to a study that found that downregulating brain activity in a specific brain area by non-invasive TMS had the effect of altering the targeted persons' political and religious beliefs; see Holbrook et al. 2016.

psychological continuity", highlighting that "mounting empirical evidence substantiates the worry that direct brain interventions might have adverse effects on such things as authenticity and personal identity by significantly altering character and personality".[37]

Klaming and Haselager also conclude that brain stimulation techniques, specifically DBS, could disrupt psychological continuity and identity.[38] They discuss a study involving a patient who underwent DBS that successfully treated his Tourette's syndrome but who, twelve months following implantation of the DBS device, developed a dissociative response under certain stimulation amplitudes, wherein he seemed disconnected from himself and his identity.[39] The patient developed an alternate, childish identity state when the amplitude of the brain stimulation increased. Yet, when the amplitude of the stimulation decreased again, the patient's responses returned to "normal" and he was unable to recall what had happened during the increased stimulation of his brain.[40] According to Klaming and Haselager, this case "demonstrates that DBS can impinge on psychological continuity (in this case by having profound effects on behavior and memory) and influence an individual's personal identity to such an extent that an alternate personality state can be observed".[41]

Meanwhile, others have challenged the idea that neurotechnological brain stimulation would plausibly induce such global and radical effects on a person's psychological connections so as to disrupt psychological continuity.[42] For example, Pugh stresses that Parfit's psychological continuity account implies a high threshold and that "whilst ruptures to numerical identity may be evinced by severe neurodegenerative diseases like Alzheimer's, persons can also lose a considerable number of psychological connections whilst retaining numerical identity with a future person".[43] Against this backdrop, Pugh considers it implausible that DBS treatment would disrupt a patient's psychological continuity, as there is "little evidence to suggest DBS would typically have global effects on patients' psychological economies of the sort that would threaten a sufficient number of psychological connections for this to be the case".[44]

We suggest that Pugh's point has heightened relevance in situations where non-invasive brain stimulation is used to modulate behaviour and reduce a convicted person's risk of recidivism. Intervention in these sorts of cases can be expected to be highly targeted and appears to lack severe side effects. Present studies focus on the

37 Vincent 2014, pp. 30, 34.

38 Klaming & Haselager 2013.

39 Goethals et al. 2008. See also Zawadzki 2021 for discussion of this case.

40 Goethals et al. 2008.

41 Klaming & Haselager 2013, p. 530.

42 DeGrazia 2005b; Schermer 2009; Lipsman & Glannon 2013; Pugh 2020; Gilbert, Viaña & Ineichen 2021.

43 Pugh 2020, p. 1661.

44 Pugh 2020, p. 1661.

use of tDCS for reducing aggression, delivering a low current to a specific brain region via electrodes on the scull for about twenty minutes.[45] The use of brain stimulation in this context does not appear to induce a global and radical effect on the person's psychological functioning.[46] Rather, it produces a targeted stimulation of a *specific* brain area associated with *specific behavioural inclinations*, such as reducing aggression. Thus far, studies on the use of tDCS for this purpose have not reported any severe psychological side effects. As Knehans et al. write in their literature review on tDCS for reducing aggressive behaviour,

> [i]n four studies, no side effects were reported by the participants. In six studies, the reported side effects included itchiness, a tingling sensation, light-headedness, a burning sensation or warmth at the electrode site, and a pinching sensation or fatigue. One study reported a minor increase in stress levels in the participants if they sensed a tingling sensation during the stimulation. Out of these side effects, itchiness and a tingling sensation were the most common, and the other side-effects occurred rarely.[47]

Given the targeted nature of this type of non-invasive brain stimulation and the absence of (severe) psychological side effects in its trial use thus far, it is difficult to envisage how such an intervention could destroy over half of the psychological connections a person holds to themselves compared to a normal, actual person. Consequently, it is hard to imagine that reducing a person's aggressive tendencies in this way will interfere with the person's numerical identity such that the person ceases to exist. Of course, we cannot exclude the possibility that wrongful application or misuse of the technology might result in less targeted outcomes for criminal justice populations. We also cannot discount the possibility that unforeseeable side effects might occur even with targeted stimulation, such that severe psychological alterations may ensue in some cases. Nonetheless, *if used as intended* – that is, to target specific brain areas and specific, justice-relevant behavioural inclinations – the changes induced by brain stimulation within criminal justice contexts are unlikely to meet Parfit's threshold for disrupting psychological continuity and destroying numerical identity. Instead, the psychological changes are likely to be more "subtle".

Yet, it still seems as though eroding or destroying merely *some* psychological connections – for instance, by inducing changes to a person's intentions, goals, beliefs, desires and character – may *diminish* or *impinge on* psychological continuity and/or identity in a way that raises normative concerns. At one level, the case of a person who retains numerical identity, but who has fewer psychological connections with their earlier (same) self after a neurointervention, may raise an issue under the right to mental or psychological integrity (discussed in Chapter 3). At another, having fewer psychological connections with one's earlier self may still affect *identity* in other ethically and legally

45 Knehans et al. 2022. See Chapter 1.

46 See also Ryberg 2020, p. 72.

47 Knehans et al. 2022, p. 12.

relevant ways, even if it does not affect Parfitian psychological continuity or numerical identity. Some have argued that concerns about brain stimulation and personal identity might be better articulated within the alternative conceptualisation of *narrative identity*.[48] We consider this line of thought in the following section.

2.2.2 *Narrative Identity*

Marya Schechtman offers an alternative understanding of personal identity, which she argues can explain, unlike the psychological continuity account, why personal identity matters in the first place – that is, explaining our intuitions about the relation between personal identity and survival, moral responsibility, self-interested concern and compensation.[49] She develops a narrative self-constitution view of identity, according to which persons create their own identity by creating a coherent, autobiographical narrative: a story of their life.[50]

Narrative identity, Schechtman explains, is not an answer to what she calls the "reidentification question": the question of whether two entities at different times are one and the same entity (which Parfit and Locke are concerned with, and which we have previously referred to as numerical identity). Rather, it is an answer to the "characterization question": the question of which actions, experiences, values, beliefs, character traits – that is, "characteristics" – can be attributed to a given person. This characterisation question concerns the kind of identity that is at stake when people have an identity crisis, looking in the mirror and asking themselves: "Who am I really?". Questions that come under the umbrella of the characterisation question, Schechtman writes, are those that ask "which characteristics are *truly* those of some person (as opposed, say, to those which are his as a result of hypnosis, brainwashing, or some other form of coercion)".[51] Schechtman, then, describes the core of narrative identity as follows:

> According to the narrative self-constitution view, the difference between persons and other individuals (…) lies in how they organize their experience, and hence their lives. At the core of this view is the assertion that individuals constitute themselves as persons by coming to think of themselves as persisting subjects who have had experience in the past and will continue to have experience in the future, taking certain experiences as theirs. Some, but not all, individuals weave stories of their lives, and it is their doing so which makes them persons. On this view a person's identity (in the sense at issue in the characterization question) is constituted by the content of her self-narrative, and the traits, actions, and experiences included in it are, by virtue of that inclusion, hers.[52]

48 Mathews 2011; Schechtman 2010; Goddard 2017; Pugh 2020.
49 Schechtman 1996.
50 Schechtman 1996, p. 93; Schechtman 2011.
51 Schechtman 1996, p. 73.
52 Schechtman 1996, p. 94.

As this quotation clarifies, what determines a person's identity within this approach largely depends on how the person *experiences* themselves. It is about how people *process* their experiences into a coherent, autobiographical story of their lives.[53] This is not to say that just any random or unrealistic story people tell or believe about themselves determines who they are.[54] Not all narratives are identity-constituting, and Schechtman identifies some general constraints on precisely which kinds of narrative *are*, the two most important constraints being the (1) articulation constraint and (2) reality constraint.[55]

The *articulation constraint* requires that for shaping and retaining narrative identity, the person (the narrator) should be able to explain why they do what they do, feel what they feel and believe what they believe.[56] To quote from Schechtman, a person should be able "to articulate both the basic features of her history and life situation – the facts of her autobiography – and the way in which her life hangs together, providing explanations for why she has acted as she has and why things have unfolded as they have".[57] Elements of a person's narrative that they cannot articulate are still theirs, according to Schechtman. But they are "less fully" theirs, playing a different role in the person's life compared to articulated aspects of their self-narrative. They are "less attributable" to the person.[58]

The *reality constraint* requires that an identity-constituting self-narrative fundamentally coheres with reality. A person's self-narrative need not be completely accurate. It may and will contain (trivial) errors and inaccuracies, such as distortions and misremembering of facts. It must, however, "exhibit a fundamental grasp of what the world is like".[59] This is because personhood, in the sense Schechtman is concerned with, requires being able to engage in activities and interactions with others, and this in turn requires fundamental agreement on the most basic features of reality.[60] Views, beliefs and other characteristics that arise from profound delusions are ruled out as genuinely identity-constituting aspects of a person's narrative. As Schechtman clarifies, this "does not force us to conclude that psychotics are not persons – rather it allows us to dismiss the elements of psychotic's narratives that are out of touch with reality, and to recognize that their delusions interfere with personhood and diminish it".[61]

Both these constraints illustrate a general feature of Schechtman's narrative identity: that it *admits of degrees*.[62] Characteristics that the person cannot explain

[53] Schechtman 2009, p. 80. And at p. 81: "Self-narration involves *shaping* one's life into a coherent story as well as *conceiving* of it as such."

[54] DeGrazia 2005, p. 85.

[55] Schechtman 2009, pp. 82–83.

[56] Schechtman 1996, p. 114.

[57] Schechtman 2009, p. 82.

[58] Schechtman 1996, p. 119.

[59] Schechtman 2009, p. 83.

[60] Schechtman 1996, p. 119.

[61] Schechtman 1996, p. 127.

[62] Schechtman 1996, pp. 76, 80–89.

are to be considered *less fully* theirs and are less attributable to that person. Gross errors of fact or interpretive inaccuracies will, moreover, *diminish* personhood. On Schechtman's view, "when a narrative is disrupted or discontinuous, the *degree* of identity is correspondingly decreased".[63] Identities are thus inherently dynamic, as individuals constantly change and evolve, while making sense of themselves by reconciling these changes into a coherent self-narrative.[64] Changes in narrative identity are consequently not necessarily problematic in and of themselves – people will always change in many different ways throughout their lives.[65]

As narrative identity is concerned with how people process their subjective experiences into a coherent, self-told story, this account seems well-equipped to capture (some of the) normative concerns regarding neurotechnology and personal identity. After all, most of these concerns reference the way people *experience* the acute or long-term (side) effects of neurotechnological brain stimulation, such as subjective experiences of self-estrangement.[66] Recall how persons have reported no longer feeling like themselves following DBS treatment – with some asserting statements like, "Now I feel like a machine, I've lost my passion. I don't recognize myself anymore"; "I feel like a robot"; "I feel like an electronic doll"; "I haven't found myself again after the operation", as well as patients perceiving sudden improvements after DBS as "my second birth".[67] Considering examples like these, Ienca and Andorno highlight that "people's *perception* of their own identity may be put at risk by inadequate uses of emerging neurotechnology" and that changing a person's brain functioning with brain stimulation may impact on "the crucial requirement of personal identity consisting in *experiencing oneself* as persisting though time as the same person".[68] As the Advisory Committee of the Human Rights Council put it: DBS patients "have reported *feeling* a changed *sense* of agency and identity".[69] On the face of it, these concerns seem to relate more to narrative identity than to psychological continuity.

After all, within the narrative self-constitution view of identity, Holmen explains, the relevant question is whether the effect of a neurointervention is a threat to the narratives that individuals construct about themselves.[70] Hence, when brain stimulation disrupts these narratives, by inducing an abrupt and radical change in how the person perceives, experiences or feels (about) themselves, it may possibly interfere with narrative identity.

63 Schechtman 2009, p. 84 (emphasis added).
64 Pugh 2020, p. 1662.
65 Schermer 2009, p. 46.
66 Gilbert et al. 2017.
67 Schüpach et al. 2006.
68 Ienca & Andorno 2017, p. 20 (emphasis added).
69 Advisory Committee, UNHRC, Impact, opportunities and challenges of neurotechnology with regard to the promotion and protection of all human rights, A/HRC/AC/31/CRP.1 (8 August 2024), par. 27, footnote 36.
70 Holmen 2022, p. 742.

Schechtman herself sees the narrative view as a particularly useful framework in relation to psychological changes induced by DBS.[71] She argues that the acute changes sometimes experienced in this regard

> can disrupt a patient's personal narrative through both the rapidity and manner of change. The psychological changes brought about are so profound and occur so quickly that they can seem to break off one narrative – the story of a depressed person – and start a new one – that of a happy person.[72]

Recalling the articulation constraint, such abrupt and radical changes require an explanation. However, in cases of neurointervention, these changes are caused by direct stimulation of the brain as opposed to developing naturally from a person's intentions, beliefs, desires, emotions, values and plans. There is thus a *prima facie* tension with the articulation constraint, as a person subject to direct modification of the brain might not be able to articulate *just why* they now hold a certain attitude or desire – that is, they might not be able to identify the reasons justifying their holding such an attitude, or account for why they endorse it – even if they can detail that they adopted this attitude following DBS. Moreover, if the person in such a case came up with a story telling that the changes are a result of personal development, rather than of DBS, they would run afoul of the *reality constraint*, as such a self-narrative would be inconsistent with the basic, observable features of reality.[73]

Furthermore, apart from acute psychological changes, Schechtman argues that the long-term effects of brain stimulation could sometimes interfere with narrative identity too. Patients who report adjustment problems following such treatment often have difficulty perceiving their lives as the continuation of the life they were living before. They must reinvent themselves. As Schechtman puts it: "The metaphor of 'second birth,' while it can signify new beginnings, also signifies the loss of one's old identity."[74]

However, considering DBS to treat patients with Parkinson's disease, Baylis thinks it is unclear why a patient cannot satisfy the articulation constraint by including their consent to DBS in the patient's self-narrative.[75] What matters for narrative identity is whether personal events and experiences can be integrated into an identity-constituting narrative. Patients suffering from mental or neurological conditions may have good reasons to choose DBS treatment, which in and of itself affects their story and contributes to the dynamic and continuously evolving self-narrative. Hence, psychological changes induced by *consented* DBS need not diminish one's narrative identity by failing the articulation or reality constraint. Rather, they may well fit within the person's story, for example, of a patient combatting depression

71 Schechtman 2009, 2010. Cf. Glannon 2009; Schermer 2009; Mathews 2011; Witt et al. 2013; Mackenzie & Walker 2015; Goddard 2017; Pugh 2020.

72 Schechtman 2010, p. 137.

73 Schechtman 2009, pp. 85–86, 2010, p. 137; Pugh 2020, p. 1662.

74 Schechtman 2010, p. 138 (emphasis added).

75 Baylis 2013, p. 522. Cf. DeGrazia 2005b.

without success so far and who decides to try DBS. The abrupt and long-term changes induced by DBS, then, could be understood as caused by the patient's "desire to rid themselves of depression and their willingness to be treated in this way to do so", as Schechtman herself puts it.[76]

This can be different, though, when changes in the person's self-narrative result from force or oppression rather than free choice.[77] Unlike in cases of consent, when a person is forced to live according to constraints set by others who have fixed ideas about who the person is and who they should become, that person may no longer be able to contribute actively to authoring their own lives in a way consistent with their own interests, values, beliefs, desires and other personal characteristics.[78]

This could be particularly relevant to the use of brain stimulation in the context of criminal justice. This context is, in and of itself, coercive. Hardly anyone finds themselves in prison or forensic psychiatry out of free choice. Although convicted persons retain the possibility of making free choices, for example, to participate in a certain treatment or research study, the coercive context of criminal justice may affect the voluntariness of such decisions in some cases, which could, in turn, render the person's informed consent invalid.[79]

In the context of criminal justice, inducing abrupt psychological change by neurointervention, such as tDCS to reduce aggressiveness or sexual drive, *without valid consent*, seems to be a clear case of contravening the articulation constraint and could, therefore, diminish narrative identity. Obviously, the persuasiveness of this claim largely depends on the precise effects of the neurointervention in question. But we think it plausible that at least some types of neurointervention might have significant impact on the subject's self-narrative by altering personal characteristics (apart from possible side effects). One could think of a person convicted of assault, who experiences aggressive tendencies and outbursts since their adolescence, in fact, perceiving themselves as the aggressive "hothead" who always runs into trouble. When tDCS induces a significant and acute alteration of these aggressive characteristics in the absence of valid informed consent, the person's self-narrative will likely be disrupted, thereby threatening the person's narrative identity.

Whether such disruptions of a person's self-narrative will eventually affect their identity may, however, also depend on the person's long-term self-narrative, how neurointerventions are administered and the kind of support offered to the person receiving them. As Schechtman stresses regarding the clinical use of consensual DBS,

[76] Schechtman 2010, p. 138.

[77] Baylis 2013, p. 523. Like in a society where "a person's experiences will be significantly affected by stories others have constructed to restrict the range of narratives that can be appropriated and successfully enacted". As an example, Baylis mentions the threat to personal identity in this sense "experienced by women in a patriarchal society, by coloured people in a racist white society, and by gay people in a homophobic society".

[78] Baylis 2013, p. 523.

[79] For a discussion on this topic in relation to neurotechnology, see Pugh 2018.

> [s]ince narrative is a dynamic notion, continuity of narrative is thoroughly compatible with even quite radical change. The important thing is that the change be understood in a way that makes it part of a coherent personal narrative, one that patients and their close associates can see as, overall, *self-expressive and self-directed*. The exact nature of the support required will vary from individual to individual.[80]

From a long-term narrative perspective, she argues, changes that "may look like a narrative break, up close, can be seen as a small segment of a continuous and self-expressive life narrative".[81]

Regarding neurointerventions in criminal justice, one can imagine a convicted person who has been trying to reduce their aggressive outbursts and to rehabilitate themselves for years without success. Whereas they tried cognitive behavioural therapy and are willing to take medication, if available, to become less aggressive, the idea of electrical stimulation of their brain frightens them. Therefore, they do, initially, not consent to treatment with tDCS. However, they are informed by the prison staff that consenting to this treatment could increase the likelihood of their being granted parole. Feeling forced, they eventually participate in tDCS. Ultimately, the intervention significantly reduces the person's aggressiveness and facilitates their successful social rehabilitation, something with which they are very happy. Or alternatively, consider that the person in this scenario *is* willing to try a tDCS treatment and *does* voluntarily submit to it, but that their consent is invalid because the information provided to them – such as about risks and (side) effects – is insufficient.

Perhaps, in these scenarios, the non-consensual neurointervention need not ipso facto diminish narrative identity, if the induced psychological changes ultimately fit within the person's broader narrative of transforming their old "criminal life" towards a new "crime-free life". Although the neurointervention might induce abrupt psychological changes in the absence of valid consent, these changes may still cohere with the person's broader aspiration and earlier efforts to attain successful rehabilitation, and may actually contribute to their attaining this personal goal – fitting within the person's self-expressive life narrative (e.g., getting rid of aggressive tendencies that have been too strong to control). Offering the appropriate support throughout the process of neurorehabilitation may prove essential in this regard, to enable the person to conceive of their life after neurotechnological treatment as a continuation of their life before the intervention.

As such, consent need not be the defining factor that determines whether neurostimulation threatens the person's narrative identity. Still, there might be cases where nonconsensual neurointerventions in a forensic context will not cohere with the person's self-narrative and, therefore, interfere with narrative identity. If that is the case, we have the question: Would such an interference be morally problematic?

80 Schechtman 2010, p. 138 (emphasis added).
81 Schechtman 2010.

Interfering with narrative identity in criminal justice seems all but unique for neurotechnology. Being convicted for committing a criminal offence – especially the first time – may already have profound effects on the person's self-narrative, as will the execution of criminal sanctions, such as imprisonment.[82] As Hardie-Bick writes, "[a]lthough there are many lifecourse transitions that produce disequilibrium and require some form of readjustment, there are few transitions as difficult and demanding as adapting to life behind bars".[83] According to Ryberg, few (if any) theorists will accept the so-called "deep freeze view" on imprisonment – the view that assumes convicted persons remain totally unaffected by periods of incarceration.[84]

For example, studies have reported that those imprisoned frequently have (potentially) traumatic experiences, for example, due to violence often occurring in prison.[85] More generally, Cunha et al. highlight that imprisonment can be inherently damaging to mental health for a variety of reasons, including the "consequent disconnection from family, society, and social support, loss of autonomy, diminished meaning and purpose of life, fear of victimization, increased boredom, the unpredictability of surroundings, overcrowding and punitiveness, experiencing and witnessing violence, negative staff-prisoner interaction, and other aversive experiences".[86]

Apart from a wide range of damaging (psychological) effects, imprisonment can also change people's narratives positively. Drawing on interviews with former detainees, Maier and Ricciardelli write that "their narratives speak how imprisonment, by providing distinct space and time for reflection, functioned as a "hook" for self-change and the adoption of new narratives".[87] The key self-changes during imprisonment reported by the interviewees include "learning patience and being calmer; developing a drug-free narrative; realizing greater appreciation for loved ones; and gaining insights into their personal role in the path that led them to their incarceration".[88]

In fact, in criminal justice, we aim to trigger and induce narrative, mental and behavioural changes all the time, deploying different methods that range from deterrence and (solitary) confinement to mandatory resocialisation programmes, cognitive behavioural therapy, psychiatric treatment and the administration of psychotropic drugs including antipsychotics and antilibidinal medication.[89] Moreover, changing people's narratives and personal characteristics "for the better" – such as through reformation or correction – is arguably one of the primary objectives

82 Flanagan 1981; Hulley, Crewe & Wright 2016.
83 Hardie-Bick 2018, p. 576.
84 Ryberg 2020, p. 73.
85 Schnittker 2014; Piper & Berle 2019; Novisky & Peralta 2020.
86 Cunha et al. 2023 (references left out).
87 Maier & Ricciardelli 2022, p. 783. See also Crewe & Ievins 2020.
88 Maier & Ricciardelli 2022, p. 779.
89 See, e.g., Stevens 2012; Forsberg 2021.

of imprisonment (in combination with rehabilitative/treatment programmes) and forensic commitment.[90] Often, these measures aim at getting the robber to stop robbing, the alcoholic to stop drinking and those with aggressive tendencies to reduce and control them. As Article 10(3) of the International Covenant on Civil and Political Rights (ICCPR) prescribes: "[t]he penalty system shall comprise treatment of prisoners the essential aim of which shall be their reformation and social rehabilitation".

Still, despite these intended and unintended changes in the convicted person's self-narrative through traditional criminal sanctions (both "positive" and "negative"), incarceration and forensic treatment are not typically conceived of as being wrong for interfering with people's personal identity. Non-consensual interferences that may lead to changes in identity in this sense are often considered justified, for instance, to punish and to prevent harm to others. Against this background, we agree with Ryberg that it is difficult to reject the non-consensual use of neurointerventions solely on the grounds of personality changes and frustrating the person's experiences and self-awareness, while at the same time accepting and adhering to the use of incarceration as a form of punishment.[91] Interestingly, a recent study on public attitudes towards incarceration and "neuronormalization" showed that the participants ($n = 248$) "were more supportive of neuronormalization and considered it more ethical" than incarceration. Also, they "considered neuronormalization to be a weaker form of mind control than incarceration and would lead to more change for the better".[92]

2.3 HUMAN RIGHTS PROTECTION OF PERSONAL IDENTITY: THE CASE OF NEUROREHABILITATION

2.3.1 *Introduction*

As mentioned earlier, neurotechnologies that enable others to modify a person's mental processes – thereby, potentially interfering with their identity – have raised concerns in view of human rights. Three questions are relevant here: (i) does human rights law protect personal identity?, (ii) if so, to what extent? and (iii) what are the implications of this protection for the use of neurointerventions in criminal justice?

With respect to the first question, protecting people's personality and identity has a profound basis in human rights law. Article 22 of the Universal Declaration of Human Rights safeguards some essential conditions for dignity and the free

[90] For instance, as Ewing 2013, p. 73 writes, "[b]y the reformatory effects of punishment are generally understood any good effects punishment has on the moral character and outward habits of the man punished himself in abstraction from its effects on individuals other than the offender". See also Goffman 1961; Foucault 1975; Ellis 2012, p. 74.

[91] Ryberg 2020, p. 73.

[92] Denson, Griffiths & Smith 2024, p. 7. The authors describe "neuronormalization" as "brain-based treatments" for rehabilitation – something akin to neurointervention or neurorehabilitation as we have defined it (see Chapter 1).

development of personality. Article 8 of the United Nations Convention on the Rights of the Child recognises children's right to preserve their identity. And in the European context, Article 1 of the Oviedo Convention (a legally binding instrument on human rights in the biomedical field) prescribes that the parties "shall protect the dignity and identity of all human beings".

Elsewhere, a right to identity is indirectly protected. In the Inter-American context, it is implicit in the right to privacy of Article 11 of the American Convention on Human Rights (ACHR).[93] The same applies to the right to privacy pursuant to Article 17 ICCPR, supporting the protection of the individual's identity and self-autonomy.[94] The Human Rights Committee has repeatedly emphasised "that the notion of privacy refers to the sphere of a person's life in which he or she can freely express his or her identity, be it by entering into relationships with others or alone".[95] The United Nations High Commissioner for Human Rights similarly recognises that "[t]he right to privacy is an expression of human dignity and is linked to the protection of human autonomy and personal identity".[96] Elaborating on the connection between privacy and identity, Nowak/Schabas write, "privacy protects the special, individual qualities of human existence, a person's manner of appearance, his or her identity. Identity includes, in addition to one's name, appearance, clothing, hair and beard style, gender, genetic code, feelings and thoughts, specific past, as well as religious belief and other convictions".[97]

In the European context, the ECtHR likewise considers the notion of private life in the meaning of Article 8 ECHR to encompass a "right to identity" and a "right to personal development", in terms of either personality or personal autonomy.[98] The protection of personal identity makes many appearances in the case law of the ECtHR,[99] ranging from the protection of gender, genetic and biological identity,[100] and also ethnic and religious identity,[101] to the protection of social and national identity.[102] Marshall observes that the case law of the ECtHR reflects, in

93 *Obligaciones Estatales en Relación Con el Cambio de Nombre, la Identidad de Género, Y los Derechos Derivados de un Vínculo Entre Parejas del Mismo Sexo*, Advisory Opinion, Inter-American Court of Human Rights (24 November 2017) par. 87.

94 Taylor 2020, p. 4. See also Mater & Murray 2025.

95 *Coeriel and Aurik* v. *The Netherlands*, CCPR/C/48/D/453/1991, 8 July 1993, par. 10.2.

96 High Commissioner, *The right to privacy in the digital age*, 13 September 2021, A/HRC/48/31, par. 7.

97 Nowak/Schabas 2019, p. 467, with further references.

98 ECtHR 15 January 2009, 1234/05 (*Reklos and Davourlis/Greece*), par. 39. Cf ECtHR 18 October 2022, 215/19 (*Basu* v. *Germany*), par. 2; ECtHR 30 January 2020, 50001/12 (*Breyer/Germany*), par. 73.

99 Marshall 2016, 2022; Tamimi 2018; Harris et al. 2023, pp. 521–524.

100 For example, ECtHR 1 December 2022, 57864/17, 79087/17 and 55353/19 (*A D and Others/Georgia*), par. 48; ECtHR 27 August 2015, 46470/11 (*Parrillo/Italy*), par. 158–159. See also Marshall 2016, p. 89 et seq.

101 For example, ECtHR 27 April 2010, 27138/04 (*Ciubotaru* v. *Moldova*), par. 53; ECtHR (GC) 10 November 2005, 44774/98 (*Leyla Şahin* v. *Turkey*), par. 104. See also Marshall 2016, p. 142 et seq.

102 For example, ECtHR 11 October 2018, 55216/08 (SV v. *Italy*), par. 54; ECtHR 25 June 2020, 52273/16 (*Ghoumid and Others/France*), par 43. See also Tamimi 2018.

general, a kind of self-determined and fluid version of identity and personal freedom.[103] It acknowledges "the importance of building and retaining an ability and capacity that is each person's domain, to enable them to think reflectively without interference, to be in control of their own faculties, to decide their own plan of life".[104]

Marshall unpacks the protection of two general conditions of identity formation in the ECtHR's case law: that is, the protection of our minds and bodies.[105] These conditions link closely to the normative concerns voiced in the literature about neurotechnology and personal identity. As discussed in section 2.2, those concerns relate to the ability of neurotechnology to induce significant changes in a person's brain (body) and mental states (mind) – which according to some could disrupt *psychological continuity*, while according to others are better understood as a potential interference with *narrative identity*. The extent to which existing human rights protect both psychological continuity and narrative identity, and the implications of this protection for the neurorehabilitation of convicted persons, is discussed in the following sections.[106]

2.3.2 *Psychological Continuity*

To what extent do human rights protect psychological continuity? Elsewhere, one of us has argued that interference with psychological continuity in the Parfitian sense is likely to infringe (1) the right to identity and (2) the right to personal integrity, both protected under Article 8 ECHR and, to some extent, Article 3 ECHR.[107] In this section, we reflect on these rights, also in view of the ICCPR.

2.3.2.1 The Right to Identity

Human rights protection of psychological continuity has been considered essential to guarantee "the continuity across a person's habitual thoughts, preferences, and choices by protecting the underlying neural functioning".[108] It has been argued that a right to psychological continuity would protect against emerging technologies that can modify brain functioning and, ultimately, guarantee the coherence of people's behaviour and the preservation of their personal identity.[109] To some extent, protection of psychological continuity seems to be covered by the general right to identity, which is inherent in the right to privacy and private life. For example, in the case of *Odièvre* v. *France*, the Grand Chamber of the ECtHR emphasised that "Article 8

103 Marshall 2009, p. 96, 2016, p. 241.
104 Marshall 2022, p. 13.
105 Marshall 2022, pp. 18–19. See also Marshall 2016, p. 237.
106 As argued in section 2.2, in our view, narrative identity seems most relevant in this context.
107 Ligthart 2024.
108 Ienca & Andorno 2017, p. 21.
109 Ienca & Andorno 2017, p. 21.

protects a right to identity and personal development, and the right to establish and develop relationships with other human beings and the outside world. (...) The preservation of *mental stability* is in that context an indispensable precondition to effective enjoyment of the right to respect for private life".[110]

As it appears, the ECtHR considers mental stability to be an "indispensable precondition" for identity under the right to respect for private life. This can be taken to mean that destabilizing a person's mental states or capacities could obstruct the effective enjoyment of the right to identity. Although "mental stability" and "psychological continuity" are not identical,[111] they do share the feature that their preservation is an indispensable precondition for the safeguarding of personal identity. As discussed in section 2.2, disrupting psychological continuity is considered to destroy numerical identity, causing the person to cease to exist. If mental stability is required for preserving identity, then for sure psychological continuity is required too, as any breaches of psychological continuity are so heavy that they will certainly count as causing mental instability.

In her work on human rights protection of identity and personal freedom, Marshall writes that our inner mind – the personal space that produces our thoughts – needs security and legal protection to enable us to be our own person. Humans need the ability to fulfil their capacities; they need a personal space to develop themselves. If that space is the brain, Marshall argues, then

> how that brain develops or is allowed to develop in and through the societies or social spaces it finds itself in, are surely included, or ought to be, in the legal protection of any right to personal identity. This is in line with the right to private life protected in human rights treaties' provisions; an understanding that we have integrity in our own thoughts and conscience, within our body. Each person is entitled to retain an ability and capacity to enable them to think reflectively without interference; to be in control of their own faculties.[112]

Put differently, the formation and development of personal identity requires, among other things, the ability to freely develop and control our personal thoughts, beliefs, desires and other mental faculties – without restrictions or interference by others. For instance, considering Article 17 ICCPR, Nowak/Schabas state that identity, as part of privacy, includes feelings and thoughts, the forceful influencing of which constitutes a rights infringement, "e.g., by way of mandatory treatment with psychoactive drugs that changes personalities, by way of 'brainwashing' or other manipulation of the subconscious without the awareness of the person concerned".[113]

[110] ECtHR (GC) 13 February 2003, 42326/98 (*Odièvre/France*), par. 29 (emphasis added). See also ECtHR 6 February 2001, 44599/98 (*Bensaid/the United Kingdom*), par. 47.

[111] They may overlap, though. The ECtHR does not specify what it means with mental stability, leaving room for interpretation.

[112] Marshall 2022, pp. 18–19.

[113] Nowak/Schabas 2019, p. 467.

If the right to personal identity covers the protection of brain development and mental stability, and if it aims to guarantee control over one's own mental faculties, then it is plausible that such a right covers the protection of a person's psychological connections to oneself, such as in terms of memories, intentions, beliefs, goals, desires and similarity of character. It is, then, plausible that the right to personal identity covers the protection of the person's psychological continuity.

The relevance of this protection for the neurorehabilitation of convicted persons may be limited, though – as far as psychological continuity is concerned. As argued in section 2.2.1, the mental effects of neurointerventions to reduce recidivism are, generally, too minor to induce a disruption of psychological continuity, at least in the Parfitian sense. That said, when in a specific case, for example, due to wrongful application or severe side effects, brain stimulation *does* induce a global and radical decline of the person's psychological connections – disrupting psychological continuity or otherwise adversely affecting a person's "mental stability" – the right to identity is plausibly infringed.

It is noteworthy that case law on the right to identity is still relatively scarce and highly casuistic. In human rights law, the concept of identity appears far less developed compared to understandings of identity in ethics and philosophy. For instance, although it is clear from the ECtHR jurisprudence that the protection of personal identity links to preserving the person's mental stability, a well-developed approach about what "mental stability" would require as a precondition of personal identity, has not yet been articulated. Hence, much is still open for interpretation – which might benefit from the philosophical discourse and conceptualisations of personal identity. While we should be careful of drawing general conclusions and overinterpreting the protective scope of the right to identity, we should remain open to the possibility that this right may protect persons against third party-induced disruptions of psychological continuity, including with the use of neurotechnologies. After all, human rights, the ECHR in particular, are to be considered a "living instrument", which should be interpreted in view of present-day conditions, including societal, bioethical and technological developments.[114] This "dynamic" or "evolutive" interpretation enables the rights and freedoms guaranteed within the ECHR to be applied to modern societies and to keep up with persisting progress in emerging technologies.[115]

2.3.2.2 The Right to Personal Integrity

The right to identity closely relates to the right to personal integrity. As Marshall observes, the interpretation of the human right to personal identity is intertwined

[114] Taylor 2020, p. 18; Gerards 2023, p. 106.
[115] Mowbray 2013, p. 17.

with the right to personal integrity as recognised under Article 8 ECHR.[116] Regarding Article 17 ICCPR, Nowak/Schabas write that "some practices of forcibly changing the identity of a human being, such as mandatory treatment with psychoactive drugs, also serves to illustrate a second manifestation of individual existence that is covered by the right to privacy: the protection of personal integrity".[117] In the same vein, Tiedemann notes that some human rights protect physical and mental integrity, "whose severe violation leads to the loss of personal identity".[118]

The right to personal integrity receives full consideration in Chapter 3. For now, it suffices to highlight that the right is usually taken to cover the protection of *physical* and *psychological* integrity.[119] In general, the right to physical integrity covers a right against non-consensual interferences with one's body.[120] The contours of the right to psychological integrity are less clear.[121] Yet, we know that it at least covers the protection of mental health as a crucial part of private life.[122]

The rights to physical and psychological integrity plausibly cover the protection of a person's "psychological continuity". Whereas the rights to physical and psychological integrity protect against non-consensual interference with, broadly speaking, the body and mind, psychological continuity is concerned with a particular aspect of the body and the mind – that is, the brain and the continuity across specific psychological features such as memories, preferences and choices.[123] The latter seems part of the former.

Ienca and Andorno acknowledge that a right to psychological continuity would partly overlap with the right to mental integrity. But they argue for the need for a specific human right to psychological continuity because they claim that a right to psychological continuity can be threatened in cases where no infringement of the right to mental integrity takes place. In their view, infringing the latter right requires the infliction of physical or psychological *harm*, while the former does not: "the right to psychological continuity also applies to emerging scenarios that do not directly

116 Marshall 2022, p. 13, also Marshall 2016, p. 41. Moreover, the Grand Chamber appears to consider the preservation of a person's physical and psychological integrity as a prerequisite for the protection of personal identity: "The concept of 'private life' is a broad term (. . .) It covers the physical and psychological integrity of a person, *and can therefore embrace* multiple aspects of the person's identity such as, for example, gender identification, sexual orientation, name and elements relating to a person's right to his or her image" ECtHR (GC) 29 March 2016, 56925/08 (*Bédat/Switzerland*), par. 72 (emphasis added). See also ECtHR (GC) 25 September 2018, 76639/11 (*Denisov* v. *Ukraine*) par. 95.

117 Nowak/Schabas 2019, p. 468.

118 Tiedemann 2015, p. 27.

119 See, e.g., Nowak/Schabas 2019, pp. 467, 468. See also ECtHR (GC) 29 March 2016, 56925/08 (*Bédat/Switzerland*), par. 72; General Comment No. 35: Article 9 CCPR/C/GC/35, par. 3.

120 ECtHR 22 July 2003, 24209/94 (*YF* v. *Turkey*), par. 33.

121 Bublitz 2020a; Michalowski 2020.

122 ECtHR 26 November 2009, 25282/06 (*Dolenec/Croatia*), par. 165; ECtHR, 6 February 2001, 44599/98 (*Bensaid/the United Kingdom*), par. 47.

123 Ienca & Andorno 2017, p. 21.

involve neural or mental harm".[124] Accordingly, Ienca and Andorno argue that the right can "be threatened not only by misused brain stimulation but also by less invasive, even unperceivable interventions. A good example is unconscious neural advertising via neuromarketing".[125]

Whether disruptions to psychological continuity will ever occur in scenarios that do not involve any neural or mental harm is, however, doubtful. This would at least depend on how one defines "psychological continuity". Recall that on the Parfitian understanding, psychological continuity means that a person has an overlapping chain of *strong* psychological connections to oneself across time, such that for an interference to disrupt psychological continuity, *more than half* the number of the person's psychological connections should be destroyed, compared to a normal, actual person. On this understanding, it seems implausible that psychological continuity will be disrupted by a mental interference without the occurrence of *any* neural or mental harm whatsoever.

Consider, for example, how the severing of a significant amount of one's psychological connections in terms of memories, intentions, beliefs and desires plausibly harms a person on a range of theories of well-being. At one level, the disruption of psychological continuity harms a person on each of mental state,[126] preferentist[127] and objective list accounts[128] of well-being,[129] insofar as the severing of intentions, beliefs, memories, desires et cetera either is experienced as distressing (mental state theories), prevents a person satisfying their desires (preferentist theories) or deprives a person of something objectively valuable such as knowledge (objective list theories). But most obviously, and insofar as significant disruption of psychological continuity implies a loss of numerical identity, the person whose psychological continuity is disrupted is harmed simply because they are made to no longer exist, and as such cannot have a level of well-being anymore.

If a neurointervention inflicts such acute and global mental deterioration – for instance, due to severe side effects or wrongful application – it may even amount to cruel, inhuman or degrading treatment, which is prohibited in absolute terms by Articles 7 ICCPR and 3 ECHR.[130] Tiedemann notes this in asserting that "[s]ome human rights protect physical and mental integrity whose severe violation leads to

124 The distinction between harmful and harmless interferences with people's brains and mental faculties may be appealing in normative evaluations of emerging neurotechnology. However, whether it adds to a compelling argument to distinguish a right to psychological continuity from the right to psychological integrity can be challenged: Ligthart 2024. For example, it is doubtful whether infringing the right to psychological integrity indeed requires the infliction of physical and/or psychological harm (see Chapter 3, section 3.3.1).

125 Ienca & Andorno 2017, p. 22.

126 Crisp 2006.

127 Heathwood 2016.

128 Fletcher 2013.

129 See Parfit 1984, appendix C for this tripartite classification of theories of well-being.

130 Ligthart 2024.

loss of personal identity. This is evidenced by the ban of torture and inhuman and degrading treatment and punishment".[131]

Illustrative in this regard is a recent statement of the UN Special Rapporteur on torture and other cruel, inhuman or degrading treatment or punishment. In their report on psychological torture and ill-treatment, the Rapporteur explicitly refers to the potential threats of neurotechnology in relation to profound disruptions of a person's "mental identity", "capacity" and "autonomy". Drawing attention to the rapid advances in medical, pharmaceutical and neurotechnological science, the Rapporteur highlights the difficulty of predicting to what extent future techniques of torture, as well as the enhancement of people's mental and emotional resilience, may allow the manipulation, circumvention or suppression of the subjective experiences of pain and suffering, while *still* attaining the dehumanising, debilitating and incapacitating effects of torture.[132] Against this background, the Rapporteur stresses that states must interpret and exercise the prohibition of torture in good faith and in light of the evolving values of democratic societies, emphasising that it would be

> irreconcilable with the object and purpose of the universal, absolute and non-derogable prohibition of torture, for example, to exclude from the definition of torture the profound disruption of a person's mental identity, capacity or autonomy only because the victim's subjective experience or recollection of "mental suffering" has been pharmaceutically, hypnotically or otherwise manipulated or suppressed.[133]

In the European context, too, it is not implausible that the ECtHR would qualify a non-consensual disruption of over half a person's psychological connections to oneself in the Parfitian sense through a neurointervention as "degrading", which the ECHR defines as a treatment that "humiliates or debases an individual, showing a lack of respect for, or diminishing, his or her human dignity, or when it arouses feelings of fear, anguish or inferiority capable of breaking an individual's moral and physical resistance".[134] We come back to this in Chapter 3.

2.3.3 *Narrative Identity*

Let us now turn to the protection of narrative identity. To what extent is the way people *experience* themselves and *process* those experiences into a coherent, autobiographical story, protected by human rights law? And what might such legal protections imply for the neurorehabilitation of convicted persons?

[131] Tiedemann 2015, p. 27.

[132] UN Special Rapporteur on Torture and other cruel, inhuman or degrading treatment or punishment, 20 March 2020, A/HRC/43/49, par. 32.

[133] UN Special Rapporteur on Torture and other cruel, inhuman or degrading treatment or punishment, 20 March 2020, A/HRC/43/49, par. 32.

[134] ECtHR (GC)17 July 2014, 32541/08 and 43441/08 (*Svinarenko and Slyadnev* v. *Russia*) par. 115.

Protecting and ensuring certain enabling preconditions for the construction of one's own narrative identity appears to be subject to human rights law, in particular to the right to respect for private life – though the term "narrative identity" is not mentioned in the relevant case law and scholarly literature.[135] Marshall highlights that human rights can be vital "in allowing identity *formation*, through creating the social conditions to enable an individual to develop their personality and identity as they wish".[136] The idea of identity formation also has affinities with the idea of narrative construction, giving the "authoring" suggested by both. Marshall stresses that freedom as self-direction and self-development is not something individuals sustain and develop on their own in isolation from the outside world. Rather, the development and preservation of identity partly takes place in relation and conversation with others, within the social environments we find ourselves in.[137] Think of how the right to freely develop, change and adhere to a certain religion or belief, and to manifest one's religious identity – for example, through dress or going to church – is protected by the right to freedom of religion and belief.[138] Consider, too, how access to information about one's origins[139] and the preservation of objects of ancestral significance[140] have each been considered to potentially be significant for identity formation and self-development and hence subject to human rights protection[141] – and also how these factors seem to pertain to narrative identity specifically.

With respect to access to information about one's origins, the Glover Report on Reproductive Technologies for the European Commission noted that "our sense of who we are is bound up with the *story* we tell about ourselves. A life where the biological parents are unknown is like a novel with the first chapter missing".[142] Such a missing chapter may frustrate the person's ability to answer the characterisation question central to narrative identity: "Who am I really?" The importance of having access to information about one's origins for identity formation is acknowledged by the ECtHR. In cases on paternity dispute, for example, the Court observed that people "have a vital interest, protected by the Convention, in receiving the information necessary to uncover the truth about an important aspect of their personal identity".[143] It further observed that respect for private life in the meaning of Article 8 ECHR "requires that everyone should be able to establish details of their identity as individual human beings", with the individual's entitlement to such information

135 Cf. Marshall 2016, p. 26.

136 Marshall 2016, p. 241 (emphasis added).

137 Cf. Marshall 2016, p. 19.

138 Cf. Nowak/Schabas 2019, p. 467; Marshall 2009, pp. 139–161, 2016, p. 21.

139 ECtHR 7 February 2002, 53176/99 (*Mikulić/Croatia*), par. 64.

140 *Hopu and Tepoaitu Bessert* v. *France*, CCPR/C/60/D/549/1993/Rev.1., 29 December 1997.

141 Marshall 2009, p. 123.

142 Glover et al. 1989, p. 37 (emphasis added).

143 ECtHR 7 February 2002, 53176/99 (*Mikulić/Croatia*), par. 64.

being "of importance because of its *formative implications* for his or her personality".[144]

With respect to the preservation of objects of ancestral significance, the Human Rights Committee in the case of *Hopu and Bessert* v. *France* interpreted the protection of identity under Article 17 ICCPR as sometimes covering the protection of objects that people see as connecting them with their ancestors. In this case, the applicants, both ethnic Polynesians, complained that the construction of a luxury hotel on the site of their ancestral burial grounds would arbitrarily interfere with their privacy in violation of Article 17 ICCPR, because these burial grounds have an important place in their history, culture and life. The Human Rights Committee noted that it "transpires from the authors' claims that they consider the relationship to their ancestors to be an essential element of their identity". The majority agreed and concluded that there had been an arbitrary interference with Article 17 ICCPR.[145] Because the applicants in this case *perceived* the relationship to their ancestors as significant to, or even constitutive of, their identity, human rights protection of identity applied.

Although there may be no direct link between these cases and narrative identity, the examples illustrate that for the human rights protection of people's identity, personal narratives matter at least sometimes. They indicate that at least some aspects of a person's narrative, and some enabling preconditions for answering the characterisation question, receive protection by the human right to personal identity as part of the rights to privacy and private life. As pointed out earlier, according to Schechtman, the most familiar examples of the characterisation question are "questions of which characteristics are *truly* those of some person (as opposed, say, to those which are his as a result of hypnosis, brainwashing, or some other form of coercion)".[146] Altering personal characteristics and behavioural traits through neurotechnology has the potential to impact on how persons experience themselves – especially when this takes places without valid – free and informed – consent (section 2.2.2). It appears safe to say that even more than receiving information about one's origins or the intactness of historic sites and cultural heritage, a person's unmanipulated brain and mental states – memories, in particular, as the psychological "equivalent" of ancient sites – are important, enabling preconditions for narrative identity formation. If the former are protected through the right to identity, then there is reason to think that the latter should be too.

Furthermore, the self-constitution and formation of personal identity may also be covered by the more general protection of *self-determination*,[147] also enshrined in Articles 8 ECHR and Article 17 ICCPR. For example, regarding Article 17 ICCPR, Nowak/Schabas note that "privacy covers the area of individual autonomy in which

144 ECtHR 7 February 2002, 53176/99 (*Mikulić/Croatia*), par. 54 (emphasis added).
145 *Hopu and Tepoaitu Bessert* v. *France*, CCPR/C/60/D/549/1993/Rev.1., 29 December 1997.
146 Schechtman 1996, p. 73.
147 Marshall 2016, p. 241.

human beings strive to achieve self-realization", which "liberty of action" is "inherent in private self-determination".[148] Taylor speaks in this context of human rights that protect the individual's "identity and self-autonomy", including in the dimensions of gender, sexuality and religion.[149] In the jurisprudence of the ECtHR, self-determination is closely linked to the notion of personal autonomy,[150] the latter being an important principle underlying the interpretation of Article 8 ECHR.[151] According to the Grand Chamber of the ECtHR, "a right to self-determination" can be derived from the umbrella right to respect for private life pursuant to Article 8 ECHR.[152] Among other things, it embraces a right to "informational self-determination" and a right to "sexual self-determination".[153] Although the ECtHR has not yet clearly articulated the meaning and scope of the right to self-determination, the right protects at least some aspects of a person's identity.[154]

This follows most evidently from the case law on sexual orientation and gender identity. According to the ECtHR, gender identity and sexual orientation are one of the most intimate aspects of private life,[155] qualifying the latter as "an essentially private manifestation of human personality".[156] The right to self-determination not only protects from interference with private sexual *behaviour* but also guarantees a freedom to self-create, reshape and develop different aspects of the person's (sexual) *identity*, for instance, by *defining* oneself as either a male or female. As the Court puts it:

> The Court further reiterates that the notion of personal autonomy is an important principle underlying the interpretation of the guarantees of Article 8 of the Convention. This has led it to recognise, in the context of the application of that provision to transgender persons, that it includes a right to self-determination, of which the *freedom to define* one's sexual identity is one of the most basic essentials.[157]

The Human Rights Committee has approached the freedom to define one's own sexual identity as part of the protection of a person's identity and gender identity under Article 17 ICCPR. For example, the complaint in G. v. *Australia* concerned an Australian law that did not allow a transgender person to change the reference to

148 Nowak/Schabas 2019, p. 472.
149 Taylor 2020, p. 4.
150 ECtHR 29 April 2002, 2346/02 (*Pretty/the United Kingdom*), par. 61.
151 ECtHR (GC) 11 July 2002, 28957/95 (*Christine Goodwin/UK*), par. 90.
152 ECtHR (GC) 27 August 2015, 46470/11 (*Parrillo/Italy*), par. 153.
153 ECtHR (GC) 27 June 2017, 931/13 (*Satakunnan Markkinapörssi Oy and Satamedia Oy/Finland*), par. 137; ECtHR 12 June 2003, 35968/97 (*Van Kück/Germany*), par. 78.
154 Marshall 2009, pp. 121–122.
155 ECtHR 12 June 2003, 35968/97 (*Van Kück/Germany*), par. 56; ECtHR 2 March 2010, 13102/02 (*Kozak/Poland*), par. 83.
156 ECtHR 27 September 1999, 33985/96 and 33986/96 (*Smith and Grady/UK*), par. 127.
157 ECtHR 11 October 2018, 55216/08 (*S.V./Italy*), par. 55 (emphasis added); ECtHR 10 March 2015, 14793/08 (*Y.Y./Turkey*), par. 102; ECtHR 12 June 2003, 35968/97 (*Van Kück/Germany*), par. 73 and 78.

her sex on the birth certificate unless she divorced from her spouse (with whom she had a happy relationship). The Human Rights Committee stressed that the right to privacy of Article 17 ICCPR includes the protection of the person's identity and gender identity and found the Australian law to constitute an arbitrary interference with the person's privacy and family life.[158] Nowak/Schabas note that identity often manifests itself in official documents, such as birth certificates.[159] Such pieces of information and official reference can play an important role in the development of people's narratives and, therefore, in the self-constitution of their identity.

Considering the case law on gender identity and sexual orientation, Marshall observes that the Court's conception of "freedom" under Article 8 ECHR could be interpreted as "self-creation or self-determination", protecting the freedom to be and become the person one chooses, "in keeping with their own sense of their identity in a self-determining sense".[160] The right to personal identity in this context allows individuals to freely change, develop and create their identities, "rather than bringing to realisation some essence within".[161] As such, personal identity as protected under Article 8 ECHR is flexible and dynamic, rather than fixed and static. As Judge Martens phrased it in a dissenting opinion dating back to 1990, "[h]uman dignity and human freedom imply that a man should be free to shape himself and his fate in the way that he deems best fits his personality".[162]

This shaping of the self can take different forms, one of them being the processing of our personal experiences into a coherent, autobiographical story of our lives. Such a self-determining interpretation of human freedom in relation to personal identity fits well within the general view that the right to respect for private life "secures to the individual a sphere within which he can freely pursue the development and fulfilment of his personality".[163] If this self-creating and self-determining freedom is interfered with by brain stimulation that disrupts a person's self-narrative, for example, in the context of neurorehabilitation, the right to self-determination, including the freedom to define one's own identity, will likely be infringed.

2.3.4 *Implications for Neurorehabilitation*

Human rights protect personal identity. Meanwhile, many of the concepts referred to in this context, such as identity, personality and mental stability, are still ill-defined in the law.[164] In addition, the theoretical underpinnings of the human rights

[158] G. v. *Australia*, CCPR/C/119/D/2172/2012, 28 June 2017. See also Report of the UN Special Rapporteur on the right to privacy, 16 October 2019, A/HRC/40/63.

[159] Nowak/Schabas 2019, p. 468.

[160] Marshall 2009, pp. 104, 122.

[161] Marshall 2009, pp. 104, 122.

[162] Dissenting opinion Judge Martens, 27 September 1990, 10843/84 (*Cossey/UK*), par. 2.7.

[163] ECtHR 28 October 2014, 49327/11 (*Gough/UK*), par. 182; ECtHR 23 March 2017, 53251/13 (*A.-M.V./Finland*), par. 76.

[164] Cf. Bou-Sfia 2024, p. 5.

protection of identity are, by and large, undefined and, thus, unclear. Contrary to philosophy, in human rights law, personal identity lacks clear conceptual consideration. The protection of identity appears to develop ad hoc, through individual cases and complaints and is, therefore, fragmented and specified to the facts of those cases. At best, scholars can interpret individual cases and decisions and relate them to specific theoretical accounts of identity, or defend a specific account they think is most appropriate to substantiate a human right to identity.[165]

We showed that under the ICCPR and ECHR, there is no explicit recognition of either Parfit's psychological continuity or Schechtman's narrative identity account. However, as argued in the previous section, there are reasons to assume that, implicitly, these types of identity receive protection from human rights. Interference with both narrative identity and psychological continuity may sometimes infringe the rights to identity and self-determination, which are inherent in the right to privacy. Disrupting a person's psychological continuity may furthermore infringe the right to personal integrity.

Let us for now assume that, to some extent, both psychological continuity and narrative identity receive protection within the established framework of human rights, in particular through the right to identity inherent in the right to privacy/private life.[166] Let us also assume that in some cases the use of brain stimulation for the rehabilitation of convicted persons can infringe the right to identity. Then, the next question is whether and under what conditions such an infringement could be justified, or whether certain neurotechnological interferences with the identity of convicted persons will be prohibited across the board.

As the protection of identity is part of the *qualified* right to privacy, it is subject to limitations. Both under Article 17 ICCPR and 8 ECHR, infringements of the right to privacy can be justified when having a (non-arbitrary) legal basis and being proportionate to a legitimate aim, such as the prevention of crime and the protection of the rights and freedoms of others.[167] For example, some types of non-consensual medical interventions, such as taking blood for DNA analysis, infringe the right to private life under Article 8 ECHR, but can still be justified for obtaining evidence of the person's involvement in the commission of a criminal offence.[168] Furthermore, non-consensual medical treatment, which would normally infringe the right to respect for private life, could be justified in case of "medical necessity".[169] Whether and when interference with a convicted person's identity through a neurointervention could be justified is hard to predict. This will depend on a range of factors that vary across individual cases, such as the induced neural, psychological and behavioural

165 See, e.g., Marshall 2009, 2016, 2022; Mater & Murray 2025.
166 The right to personal integrity will be further elaborated upon in Chapter 3.
167 Lavrysen 2018; Nowak/Schabas 2019, pp. 463–446.
168 ECtHR 15 May 2018, 41079/16 (*Caruana/Malta*), par. 31; ECtHR (GC) 11 July 2006, 54810/00 (*Jalloh/Germany*), par. 70.
169 Buelens, Herijgers & Illegems 2016; Harris et al. 2023, p. 528.

changes, and the purpose of the intervention, for example, whether it is employed for medical reasons or to prevent severe or less severe crimes.

Here, we will not estimate which types of identity change caused by neurointerventions may or may not be permissible under different conditions. Rather, we wish to highlight a more general feature of identity interference that emerges, specifically, from the ECtHR case law – which may inform our thinking about the (im)permissibility of identity-affecting neurointerventions in criminal justice more broadly. This particularity relates to the margin of appreciation doctrine developed in the jurisprudence of the ECtHR.

In determining whether an infringement of the right to respect for private life is proportionate to the legitimate aim it pursues, the national authorities enjoy a *margin of appreciation*, which can either be "wide", "certain" or "narrow".[170] The narrower this margin, the stricter the ECtHR's review of the proportionality of a rights infringement.[171] The broader this margin, the more discretion states enjoy in striking a "fair balance" between the competing personal and public interests at stake.[172] The breadth of this margin of appreciation varies across individual cases and depends on a number of relevant factors,[173] such as the context of the interference and the level of consensus among the member states of the Council of Europe, either as to the relative importance of the interest at issue or as to the best way of protecting it.[174]

Another relevant factor concerns the *importance* of the right at stake. In principle, the margin of appreciation will be narrow when the "essence" or "core" of a convention right is affected. Gerards explains this approach from the perspective of effective protection of the ECHR in relation to the principle of subsidiarity: the more important a right, the more reason for supervision on how that right is guaranteed on the national level.[175] The ECtHR has identified four central values underlying the ECHR: democracy and the rule of law, pluralism, human dignity, and personal autonomy. According to Gerards,

> core rights reasoning generally implies that the closer a certain aspect of a right is related to these central values, the more important it can be considered to be. By contrast, the more a certain aspect is in the periphery of the right, the less weighty it is. It is precisely because restrictions of core rights might endanger the achievement of the Convention's central objectives that the Court finds it justified to apply strict scrutiny.[176]

170 Lavrysen 2018, p. 328.

171 For example, adopting a strict review could imply that the ECtHR requires an infringement not simply to pursue a "legitimate aim" but is grounded in "compelling" or "very weighty" reasons.

172 Gerards 2023, Ch. 8.

173 Gerards 2023, p. 255.

174 ECtHR (GC) 24 January 2017, 25358/12 (*Paradiso and Campanelli/Italy*), par. 182; ECtHR 13 February 2020, 45245/15 (*Gaughran/UK*), par. 77 and 84.

175 Gerards 2023, p. 272.

176 Gerards 2023, pp. 272–273.

Under Article 8 ECHR, the ECtHR has repeatedly stated that when "a particularly important facet of an *individual's existence* or *identity* is at stake, the margin allowed to the State will be restricted".[177] For example, in a case on the legal recognition of a parent-child relationship after surrogacy, the ECtHR held that "regard should also be had to the fact that an essential aspect of the identity of individuals is at stake where the legal parent-child relationship is concerned. The margin of appreciation afforded to the respondent State in the present case therefore needs to be reduced".[178] In another case, the ECtHR explained that the "extent of the State's margin of appreciation depends not only on the right or rights concerned but also, as regards each right, on the very nature of the interest concerned. The Court considers that the right to an identity (...) is an integral part of the notion of private life. In such cases, particularly rigorous scrutiny is called for when weighing up the competing interests".[179]

In the same vein, when the non-consensual stimulation of a convicted person's brain changes personal characteristics that are to be considered an essential aspect of the person's identity – which we conceive as plausible in at least some cases (section 2.2) – the margin of appreciation will most likely be narrow too. In those cases, the national authorities have less discretion in balancing the convicted person's private interests against the public interest of crime prevention (e.g., by lowering recidivism risks). Consequently, the ECtHR could then apply a strict test of necessity and proportionality, critically assessing the availability of less intrusive means, and may require additional procedural safeguards in domestic law to guarantee careful and individualised decision-making and access to judicial remedies.[180]

2.4 CONCLUDING REMARKS

The use of neurointerventions for the rehabilitation of convicted persons raises concerns in view of their identity. In general, non-invasive brain stimulation for neurorehabilitation is unlikely to induce such radical psychological change so as to disrupt the person's psychological continuity and destroy their numerical identity. However, depending on their precise application and on the broader self-narrative of the convicted person involved, brain stimulation may interfere with narrative identity. A clear conceptual foundation of personal identity is lacking in human rights law. Yet, to some extent, human rights appear to protect, implicitly, (certain enabling preconditions of) narrative identity, in particular through the right to identity that is inherent in the right to privacy (Article 17 ICCPR) and, in Europe, the right to respect for private life (Article 8 ECHR). We have argued that,

177 ECtHR (GC) 10 April 2007, 6339/05 (*Evans/UK*), par. 77 (emphasis added); ECtHR (GC) 4 December 2007, appl.no. 44362/04 (*Dickson/UK*), par. 78. See also Bou-Sfia 2024, pp. 27–29.

178 ECtHR 26 June 2014, 65192/11 (*Mennesson/France*), par. 80.

179 ECtHR 13 July 2006, 58757/00 (*Jäggi/Switzerland*), par. 37.

180 Gerards 2023, pp. 248–249; Bou-Sfia 2024, p. 29.

in general, non-consensual neurointerventions that disrupt a person's identity-constituting narrative by inducing significant behavioural change can infringe these rights. Given the qualified nature of these rights, infringements may sometimes be justified, for instance to prevent severe crime. However, from the European perspective, we showed that the protection of people's identity appears to circle around the essence of Article 8 ECHR. This provides a strong reason to assume that, when a person's identity is interfered with, the margin of appreciation of states will be narrow, and that, therefore, the discretion of states to employ identity-affecting neurointerventions in criminal justice will be limited.

3

The Right to Personal Integrity

Protecting Bodies and Minds

3.1 INTRODUCTION

For a long time, criminal justice typically operated through the human body.[1] Historically, the intentional infliction of severe physical harm, such as through quartering and the rack, has been central to both criminal investigation and punishment. This centrality of the human body in criminal justice arguably changed with the rise of carceral punishment and, as of the mid 1900s, with the emergence of human rights protection to the integrity of persons. Yet, it is still the case that nowadays the use of physical force by state officials makes many appearances in modern criminal justice, ranging from handcuffing, taking bodily material for DNA analysis and using pepper spray on arrest, to physical force strip searches in prison and mechanical restraint in forensic hospitals.[2] Moreover, capital punishment, as the supreme corporal sanction,[3] is permitted under international human rights law[4] and still applies in many jurisdictions worldwide.

Given the particularly vulnerable position of the human body when in the hands of the powerful State, it is not surprising that human rights offer strong and robust protection to the integrity of the body, such as through the absolute prohibition of torture, inhuman and degrading treatment and the right to security of person. These rights play a central role in delimiting permissible state interference with the body, including within prison settings. In fact, a considerable portion of the violations of human rights over the body arise from the criminal justice context, such as through the forced feeding of prisoners, beating up defendants and employing medical interventions to obtain physical evidence of a crime.[5]

Apart from the body, modern criminal justice systems also operate through the human mind. As Foucault argued, disciplinary mechanisms of imprisonment have shifted focus from the body to the "soul", transforming punishment into an

1 Foucault 1975.
2 See, e.g., Guide on Article 3 of the European Convention on Human Rights, 31 August 2024.
3 Nowak & Schabas 2019, p. 196.
4 See, e.g., Article 6 ICCPR. See, in contrast, Protocol No. 6. to the ECHR.
5 See, for example, Taylor 2020, Ch. 7; Harris et al. 2023, Ch. 6.

instrument of control over the convicted person's mind and, ultimately, their behaviour.[6] As briefly touched upon in the previous chapter, according to some theories of criminal punishment, its very aim is to reform convicted persons, for example, by improving their moral character and setting their minds free to realise the immorality of their behaviour.[7] In addition, imprisonment is notoriously known for its adverse psychological side effects. Furthermore, next to punishment, modern criminal justice systems employ a variety of preventive measures aiming to reduce the risk of future harm, by interfering with the convicted person's mental states and capacities.[8] These measures range from rehabilitation programmes and cognitive behavioural therapy to antilibidinal medication as a mandatory condition for parole and coercive psychiatric interventions, including the administration of neuropharmaceuticals. In the future, this may also include some forms of brain stimulation, such as transcranial direct current stimulation (tDCS) or transcranial magnetic stimulation (TMS).

Although human rights protect the integrity of the mind next to the body, *mental* changes induced through the criminal justice system via (proportionate) punishment or preventive measures are seldom conceived of as infringing or violating human rights that pertain to the mind. This may, in part, be explained by the lack of clarity and controversy surrounding the question of how human rights regulate – or should regulate – interferences with people's inner mental processes, feelings and emotions.[9] For example, the contours of a right to mental integrity are still relatively underdeveloped and, therefore, less clear compared to the right to bodily integrity, which may hamper its application in concrete cases and policy-making. However, this may soon change. With the emergence of brain-stimulating technologies that aim to influence mental processes, scholars are increasingly endeavouring to define the meaning, scope and permissible limitations of the right to mental integrity.

In this chapter, we investigate the relevance and implications of the right to personal integrity – that is, the right to bodily and mental integrity – for the neurorehabilitation of convicted persons. How could neurotechnological brain stimulation in this context infringe these rights? And could such infringements be permissible in some instances? Regarding the right to bodily integrity, we closely stick to the interpretation of the right as follows from human rights law, particularly the International Covenant on Civil and Political Rights (ICCPR) and the European Convention on Human Rights (ECHR). Under both treaties, a right to bodily integrity is clearly defined and developed. For our analysis of the right to mental integrity, we also rely on the philosophical literature aiming to define a moral right to mental integrity and explore some possible understandings of the

6 Foucault 1975.

7 Ellis 2012, p. 74; Ewing 2013, p. 83.

8 Ashworth & Zedner 2014.

9 For debate, see Bublitz & Merkel 2014; Ienca & Andorno 2017; Ligthart et al. 2023a; Istace 2024.

right in human rights law, using insights from this literature. Along the way, we consider the implications of the right to bodily and mental integrity for the neurorehabilitation of convicted persons.

We proceed as follows. In section 3.2, we discuss the right to personal integrity's legal foundations and consider its meaning, scope and permissible limitations under established human rights law – also in relation to neurorehabilitation in criminal justice. In section 3.3, we explore possible constructions of the human right to mental integrity and consider the possibility of brain stimulation of convicted persons in that regard. Section 3.4 draws conclusions.

3.2 HUMAN RIGHTS PROTECTION OF PERSONAL INTEGRITY

The protection of personal integrity makes many appearances in human rights law. For example, a "right to integrity of the person" is laid down in Article 3 of the European Charter of Fundamental Rights, prescribing that "Everyone has the right to respect for his or her physical and mental integrity." Likewise, Article 5(1) of the American Convention on Human Rights states that "Every person has the right to have his physical, mental, and moral integrity respected." A similar right to the protection of the integrity of the person follows from Article 17 of the Convention on the Rights of Persons with Disabilities, stating that "Every person with disabilities has a right to respect for his or her physical and mental integrity on an equal basis with others."

Neither the ICCPR nor the ECHR explicitly recognises a right to personal (i.e., bodily and mental) integrity. Meanwhile, implicitly, they offer robust protection to the integrity of both the human body and mind, via other rights. We consider the protection provided by, respectively, (1) the right to security of person, (2) privacy rights, (3) the prohibition of torture, inhuman and degrading treatment, and (4) the right to freedom of thought and opinion.

3.2.1 *The Right to Security of Person*

Looking first to the right to personal security pursuant to Article 9 ICCPR, it is clear that both bodily and mental integrity are protected. According to General Comment No. 35, this right "concerns freedom from injury to the body and the mind, or bodily and mental integrity".[10] It protects individuals "against intentional infliction of bodily or mental injury" but also against "foreseeable threats" to the same.[11] Physical and mental integrity in this context are understood quite narrowly: infringements require at least some kind of physical or mental *injury*, which we can

[10] CCPR General Comment No. 35, par. 3.

[11] CCPR General Comment No. 35, pars. 3, 9. Primarily by private persons. States should take appropriate measures to ensure the security of person: Nowak & Schabas 2019, pp. 24–242.

understand as physical or mental *harm* or *damage*.[12] 'Injury' under Article 9 ICCPR is understood as denoting only harms or damage that pass a certain level of severity. The above mentioned General Comment stipulates that "the right to security of person does not address *all* risks to physical or mental health".[13] This Comment also specifically refers to *violent behaviours* when discussing security of the person.[14]

A wide range of actions can, however, still pass this threshold of severity. Think of a gunshot wound, a death threat or an assassination attempt.[15] Deep brain stimulation (DBS) also plausibly causes physical injury in the sense required for Article 9 ICCPR, in that it requires surgery for the implantation of electrodes in a person's brain – which involves making a small hole in the skull and placing a neurostimulator under the collarbone. Consequently, if performed in the absence of valid consent, this physical injury caused by DBS *could* infringe Article 9 ICCPR. Whether DBS also inflicts *mental* harm or injury is less clear. This probably depends on the precise stimulation and its accompanied (side) effects. But insofar as the placement of electrodes in a person's brain is non-consensual, it seems plausible that undergoing such a procedure could in and of itself be mentally distressing in a way that infringes Article 9 ICCPR, on at least some occasions.[16]

Non-invasive interventions such as tDCS and TMS, on the other hand, seem less likely to infringe the right to security of the person by causing physical or mental injury, though infringements are not impossible. The direct physical side effects of these interventions are minor, such as causing itchiness and a tingling sensation.[17] The intended mental effects, meanwhile, may be substantial, such as reducing depression, aggressiveness or increasing emphatic abilities. However, in our view, such mental effects can hardly be considered mental *injury* of the kind protected under Article 9 ICCPR. We say this because the abovementioned mental effects are not obviously antithetical to mental/psychological health or well-being, or detrimental to a person's mental or cognitive capacities – features that we might expect to be required for something to constitute a mental *injury*. That said, we cannot rule out the possibility of mental injury even with these non-invasive approaches. If delivered non-consensually, these interventions may cause mental distress in at

12 Note that this right applies regardless of whether the person is detained or not, despite the reference to arrest and detention within Article 9 (CCPR General Comment No. 35, par. 9). As the Human Rights Committee has stressed, "[a]n interpretation of article 9 which would allow a State party to ignore threats to the personal security of non-detained persons within its jurisdiction would render totally ineffective the guarantees of the Covenant": *Páez/Colombia*, No. 195/1985, CCPR/C/39/D/195/1985 (1990).

13 CCPR General Comment No. 35, par. 9.

14 CCPR General Comment No. 35, par. 9.

15 *Leehong/Jamaica*, No. 613/1995, CCPR/C/66/D/613/1995 (12 August 1999); Nowak & Schabas 2019, p. 242 with further references. Note that the right is broader than the right to life, as it also addresses injuries that are not life-threatening, such as the use of excessive force by law enforcement officials: Taylor 2020, p. 247.

16 And perhaps also qualify as inhuman or degrading treatment (see section 3.2.3).

17 Knehans 2022.

least some circumstances, particularly if the recipient failed to identify with the mental changes these techniques brought about.[18] There is also the possibility of unforeseen, harmful side effects with tDCS and TMS, as with DBS.

3.2.2 *Privacy Rights*

The scope of the protection of personal integrity by the right to privacy (Article 17 ICCPR) and the right to respect for private life (Article 8 ECHR) is arguably broader, in that these rights also seem to protect against actions that can be expected to induce smaller physical or mental changes, without the necessary requirement of causing physical or mental injury.[19] Regarding Article 17 ICCPR, Nowak/Schabas write that the right to privacy covers "the protection of personal integrity", which, for example, is at stake in cases of body searches, withdrawal of blood samples, non-consensual medical treatments, national prohibitions of pregnancy termination, intentional trivial insults by executive organs and minor quarrels.[20] Although these interventions could all potentially cause minor physical or mental harm, in most of these examples, severe bodily or mental injury seems unlikely or at least is not foreseeable.[21] Infringements of personal integrity under Article 17 ICCPR thus do not seem to be limited to actions that induce severe bodily or mental injury.

The ECtHR has explicitly stated that the right to respect for private life pursuant to Article 8 ECHR "provides for the protection of physical and mental integrity".[22] For the interpretation of these Article 8 guarantees, the ECtHR considers personal autonomy an "important principle".[23] The right to physical integrity under Article 8 ECHR covers a variety of severe and less severe interferences with the body, ranging from minor non-consensual medical interventions, such as taking saliva with a buccal swab[24] and withdrawing blood samples,[25] to more serious interferences, including forced medication,[26] strip searches[27] and gynaecological examination in prison.[28] The right to mental integrity, also referred to as "psychological" and

[18] Recall our discussion of identity and self-estrangement in the previous chapter.
[19] Cf. Nowak 2006, p. 36.
[20] Nowak & Schabas 2019, p. 469.
[21] To clarify, although some of these examples may sometimes cause mental distress, causing physical or mental injury is not an explicit requirement for the right's application – like in cases of "trivial insults".
[22] ECtHR 11 May 2023, 11148/18 (*Bojar/Poland*), par. 12. See also: ECtHR 12 October 2006, 3178/03 (*Mayeka and Kaniki Mitunga/Belgium*), par. 83.
[23] ECtHR (GC) 5 September 2017, 61496/08 (*Bărbulescu/Romania*), § 70; ECtHR (GC) 15 March 2012, 4149/04 and 41029/04 (*Aksu/Turkey*), § 58.
[24] ECtHR 14 April 2020, 75229/10 (*Dragan Petrović/Serbia*); ECtHR 15 May 2018, 41079/16 (*Caruana/Malta*).
[25] ECtHR 5 January 2006, 32352/02 (*Schmidt/Germany*).
[26] ECtHR 3 July 2012, 34806/04 (*X/Finland*).
[27] ECtHR 26 September 2006, 12350/04 (*Wainwright/UK*).
[28] ECtHR 13 May 2008, 52515/99 (*Juhnke/Turkey*).

"moral" integrity,[29] is associated with the protection of mental health.[30] But its protective scope is arguably broader,[31] as the right also pertains to bullying at school,[32] well-founded fear for physical abuse,[33] and loss of honour and reputation, for example, by others publishing defamatory statements and erotic pictures of a person in the media.[34]

Still, application of the right to *mental* integrity specifically in court cases is yet relatively scarce. Consequently, much remains unclear about the right's meaning and scope under Article 8 ECHR. For example, it is unsettled whether the infliction of mental harm or distress is required for infringing the right; or whether the right also covers interferences that do not directly harm mental well-being (such as making a person happier through secretly administering antidepressants, or changing their preferences or beliefs through subliminal advertising).

One guiding point is that Article 8 ECHR applies when the effects of an interference on personal integrity are "sufficiently adverse".[35] As De Vries explains, "Article 8 only applies when a person's physical or psychological integrity is adversely affected to a certain degree. Thus, the obligation to wear a seatbelt does not come within the scope of the right to private life."[36] Yet, this jurisprudential criterion is still vague and has not been further developed in case law yet.[37] What does the ECtHR mean by *adverse* effects? Would making people happier, less aggressive or more emphatic qualify as such? And when are the effects of an interference *sufficiently* adverse so as to infringe the right to personal integrity?

Regarding bodily integrity, many interferences seem to meet this 'sufficiently adverse' requirement: "even a minor interference with the physical integrity of an individual must be regarded as an interference with the right to respect for private life under Article 8 if it is carried out against the individual's will".[38] Taking a buccal swab, for instance, infringes the right to bodily integrity under Article 8 ECHR if performed non-consensually, although it "is an act of a very short duration, it usually causes no bodily injury or any physical or mental suffering, and thus is of minor importance".[39] Mandatory x-ray for tuberculosis screening and the obligation of imprisoned persons to provide a urine sample for drug testing also infringe this

29 These terms are used interchangeably, without any further general definition: De Vries 2018, p. 690.

30 ECtHR 6 February 2001, 44599/98 (*Bensaid/UK*), par. 47; ECtHR 26 November 2009, 25282/06 (*Dolenec/Croatia*), par. 165; Marshall 2009, p. 184; Ienca & Andorno 2017, p. 18; Istace 2023, p. 329.

31 De Vries 2018, pp. 690–691; Michalowski 2020.

32 ECtHR 24 July 2012, 41526/10 (*Đorđević/Croatia*), par. 97–98.

33 ECtHR 30 November 2010, 2660/03 (*Hajduová/Slovakia*), par. 49.

34 ECtHR 28 October 2014, 531/06 (*Ion Cârstea/Romania*), par. 38; ECtHR 21 November 2013, 16882/03 (*Putistin/Ukraine*), par. 32.

35 ECtHR 6 February 2001, 44599/98 (*Bensaid/UK*), par. 46.

36 De Vries 2018, p. 691, referring to EComHR 13 December 1979, 8707/79 (*X./Belgium*). See also ECtHR 25 March 1993, 13134/87 (*Costello-Roberts/UK*).

37 Harris et al. 2023, p. 525.

38 ECtHR 16 June 2005, 61603/00 (*Storck*/Germany), par. 143.

39 ECtHR 15 May 2018, 41079/16 (*Caruana/Malta*), par. 41.

right.[40] Furthermore, regarding medical treatment, Harris et al. write that without consent such treatment raises serious issues within the scope of private life, "however slight the intervention".[41] Apparently, "slight" interferences with the body that are "of minor importance" can still qualify as "sufficient" and thus infringe the right to bodily integrity. Perhaps the implicit reasoning behind this is that non-consensual bodily interference, although minor, reduces the person's control over their body, thus interfering with personal autonomy in that regard, which is, as said, an important principle underlying the interpretation of Article 8 ECHR.

Non-consensual brain stimulation thus may infringe the right to *bodily* integrity as protected by the right to privacy and private life, even if the physical effects of the intervention are minor (as they would likely be in the case of tDCS or TMS).[42] We say "may infringe" because clearly not all bodily interferences of minor significance infringe this right. We often cause non-consensual yet minor effects in other people's bodies that cannot plausibly be held to infringe the right to bodily integrity – for instance, tapping someone on the shoulder, raising the room temperature significantly[43] or telling a disgusting story that causes one to wretch or vomit.[44] Yet, given that the case law pertaining to the right to bodily integrity under Article 8 ECHR and Article 17 ICCPR indicates that (very) minor bodily interferences performed non-consensually (e.g., mandatory x-ray and the obligation to provide urine samples) *can* infringe the right, it is not too far of a stretch to expect human rights courts to find non-invasive, non-consensual brain stimulation to infringe the right to bodily integrity too. DBS would certainly be judged to infringe this right, given that, as said, the physical interference involved in DBS is significant.

Still, that the right to bodily integrity is *infringed* need not imply that the right is *violated*. Recall that the right to privacy (Article 17 ICCPR) and the right to respect for private life (Article 8 ECHR) are qualified rights. Infringements can be justified when, generally speaking,[45] they have an accessible and foreseeable legal basis, pursue a legitimate purpose – such as preventing crime and disorder – and are proportionate in relation to that purpose.[46] The slightness of a bodily interference through non-invasive brain stimulation is legally significant here, particularly with regard to the requirement of proportionality.

In general, the more severe an infringement of a human right, the more substantial the reasons must be to justify such an infringement.[47] Conversely, less intrusive

[40] EComHR 10 December 1984, 10435/83 (*Acmanne and others/Belgium*); EComHR 6 April 1994, 21132/93 (*Peters/The Netherlands*).
[41] Harris et al. 2023, p. 528. See also De Vries 2018, p. 693.
[42] Note that TMS, unlike tDCS, does not even require physical touching, operating via a magnetic field placed close to the head.
[43] Bublitz 2024, p. 786, footnote 31.
[44] Douglas & Forsberg 2021, p. 186.
[45] Indeed, this is very general and rather simplified.
[46] Lavrysen 2018; Nowak & Schabas 2019, p. 465.
[47] Christoffersen 2009, p. 208; Gerards 2023, p. 355.

interferences require less weighty reasons for their justification. Minor bodily interference caused by non-invasive brain stimulation thus can plausibly be held proportionate for the prevention of serious criminal offences – including abuse, murder and rape – *even if* they infringe the qualified right to bodily integrity. Many criminal justice practices that interfere with the body (e.g., handcuffing and strip searches) are not typically conceived of as violating the right to bodily integrity as they aim to prevent harm to others and can therefore be justified.[48] Sometimes even more severe bodily effects are considered proportionate to prevent harm, at least in some jurisdictions (for instance, the oft-severe physical effects and side effects of antilibidinal medication), though this is controversial.[49] Moreover, although the Human Rights Committee was "concerned at the lack of clarity on the frequency and circumstances surrounding the use of coercive electroconvulsive treatment" in Norwegian mental health-care institutions, it did not rule out the permissible use of these coercive interventions, concluding that Norway "should increase procedural safeguards for patients and stipulate in law the circumstances allowing for the limited use of coercive electroconvulsive treatment".[50]

Does this mean that the right to personal integrity under Articles 17 ICCPR and 8 ECHR only offers *weak* protection against non-invasive brain stimulation? Not necessarily. While the *bodily* interference might be of minor gravity, the *mental* interference may – at least in some instances – be much more severe.[51] As Bublitz stresses, what really matters are the *mental effects* of brain stimulation, encompassed by the right to mental integrity.[52] Likewise, according to Craig, "there are strong reasons to believe that the most compelling arguments against non-consensual [direct brain interventions] do not rest on the right to bodily integrity, but on the more fundamental right to 'mental integrity'".[53]

As said, the right to mental integrity as covered by the abovementioned privacy rights is relatively underdeveloped. We therefore do not yet have the legal resources to assess whether the right to mental integrity might afford persons greater protection against non-consensual brain stimulation than that which is afforded by the right to

48 Provided that they have an accessible and foreseeable basis in the law.

49 As earlier indicated, in some jurisdictions, antilibidinal interventions can be administered as a mandatory condition of parole or probation, where the validity of consent is open to debate; see Sifferd 2020; Forsberg 2021; Shaw 2022, pp. 1414–1416, for discussion. Traditional forms of punishment, such as incarceration, also sometimes appear to give rise to non-consensual alterations of neural processes in the brain, and these alterations are not typically thought to violate the right to bodily integrity.

50 Concluding Observations, Norway, CCPR/C/NOR/CO/7, pars. 22–23. Cf. Concluding Observations, Latvia, CCPR/C/LVA/CO/3, par. 16; Concluding Observations, USA, CCPR/C/USA/CO/4, par. 18.

51 Also, how significant the interference is may depend on how one measures "significance" in this regard. For example, Tesink et al. 2023 have argued that the mental and behavioural effects of neurointerventions could in some cases be relevant to determining the severity of infringements of the right to bodily integrity.

52 Bublitz 2024, pp. 785–786. See also Mendlow 2018, p. 2368; Ryberg 2020, p. 83; Shaw 2022.

53 Craig 2016, p. 111.

bodily integrity, under Articles 17 ICCPR and 8 ECHR. Nonetheless, if the scope of the right to mental integrity turns out to be *analogous* to the scope of the right to bodily integrity under these provisions – that is, as a right against sufficiently adverse effects on the mind – neurointerventions that alter mental states or processes may be considered to regularly infringe the right to mental integrity.[54] We delve deeper into this issue in section 3.3, discussing three different approaches to further construct the protective scope of the right to mental integrity, and consider some of their implications for the right's permissible limitations.

3.2.3 *The Prohibition of Torture, Inhuman, and Degrading Treatment*

On top of the qualified protection offered by the right to personal integrity pursuant to Articles 17 ICCPR and 8 ECHR, some severe interferences with physical and mental integrity could also breach the *absolute* and non-derrogable prohibition of torture, inhuman and degrading treatment and punishment. Nowak/Schabas equate the prohibition of torture of Article 7 ICCPR with "the right to physical and spiritual integrity".[55] In the General Comment on Article 7 ICCPR, the Human Rights Committee clarifies that the aim of this provision "is to protect both the dignity and the physical and mental integrity of the individual" and that it "relates not only to acts that cause physical pain but also to acts that cause mental suffering".[56] The ICCPR does not provide a clear definition of the concepts covered by Article 7 ICCPR, "nor does the [Human Rights] Committee consider it necessary to draw up a list of prohibited acts or to establish sharp distinctions between the different kinds of punishment or treatment".[57] In general, the distinction between torture, cruel, inhuman and degrading treatment and punishment depends on the nature, purpose and severity of the treatment inflicted.[58] The assessment of what constitutes inhuman or degrading treatment as prohibited by Article 7 ICCPR "depends on all the circumstances of the case, such as the duration and manner of the treatment, its physical or mental effects as well as the sex, age and state of health of the victim".[59]

The same applies *mutatis mutandis* to the prohibition of torture, inhuman and degrading treatment of Article 3 ECHR, which prohibits, in absolute terms, serious interferences with bodily and mental integrity,[60] ranging from the intentional

54 Bublitz 2024, p. 788. See Advisory Committee, UNHRC, Impact, opportunities and challenges of neurotechnology with regard to the promotion and protection of all human rights, A/HRC/AC/31/CRP.1 (8 August 2024), par. 27: "Neurotechnologies can lead to violations of the right to personal integrity (…) when endangering individuals' autonomous control over their body and mind."

55 Nowak & Schabas 2019, p. 170. Cf. Taylor 2020, p. 199.

56 CCPR General Comment No. 20, par. 2 and 5.

57 CCPR General Comment No. 20, pars. 2–5.

58 CCPR General Comment No. 20, pars. 2–5.

59 *Vuolanne/Finland*, No. 265/1987, CCPR/C/35/D/265/1987 (8 July 1987), par. 9.2.

60 For the use of these terms, see, e.g., ECtHR (GC) 11 July 2006, 54810/00 (*Jalloh/Germany*), par. 82. See also ECtHR (GC) 2 February 2021, 22457/16 (*X and Others/Bulgaria*), par. 179.

infliction of severe physical and mental suffering (i.e., torture) to treatment that arouses feelings of fear, anguish and inferiority, capable of humiliating and debasing the person (i.e., degrading treatment).[61] To infringe – and therefore violate – Article 3 ECHR, treatment or punishment must attain a "minimum level of severity".[62] Whereas the prohibition of ill-treatment is itself absolute, this severity threshold is relative. It depends on all the circumstances of the individual case, including the nature and context of the treatment, the manner and method of its execution, its duration, its purpose, its physical or mental effects and, sometimes, the sex, age and state of health of the victim and their vulnerable status.[63]

No doubt the surgical implantation of electrodes in a person's brain to control some of their brain processes will, without valid consent, qualify as inhuman or degrading treatment (and perhaps even torture). Such practices are likely prohibited across the board by Articles 7 ICCPR and 3 ECHR. Meanwhile, regarding *non-invasive* neurointerventions, including tDCS and TMS, the relevance of the absolute prohibition of ill-treatment is plausibly far more limited.[64] After all – provided that these interventions are safe and effective – their application should not typically cause bodily injury, physical pain or mental suffering. Rather, they are of short duration and may influence mental features, such as empathic abilities, through minor and painless bodily alterations (an effect that future technologies may have). These 'subtle' interferences with the body and mind are, in and of themselves, unlikely to attain the severity threshold of the prohibition of ill-treatment.[65] They are plausibly not severe enough to elicit the absolute protection of physical and mental integrity from Articles 7 ICCPR and 3 ECHR.

However, next to physical and mental integrity, the prohibition of ill-treatment also aims to protect human dignity. Regarding Article 3 ECHR, Harris et al. observe that for "degrading treatment" the emphasis is on humiliation and debasement, rather than on physical and mental suffering.[66] According to the ECtHR there is a strong link between respect for human dignity and the concept of "degrading" treatment.[67] The latter being defined sometimes as treatment that "humiliates or debases an individual, showing a lack of respect for, or diminishing, his or her

61 Harris et al. 2023, pp. 247–264.

62 ECtHR (GC) 1 June 2010, 22978/05 (*Gäfgen/Germany*), par. 101; ECtHR (GC) 26 October 2000, 30210/96 (*Kudła/Poland*), par. 91.

63 Harris et al. 2023, p. 243; ECtHR (GC) 1 June 2010, 22978/05 (*Gäfgen/Germany*), par. 88.

64 For a more nuanced analysis, see Van de Pol 2023, highlighting, among other things, that "If a medical necessity exists, the treatment will most likely fail to reach the minimum level of severity, even when the person involved did not consent to the treatment" (p. 469).

65 Cf. Vermeulen & Battjes 2018, p. 400, considering some examples of "unpleasant or even harsh" treatments that did not amount to inhuman or degrading treatment. Cf. also Duffy 1983, p. 319, stating that although views and reactions of the victim are important considerations, States should not be liable for actions that a victim finds degrading "merely because of his own unreasonable attitudes or exceptionally sensitive nature".

66 Harris et al. 2023, p. 264.

67 ECtHR (GC) 28 September 2015, 23380/09 (*Bouyid/Belgium*), par. 90.

human dignity, or when it arouses feelings of fear, anguish or inferiority capable of breaking an individual's moral and physical resistance".[68] At the international level, the protection of human dignity by Article 7 ICCPR[69] is complemented by the right of detainees to be treated with humanity and dignity pursuant to Article 10 ICCPR.[70] In human rights law, human dignity features different understandings, including "inherent dignity" – that is, the worth of every person by virtue of being a human.[71] One core aspect of human dignity is the care for and protection of human beings as subjects and as specific individuals with personality.[72]

Subjecting a convicted person to brain stimulation in order to change their behaviour by modifying their neural and mental functioning could be argued to reduce the person to an object rather than a subject, which disrespects human dignity and could therefore violate the legal norms laid down in Articles 7, 10 ICCPR and 3 ECHR.[73] The ECtHR, in *Tyrer/UK* – a case about the infliction of corporal punishment by the police – considered that treating a person as an object could indeed interfere with human dignity, stating that

> although the applicant [in this case] did not suffer any severe or long-lasting physical effects, his punishment – *whereby he was treated as an object in the power of the authorities* – constituted an assault on precisely that which it is one of the main purposes of [Article 3 ECHR] to protect, namely a person's dignity and physical integrity.[74]

One way of objectifying persons, Bublitz argues, is by reducing them to their corporal existence, to their bodies, such as through "reductive forms of neuroscience which seek to explain and address mental aspects exclusively at the level of the brain".[75]

If we follow this line of thought, the use of non-consensual brain stimulation to induce behavioural change in convicted persons can at least in some situations raise concerns about human dignity. For example, this could be the case when forensic behavioural interventions would *exclusively* operate through modifying a convicted person's brain, purely treating the person as a means, rather than as an end in themselves.[76] Meanwhile, concerns about objectification and disrespecting

68 ECtHR (GC) 17 July 2014, 32541/08 and 43441/08 (*Svinarenko and Slyadnev/Russia*), par. 115.

69 CCPR General Comment No. 20, par. 2.

70 Taylor 2020, p. 174. To infringe Article 10, a minimum level of severity is also required: *Brough/Australia*, No. 1184/2003, CCPR/C/86/D/1184/2003 (2006), par. 9.2.

71 Le Moli 2021.

72 Bublitz 2024, pp. 793–795. Meanwhile, the meaning and scope of inherent dignity protection have not comprehensively been specified, and it is often criticized for being (too) vague and abstract.

73 Cf. Bublitz & Merkel 2014, p. 73; Kirchmair 2019.

74 ECtHR 25 April 1978, 5856/72 (*Tyrer/UK*), par. 33 (emphasis added). See also ECtHR (GC) 28 September 2015, 23380/09 (*Bouyid/Belgium*), par. 90.

75 Bublitz 2024, p. 794. See also Bublitz & Merkel 2014, p. 73.

76 We doubt whether neurointerventions would ever acquire such a unique and absolute position within rehabilitation practice though.

human dignity may diminish when the use of neurointerventions complements – or is complemented by – rehabilitation programmes that respect subjectivity.[77]

Often, rehabilitation programmes in criminal justice entail a wide spectrum of services and activities that engage with the convicted person.[78] These include education, work training, therapy and probation on a variety of conditions, ranging from substance abuse counselling to pharmacological interventions for reducing sexual drive. Embedding non-invasive brain stimulation as a complementary element in such larger and diverse rehabilitation programmes would likely negate or at least diminish concerns about objectification and human dignity.

Interestingly, for a treatment or punishment to violate Article 3 ECHR, the ECtHR holds that the suffering and humiliation involved "must in any event go beyond that inevitable element of suffering or humiliation connected with a given form of legitimate treatment or punishment",[79] such as imprisonment or, in this context, existing accepted pharmacotherapeutic practices. Regarding present forms of non-invasive brain stimulation, such as tDCS and TMS, we do not see a clear and compelling reason why the suffering or humiliation involved would exceed the level of suffering and humiliation entailed by accepted pharmacological interventions – provided that they are incorporated within a broader rehabilitation programme.

3.2.4 *The Right to Freedom of Thought and Freedom of Opinion*

Finally, depending on its conceptualisation, *mental* integrity could also be implicitly protected by the right to freedom of thought and, to some extent, by the right to freedom of opinion. Under Articles 18 ICCPR and 9 ECHR, the right to freedom of thought is generally considered an absolute right.[80] Infringements are never permissible. The same applies to the right to freedom of opinion in the meaning of Article 19 ICCPR.[81] Whether the freedom to hold opinions under Article 10 ECHR is also absolute is less clear. Whereas the text of Article 10 ECHR suggests qualified protection, it has been argued that the freedom of opinion in this provision "enjoys an almost absolute protection in the sense that the possible restrictions set forth in paragraph 2 are inapplicable".[82]

The right to *freedom of thought* is typically taken to protect against the "impermissible alteration" of thought, thereby protecting some aspects of persons' "mental autonomy".[83] According to the Council of Europe's *Human rights handbooks*, the internal dimension of Article 9 ECHR seeks at its most basic level "to prevent state

77 Cf. Bublitz 2024, pp. 794–795 and footnote 86.

78 McNeil 2012; Ugwudike et al. 2020; Coppola & Martufi 2024.

79 ECtHR (GC) 26 October 2000, 30210/96 (*Kudła/Poland*), par. 92.

80 CCPR General Comment No. 22, par. 3; Vermeulen & Roosmalen 2018, p. 738. But the absolute nature of the right has recently been challenged: Ligthart 2025c.

81 CCPR General Comment No. 34, pars. 5 and 9.

82 Bychawska-Siniarska 2017, p. 13. See also Van Rijn 2018, p. 811.

83 UN Special Rapporteur on the Freedom of religion or belief, 5 October 2021, A/76/380, par. 28.

indoctrination of individuals by permitting the holding, development, and refinement and ultimately change of personal thought, conscience and religion".[84] Vermeulen and Roosmalen write that the internal dimension of Article 9 ECHR guarantees that States may never interfere with the most intimate and inner sphere of their citizens. They are not allowed to dictate what people should believe, nor may they use coercion to make individuals change their beliefs, such as through "brainwashing".[85] As examples of possible infringements of the right to freedom of thought pursuant to Article 18 ICCPR, the Special Rapporteur on Freedom of Religion or Belief has considered, among other things, psychological torture, re-education of political prisoners, involuntary treatment for mental disorders, non-consensual conversion practices and – interestingly for our present purposes – neurotechnological interventions that alter mental states.[86]

An essential element of the right to *freedom of opinion* is the freedom to form and develop opinions by way of reasoning.[87] It protects the holding of an opinion without interference,[88] which requires among other things freedom from coercion in the development of beliefs, ideologies, reactions and positions.[89] The Special Rapporteur on Freedom of Opinion and Expression writes that violations of Article 19(1) ICCPR could consist in "forced neurological interventions, indoctrination programmes (such as 're-education camps') or threats of violence designed to compel individuals to form particular opinions or change their opinion".[90]

According to Bublitz, taken together, the essence of the rights to freedom of thought and opinion "lies in the protection of the most important mental states, processes, and abilities, i.e. in mental actions such as thinking, reasoning, decision-making, imagining, or remembering, as well as forming and revising of beliefs, opinions, attitudes, and related mental states and processes".[91] Regarding both Articles 18 and 19 ICCPR, Nowak/Schabas consider that they require "[s]tate parties to refrain from interfering with an individual's spiritual and moral existence – whether this be through indoctrination, 'brainwashing', influencing of the conscious or subconscious mind with psychoactive drugs or other means or manipulation".[92]

84 Murdoch 2012, p. 18.
85 Vermeulen & Roosmalen 2018, p. 738.
86 UN Special Rapporteur on the Freedom of religion or belief, 5 October 2021, A/76/380.
87 UN Special Rapporteur on the promotion and protection of the right to freedom of opinion and expression, 29 August 2018, A/73/348, par. 23.
88 CCPR General Comment No. 34: Article 19, par. 9.
89 *Yong Joo-Kang/Republic of Korea*, CCPR/C/78/D/878/1999, 16 July 2003. CCPR General Comment No. 34, par. 9.
90 UN Special Rapporteur on the promotion and protection of the right to freedom of opinion and expression, 29 August 2018, A/73/348, par. 23.
91 Bublitz 2024, p. 792.
92 Nowak & Schabas 2019, pp. 503, 546. In this context, Nowak & Schabas highlight the difficulty of delineating between impermissible interferences and permissible means of influence to which we are regularly exposed in daily life, such as by the media, advertising and propaganda. We come back to this in section 3.3.

In the literature on the human rights implications of neurotechnology, the main focus is on the freedom of thought (rather than the freedom of opinion). Non-consensually modifying mental states and processes through neurointerventions in criminal justice has been argued in the scholarly literature to infringe the absolute right to freedom of thought such that it should be "prohibited across the board".[93] The plausibility of this claim, however, very much depends on how one defines the scope of the right,[94] which partly depends, in turn, on how one interprets "thought" in this context – a question that is currently under debate.[95] Roughly, three interpretations can be distinguished.[96]

First, according to what we could call the "narrow view", "thought" under Article 18 ICCPR and Article 9 ECHR is confined to thoughts originating from religion.[97] This narrow understanding does not receive much (if any) support in recent scholarly literature – even if, in past practice, Article 18 ICCPR "had been generally interpreted as safeguarding only the freedom of religion and the freedom of thought and belief associated with religion".[98]

A second position, referred to as the "moderate view",[99] holds that "thought" denotes especially significant thoughts, with great personal importance.[100] On this view, the right to freedom of thought offers absolute protection not to just *any* thought, opinion, idea or other mental state. Rather, it protects those thoughts that have a major impact on a person's way of living, including political, cultural, philosophical and scientific thought, and, arguably, a person's deepest wishes and sexual desires.

According to a third position, referred to as the "robust-scope view", thought means *any* mental state with content as well as thinking as a mental process.[101] On this view, all thoughts and thinking are protected, including political thoughts, a person's thought to have a cup of coffee, and their thoughts about what colour socks to wear.[102]

On the first two positions, brain stimulation for the rehabilitation of convicted persons is unlikely to infringe the right to freedom of thought in most cases, as these interventions do not typically interfere with a person's religious adherence nor with significant personal conceptions such as their political or philosophical views. There may be an infringement of the right to freedom of thought on the moderate view,

93 Bublitz 2014, 2018, p. 301.

94 Cf. Advisory Committee, UNHRC, Impact, opportunities and challenges of neurotechnology with regard to the promotion and protection of all human rights, A/HRC/AC/31/CRP.1 (8 August 2024), par. 22.

95 See for example Bublitz 2025 and Ligthart 2025b.

96 Cf. Bublitz 2025, who considers six possible understandings.

97 De Jong 2000, p. 22.

98 CCPR/C/SR.1162, par. 43. Cf. EComHR 23 March 1993, 19459/92 (*F.P./Germany*).

99 Ligthart 2025a.

100 Partsch 1981, pp. 213–214; Istace 2024, p. 28; Ligthart 2022, 2025a, 2025b; De Jong 2000, pp. 23–33.

101 Bublitz 2025.

102 Alegre 2017, 2022; McCarthy-Jones 2019; O'Callaghan et al. 2024; Bublitz 2025; Hertz 2025.

however, if an intervention interferes with, for example, sexual desires – insofar and to the extent that a person's sexual desires are of great personal importance to them.

On the robust-scope view, neurointerventions may more regularly infringe the right, given that this view sees all thoughts as coming under the scope of freedom of thought. So, brain stimulation to change a person's antisocial attitude towards criminality, for example, would constitute an infringement on this view.[103]

Note, however, that also on this view, interference with mental phenomena that are not considered "thoughts" in ordinary language will not reasonably infringe the right.[104] One could think of *feelings, tendencies, behavioural control, risk taking, empathic abilities* and *emotional responses* – typical targets for the rehabilitation of convicted persons. The general rule of interpretation of Article 31(1) of the Vienna Convention seems to oppose the qualification of such mental phenomena as protected "thoughts", prescribing that "ordinary meaning" should be given to the terms of a treaty in light of its object and purpose. As Bublitz writes when defending the robust-scope view, "[i]n common usage, 'thought' refers to specific mental entities. This meaning must therefore be integrated into the interpretation of Article 18(1) ICCPR".[105] Since mental phenomena such as feelings, behavioural inclinations and emphatic abilities are not normally captured by the common understanding of "thought", interfering with such mental phenomena through neurotechnology will plausibly fall *outside* the scope of the right to freedom of thought.

To substantiate a broad interpretation of "thought", proponents of the robust-scope view often refer to the General Comment on Article 18 ICCPR, highlighting that "[t]he right to freedom of thought (...) is far-reaching and profound; it encompasses freedom of thought on all matters".[106] Furthermore, a recent report on the right to freedom of thought by the UN Special Rapporteur on Freedom of Religion and Belief can be interpreted as endorsing a robust understanding of thought.[107]

Whereas the robust-scope view gets arguable support regarding the interpretation of Article 18 ICCPR, it appears to lack support with regard to Article 9 ECHR. Rather, the case law on Article 9 ECHR suggests an interpretation along the lines of the moderate view.[108] For example, in *F.P./Germany*, the EComHR considered that Article 9 ECHR "is essentially destined to protect religions or theories on

103 Bublitz 2014, 2018.

104 Bublitz 2025, stating that the robust-scope view may exclude "mental states and processes without intentional objects such as moods or activities such as feeling".

105 Bublitz 2025, p. 8.

106 CCPR General Comment No. 22, par. 1. Whether this statement is indeed compelling for supporting the Robust-scope view can be challenged: Ligthart 2025a.

107 UN Special Rapporteur on the Freedom of religion or belief, 5 October 2021, A/76/380; Ligthart et al. 2022; O'Callaghan et al. 2023.

108 Ligthart 2022, 2025b.

philosophical or ideological universal values".[109] Moreover, the ECtHR's Grand Chamber has repeatedly considered that, in general,

> as guaranteed by Article 9 of the Convention, the right to freedom of thought, conscience and religion denotes only those views that *attain a certain level of cogency, seriousness, cohesion and importance*.[110]

This means that Article 9 ECHR does not protect just any thought, opinion or idea.[111] To be protected by this provision, personal or collective views must meet a certain threshold, which supports the moderate view.

One could argue that this threshold only applies to the freedom to *manifest* thought, conscience and religion.[112] However, this is unlikely for at least two reasons.[113] First and foremost, in the above quote the ECtHR clearly refers to Article 9 ECHR, and Article 9 ECHR does not protect *external manifestations* of thought. The manifestation/expression of thought is instead protected by the right to freedom of expression.[114] Hence, referring to "thought" in the meaning of Article 9 ECHR can only pertain to *unexpressed* thought.

Second, the very first sentence of Article 9 ECHR – Everyone has the right to freedom of thought, conscience and religion – is generally taken to comprise *forum internum* protection.[115] This right is "largely exercised inside the individual's heart and mind" and receives absolute protection.[116] The *forum externum* protection is encompassed by the addition that "this right includes freedom (...) to manifest his religion or beliefs".[117] Hence, if the ECHR refers to "the right to freedom of thought, conscience and religion", as it does in the quotation above, then this must at least cover *forum internum* protection. If the ECHR's consideration on cogency, seriousness, cohesion and importance would only have applied to the *forum externum*, they would not have referred to the right to "freedom of thought, conscience and religion" but rather to the "freedom to manifest one's religion or beliefs".

The ECtHR, admittedly, has provided little guidance on how to understand and apply the threshold requirements of cogency, seriousness, cohesion and importance.[118] Neither has it applied them in cases concerning the protection of inner "thought", instead

109 EComHR 23 March 1993, 19459/92 (*F.P./Germany*). See also EComHR 15 December 1983, 10358/83 (*C./UK*), par. 147; EComHR 11 October 1991, 16311/90, 16312/90 and 16313/90 (*Hazar and Açik/Turkey*).

110 ECtHR (GC) 26 April 2016, 62649/10 (*İzzettin Doğan and others v. Turkey*), par. 68 (emphasis added). See also ECtHR (GC) 1 July 2014, 43835/11 (*S.A.S./France*), par. 55; ECtHR 8 June 2021, 48329/19 (*Ancient Baltic religious association Romuva/Lithuania*), par. 125; ECtHR 9 November 2021, 9476/19 (*De Wilde/the Netherlands*), par. 51; ECtHR 22 November 2022, 20921/21 (*Nikolaus ALM/Austria*), par. 9.

111 Unlike Article 10 ECHR, which has a very broad scope.

112 Bublitz 2025; Hertz 2025.

113 Ligthart 2025b.

114 Evans 1997, p. 285.

115 Harris et al. 2023, p. 578.

116 Godien 2005, p. 95.

117 Harris et al. 2023, p. 578.

118 Wolff 2023.

focusing on the *manifestation* of religion and beliefs. The precise implications of this threshold are thus largely uncertain and we are left to speculate. Nonetheless, some remarks voiced within the United Kingdom's House of Lords on the matter may prove at least somewhat instructive. In the case of *R. (Williamson)* v. *Secretary of State for Education and Employment*, Lord Nicholls observes that, with respect to "seriousness" and "importance", a manifested view or belief that comes under the protective scope of Article 9 ECHR "must be a belief on a fundamental problem".[119] And with respect to "cogency" and "cohesion", Lord Nicholls observes that these requirements relate to "being intelligible and capable of being understood", while also emphasising that "being intelligible" is not the same as being "susceptible to (…) rational justification".[120]

These observations arguably only push the problem back, given that we still have to figure out what "a fundamental problem" and "intelligible" mean. But it is plausible that some thoughts, views and beliefs more obviously pertain to fundamental problems – again, philosophical and religious beliefs about how, for example, (one ought) to live one's life or organise society. Everyday thoughts about the kind of socks to wear or whether to grab a cup of coffee, on the other hand, seem far less likely to do so (and hence seem unlikely to be covered by Article 9 ECHR) – notwithstanding that these thoughts relate in some small way to how the relevant individual chooses to live their life.[121]

When it comes to mental phenomena that might be relevant targets for neurorehabilitation, such as certain desires or preferences, their relation to fundamental problems is not entirely clear. One perspective, again voiced by Lord Nicholls, might be that these mental phenomena only pertain to fundamental problems if they "relate to an aspect of human life or behaviour of comparable importance to that normally found with religious beliefs".[122] A similar idea is voiced by Cecile Laborde in her interpretation of the "importance" requirement as being reached when a given thought or belief "actually occupies a pivotal place in [individuals'] lives as they want to live it, and is not simply a peripheral, incidental or occasional commitment".[123] These comments suggest that what is at issue is whether a given view is something its bearer strongly identifies with or holds dear.[124]

Some desires or predilections that are relevant from a rehabilitation perspective – for example, paedophilic or violent sexual desires – may assume as important a role in a person's life as their political or religious beliefs. If these kinds of thoughts or desires sometimes assume such importance, then it may be that, on the

119 R. *(on the application of* Williamson) *v Secretary of State for Education and Employment*; UKHL 15 [2005] 2 A.C. 246, par. 23. Cf. EComHR 10 March 1981, 8741/79 (*X/Germany*), p. 138.

120 R. *(on the application of* Williamson) *v Secretary of State for Education and Employment*; UKHL 15 [2005] 2 A.C. 246, par. 23. Cf. EComHR 10 March 1981, 8741/79 (*X/Germany*), p. 138.

121 Which could depend on the precise context: Ligthart & Van de Pol 2025. Cf. Bublitz 2025, p. 13.

122 R. *(on the application of* Williamson) v. *Secretary of State for Education and Employment*; UKHL 15 [2005] 2 A.C. 246, par. 24.

123 Laborde 2017, p. 207.

124 Cf. ECtHR (GC) 8 April 2021, 47621/13 (*Vavřička and Others/the Czech Republic*), pars. 334–335.

moderate-scope view, some sexual preferences enjoy absolute protection under Article 9 ECHR.

That said, the mental states and processes typically targeted by neurointerventions for purposes of rehabilitation may often fall short of engaging absolute protection form Article 9 ECHR: either because they do not meet its threshold or because they cannot be considered "thoughts" in the first place (e.g., empathic abilities, behavioural control, risk-taking tendency).

3.2.5 *Brief recap*

The integrity of the person consists of two elements: the protection of the human body and mind. Grave interferences that cause severe physical or mental suffering can elicit *absolute* protection from the prohibition of ill-treatment. The same applies to interferences that are humiliating or disrespect human dignity. Regarding the neurorehabilitation of convicted persons, this protection seems especially relevant in relation to invasive forms of brain stimulation, such as DBS. Non-invasive interventions are, by contrast, generally less likely to meet the severity threshold of this absolute prohibition. Still, they could engage absolute protection by infringing the right to freedom of thought. Whether they do, largely depends on how "thought" is defined in the meaning of the right, which is yet unsettled.

The broadest protection against unsolicited bodily and mental interference is offered by the right to privacy and respect for private life, providing *qualified* protection against severe and less severe interferences with physical and mental integrity. Presumably, the right to bodily integrity will not offer strong protection against non-invasive brain stimulation for rehabilitation purposes, as the bodily interference of these interventions will often be minor. Meanwhile, their mental effects could be significant. Hence, non-invasive brain stimulation may well severely infringe the right to mental integrity. Whether they do not only depends on the mental effects of a specific neurointervention, but also on our understanding of the right to mental integrity, in particular its scope and permissible limitations. In the next section, we explore three possible constructions of the right's scope and consider some of their implications for the right's permissible limitations.

3.3 CONSTRUCTING THE RIGHT TO MENTAL INTEGRITY: SCOPE AND PERMISSIBLE LIMITATIONS

3.3.1 *Meaning and Scope*

While the right to mental integrity has received little attention in the law so far,[125] in philosophical literature, constructing the right is an important topic in discussions

[125] Bublitz & Merkel 2014; Michalowski 2020; Ligthart 2025d.

concerning the regulation of neurotechnologies.[126] Whereas some philosophers are especially interested in the moral underpinnings of a *legal* right to mental integrity,[127] others consider the contours and significance of mental integrity as a *moral* right.[128] We acknowledge that a moral right to mental integrity need not straightforwardly imply nor correspond to its legal counterpart, even though human rights are often considered to reflect moral guarantees. Still, when aiming to construct the meaning and scope of a legal right to mental integrity, the philosophical literature could provide some guidance.[129] In what follows, drawing from both legal and philosophical perspectives, we distinguish three general understandings of a right to mental integrity and consider their suitability for constructing the right within human rights law.[130] Consecutively, we consider the right to mental integrity as (1) a freedom to control mental states and processes, (2) a freedom from direct and harmful mental interference and (3) a freedom from significant mental interference.[131]

3.3.1.1 Freedom to Control Mental States and Processes

A first way of constructing the right to mental integrity holds that every person has the liberty to *control* what happens to their own mind and the neural parameters of mental states and processes – focusing more on how a right to mental integrity might be justified rather than on delineating its scope. For example, Lavazza defines mental integrity as "the individual's *mastery* of his mental states and his brain data so that, without his consent, no one can read, spread, or alter such states and data in order to condition the individual in any way".[132] In the same vein, Hildt holds that the "right to mental integrity stresses a person's right to *control* their brain states".[133] According to the Advisory Committee of the UN Human Rights Council, "neurotechnologies could violate the right to personal integrity (...) when endangering individuals' *autonomous control* over their body and mind".[134]

Such understandings of the right to mental integrity come close to the right to "mental self-determination" defended by Bublitz and Merkel. The principal

126 Douglas 2024; Ryberg 2020; Shaw 2022; Lavazza & Giorgi 2023; Tesink et al. 2024; Cassinadri 2025.
127 Douglas & Forsberg 2021; Douglas 2024.
128 Lavazza 2018; Craig 2016; Zohny et al. 2023; Ratoff 2024.
129 Cf. Ligthart et al. 2023a.
130 That is, as part of the qualified right to privacy and respect for private life.
131 The discussion in the next section draws on Ligthart 2025d.
132 Lavazza 2018, p. 4 (emphasis added). Cf. Committee on Bioethics, Strategic Action Plan on Human Rights and Technologies in Biomedicine, 19–21 November 2019, par. 22, where they state regarding the person's integrity that this "is understood as the ability of individuals to exercise control over what happens to them with regard to, inter alia, their body, their mental state, and the related personal data". See also Lwoff 2020.
133 Hildt 2022, p. 88 (emphasis added).
134 Advisory Committee, UNHRC, Impact, opportunities and challenges of neurotechnology with regard to the promotion and protection of all human rights, A/HRC/AC/31/CRP.1 (8 August 2024), par. 27 (emphasis added).

premise of this right is that one has a right to control one's own state of mind.[135] In the negative dimension, the right to mental self-determination protects *from* severe mental interference by others: anyone should "refrain from interventions severely interfering with another's mental integrity by undermining mental control or exploiting pre-existing mental weaknesses".[136]

Bublitz and Merkel ground this right to mental self-determination partly in the idea of self-ownership over our minds: "what is even more constitutive of a subject than her body is her mind. So, whoever grants self-ownership of persons over their bodies has a compelling reason to concede self-ownership over minds".[137] Douglas and Forsberg likewise state that "we might think that considerations of self-ownership and personal sovereignty in fact provide stronger support to a moral right to mental integrity than to a moral right to bodily integrity".[138]

Whereas "self-ownership" and "control" might be plausible moral *justifications* for the right to mental integrity,[139] referring to these notions will not clarify much about the right's *scope*. Which interferences would infringe a right to "the individual's mastery of his mental states" or to "control their brain states"? And what exactly would qualify as a control-undermining interference?

As Zohny et al. write, there are numerous possible interpretations of what "full control" over one's own mental states, or of controlling one's own consciousness, means.[140] One such interpretation, which they take to be the least plausible, is that "full control" means the ability to organise and deliberately select our mental states, such as thoughts, and the broader contents of our consciousness. However, they argue, this seems an incorrect description of how mental states arise from a subjective standpoint. We do not consciously select our thoughts, desires and emotions. Rather, they usually arise unbidden in the mind.[141] This process can be considered *spontaneous*, rather than under full control. Likewise, Bublitz and Merkel highlight that our factual powers to control our minds are much more limited than we may often assume. We cannot concentrate as we wish, remember all we may want or alter our preferences by efforts of will. Neither can we avoid hating, liking or loving someone else nor change our beliefs just by wanting them to be different.[142]

Against this background, Zohny et al. assume that for the interpretation of mental integrity, any reference to "full control" of mental states cannot pertain to mental

135 Bublitz & Merkel 2014. It aims to guarantee to its right-holder the "liberty to self-determine or control what is in and on her mind" (Bublitz 2020b, p. 69, emphasis added).

136 Bublitz & Merkel 2014, p. 68. In the positive dimension, meanwhile, the right protects the freedom to self-determine one's inner realm, such as the content of one's thoughts and other mental phenomena, which we will discuss in Chapter 5.

137 Bublitz & Merkel 2014, p. 62. Cf. Vallentyne 2018.

138 Douglas & Forsberg 2021, p. 191.

139 Identifying moral justifications of a legal right to mental integrity is not our primary aim here. See for this Douglas & Forsberg 2021; Lavazza & Giorgi 2023; Douglas 2024. See also Zuk 2024, p. 2.

140 Zohny et al. 2023, p. 3.

141 Zohny et al. 2023, p. 3.

142 Bublitz & Merkel 2014, p. 65.

control in a comprehensive sense, "because this is the kind of control that we lack anyway".[143] More plausibly, they argue, reference to control in the context of mental integrity relates to the more modest interpretation of being free from others *interfering* with our mental states. Such an understanding of the right to mental integrity – which aligns with the legal interpretation of a right to bodily integrity – seems to reflect the majority view in the literature on constructing the right,[144] to which some explicitly refer as a "right against mental interference".[145]

So, a first way of constructing the right to mental integrity justifies the right by arguing that our putative rights of self-ownership and control entitle us to *freedom from unsolicited mental interference*. Such a conceptualisation, however, still leaves us with many questions about the right's scope. For example, *what types* of interference would count as an infringement? And *which kinds of mental phenomena* may not be interfered with?[146] The next two possible ways of constructing the right tell us more about the right's potential scope (and less about its justificatory underpinnings).

3.3.1.2 Freedom from Direct and Harmful Mental Interference

In view of emerging neurotechnology, Ienca and Andorno have suggested understanding the human right to mental integrity as a right to protect people's mental dimension from potential harm.[147] They propose:

> For an action X, to qualify as a threat to mental integrity, it has to: (i) involve the direct access to and manipulation of neural signalling (ii) be unauthorized – i.e. must occur in absence of the informed consent of the signal generator, (iii) result in physical and/or psychological harm.[148]

Thus, to infringe the right to mental integrity on this account, a non-consensual mental interference must operate *directly* through the brain and result in physical and/or psychological *harm*. Apart from providing examples of neurotechnological interference that may infringe the right this way, including malicious brain-hacking, BCI technology for soldier enhancement, invasive brain-washing interventions and DBS in medicine, Ienca and Andorno do not further elaborate upon the meaning and normative significance of the two central aspects of their construction of the right, that is, "directness" and "harm".[149] What exactly is meant by "direct" access

143 Zohny et al. 2023, p. 3.
144 Bublitz & Merkel 2014; Douglas & Forsberg 2021; Ligthart et al. 2023a; Lavazza & Giorgi 2023; Bublitz 2024.
145 Ryberg 2020, p. 83; Douglas 2024; Ratoff 2024, p. 258.
146 Ryberg 2020, pp. 84–89; Douglas 2024; Tesink et al. 2024.
147 Ienca & Andorno 2017, p. 18.
148 Ienca & Andorno 2017, p. 18. See also Cassinadri 2025, who aims to expand and refine Ienca and Andorno's conceptualization of the right to mental integrity.
149 They do mention that the right would probably be qualified rather than absolute.

and manipulation? Why should the right to mental integrity only protect from *direct* interferences but not from *indirect* alterations of mental states?[150] And against what types of physical or psychological "harm" would the right protect? Moreover, why should the infliction of physical and/or psychological harm be a condition for infringing the right in the first place?[151]

Let us start by considering the requirement of directness, which refers to the *manner* through which an interference causes mental effects. There has been a discussion about the moral and legal significance of direct versus indirect interventions in a person's mental states and processes. Bublitz and Merkel describe these two different ways of intervening with the mind as follows:

> Tentatively, indirect (or external) interventions are those stimuli which are perceived sensually (i.e. heard, seen, smelled, felt, even if not apprehended or reflected upon consciously) and pass through the mind of the person, being processed by a host of psychological mechanisms. Thus, conscious communication in all its forms is an indirect intervention. By contrast, direct (or internal) interventions are stimuli reaching the brain by other routes than sensual perception. The main difference is that direct interventions can be primarily understood as electro-chemical or physical reactions following the laws of nature whereas indirect interventions involve psychological laws (or dynamics) and relate to what is being perceived.[152]

Arguments over the normative significance of this distinction typically appeal to the *level of control* people have over either direct or indirect interventions – that is, the extent to which people can resist their influence. The general assumption is that people have greatest control over *indirect*, sensory interventions that are *consciously perceived*.[153] Such interventions give people the opportunity to (critically) think about what they hear, see or smell, reflect upon those stimuli and process them – as one is consciously aware of them. This process opens the possibility to decide about how one integrates perceived information into one's own psychological framework, for example, by deliberating, questioning or challenging the information, before it will shape the person's beliefs, desires or traits.[154]

The level of control is generally thought to be reduced when stimuli operate indirectly and are *subconsciously* processed, such as through subliminal stimuli in advertisement or political campaigns. At the most extreme end of the spectrum, non-sensory *direct* interventions are considered to *bypass* any psychological process. They operate via purely physical-biological processes in the brain, such as psychopharmaceuticals and brain stimulation, over which the amount of conscious control people have is typically low (if any).[155]

150 Douglas 2018; Bublitz 2020b; Zohny et al. 2023.
151 Zohny et al. 2023.
152 Bublitz & Merkel 2014. See also Bublitz 2020b.
153 Though see Douglas 2018 and Levy 2020 for scepticism about this assumption.
154 Bublitz & Merkel 2014; Bublitz 2020b; Zohny et al. 2023, p. 7.
155 Bublitz & Merkel 2014; Bublitz 2020b.

These distinctions in levels of control are in turn considered normatively relevant in relation to rights that aim to protect the *autonomy* over mental states and processes, including the right to mental integrity.[156] For example, according to Ratoff, the moral "right to mental autonomy (...) is your right to form attitudes in light of overt reasons – that is, in light of reasons that have their influence on your thinking without circumnavigating your consciousness or awareness".[157] Considering the moral right to mental integrity, Zohny et al. argue that the threat to mental integrity posed by some neurotechnologies "is that they stimulate the nervous system in a way that side-steps the opportunity to rationally evaluate their potential influence on mental states or traits, and thereby to control the degree to which they do in fact influence (or interfere with) them".[158] From a legal point of view, Bublitz argues that

> the scope of the right against mind-interventions has to be confined to interferences that undermine mental self-determination to a degree that fails a test of what is reasonable in a highly cooperative, interactive, and communicative society. And this, I claim, is true of interventions that bypass mental control. (...) In light of this premise, the relevance of mental control and integrity – and the direct versus indirect distinction – becomes evident. The more control, the better.[159]

In view of a legal "right against unwanted mind-interventions", Bublitz considers interventions that undermine or bypass mental control "particularly troublesome".[160]

Note that not everyone agrees upon the moral significance of this direct-indirect distinction. For example, considering neural and environmental modulation of mental states, Douglas has challenged the idea that non-perceptual interventions are more objectionable in terms of the mental interference they involve than perceptual interventions.[161] According to Levy, indirect interventions often produce effects that bypass a person's capacity to control as well. Moreover, he argues that, generally, indirect interventions are responsible for far more injustice, harm and inequality than direct interventions.[162]

Here, we will not embark upon discussing the arguable moral significance of direct versus indirect mental influence. For our present purpose, we just assume that, in general, direct interventions, such as brain stimulation, leave less room for mental *control* than indirect interventions, such as cognitive behavioural therapy. The extent to which an intervention impairs rational or conscious control can be

156 As Zuk 2024, p. 2 writes: "According to most theorists, MI [mental integrity] is principally about autonomy or something in the near vicinity, such as self-determination, authentic choice, or self-ownership and personal sovereignty."

157 Ratoff 2024, p. 282.

158 Zohny et al. 2023, p. 8. Cf. Focquaert & Schermer 2015.

159 Bublitz 2020b, p. 70.

160 Bublitz 2020b, p. 70.

161 Douglas 2018.

162 Levy 2020. See also Levy 2007. Cf. Ryberg 2020, pp. 90–91.

relevant to human rights that protect the *autonomy* over mental states and processes, including the right to mental integrity.

However, in our view, the legal relevance of this distinction does not so much relate to the *scope* of a right to mental integrity – that is, to the question of whether an intervention infringes the right – but rather to the right's *permissible limitations*: the question of whether infringements of the right can be justified or, rather, constitute a violation (see section 3.3.2). For example, as it emerges from the case law of the ECtHR, inducing psychological effects in others through *indirect* means *can* infringe the right to mental integrity. For instance, causing well-founded anxiety or fear by threats of violence or harassment against a person themselves or their close relatives can infringe the right to psychological and moral integrity protected under Article 8 ECHR.[163] Furthermore, publishing defamatory statements and sexual photographs of a person in the media can harm the person's psychological integrity.[164] These are clearly no direct interferences with a person's mental states and feelings, but they nevertheless infringe the right to mental integrity under Article 8 ECHR.

Hence, apparently, for infringing the right to mental (moral or psychological) integrity under Article 8 ECHR, it appears not decisive whether the mental effects have been induced by either direct or indirect means. The same appears to apply to other human rights that protect mental autonomy, such as the right to freedom of thought. Various *indirect* means of influencing mental states are often referred to as paradigmatic violations of this right, including indoctrination, brainwashing and re-education camps.[165] Moreover, the Special Rapporteur on Freedom of Religion or Belief has highlighted that "[a] growing body of legal scholarship supports the claim that freedom of thought includes freedom from manipulation. While modification bypasses psychological processes to directly alter biological function, manipulation engages and controls psychological processes".[166] In other words, next to directly interfering with a person's thoughts, indirect interventions into a person's psychological processes fall within the scope of the right to freedom of thought too.

In sum, for determining the scope of human rights that protect mental autonomy, including the right to mental integrity, the direct-indirect distinction appears not particularly helpful. This distinction may be relevant to the permissible limitations of the right, however (section 3.3.2).

Let us now turn to the other central requirement of Ienca and Andorno's proposal to construct the right to mental integrity: for an infringement, the interference must result in physical and/or psychological *harm*. As Zohny et al. point out, what counts

163 ECtHR 30 November 2010, 2660/03 (*Hajduová/Slovakia*), par. 49 ECtHR 24 July 2012, 41526/10 (*Đorđević/Croatia*), par. 97.

164 ECtHR 28 October 2014, 531/06 (*Ion Cârstea/Romania*) par. 38.

165 Vermeulen & Roosmalen 2018, p. 738; Nowak & Schabas 2019, p. 503.

166 UN Special Rapporteur on the Freedom of religion or belief, 5 October 2021, A/76/380, par. 35.

as being harmed or made worse of in this regard, is, however, hard to settle: "[f]or instance, it cannot be that the concern over mental integrity comes down to being protected from any harmful mental interference. People interfere with our mental states all the time in ways that harm us on any plausible sense of that term, and in ways no one thinks we have a moral or legal right to be protected from".[167] Zohny et al. mention the example of being sincerely told by a loved one that you are a disappointment. Although these words likely lead to mental suffering in devastating ways, it does not follow that a right to mental integrity protects against others telling us things like these. By contrast, some brain interventions may well induce significant mental change, bypassing rational control, though without causing any physical or psychological harm. Think, for example, of non-consensual tDCS or TMS to increase a convicted person's emphatic abilities and reduce aggressive traits. Such interventions, which we might conceive of as paradigmatic infringements of the right to mental integrity,[168] would likely fall outside of the right's scope if infringements require either physical or psychological harm, as Ienca and Andorno suggest.

From a legal point of view, it is doubtful whether the right to mental integrity would only cover interferences that result in some kind of physical and/or psychological harm.[169] Indeed, the *absolute* protection of bodily and mental integrity as part of the prohibition of torture and ill-treatment only applies in cases of severe physical or mental suffering.[170] However, harm does not appear to be required for the application of the *qualified* right to personal integrity, inherent in Article 8 ECHR and 17 ICCPR. For instance, according to Bublitz, the right to mental integrity in the meaning of Article 8 ECHR seems conceptually broader, capturing interferences that do not amount to setbacks to mental health, like in cases of prejudiced honour and reputation, for example, through defamation.[171] Likewise, Biber and Capasso write that "the ECtHR has broadly interpreted the terms mental and psychological integrity. According to the case-law, these terms do not cover only the setbacks in mental capabilities but also situations in which no clinical-pathological mental disorders occur".[172]

Against this backdrop, we ought to be careful not to exclude too quickly the possibility that interferences with people's minds could infringe the right to mental integrity without causing physical or psychological harm.[173] This is, however, not to say that the harm caused by a mental interference is legally irrelevant to the right to mental integrity. Similar to the direct-indirect distinction, we think that its relevance primarily relates to the right's permissible limitations and the ultimate balancing of

[167] Zohny et al. 2023, p. 4.
[168] Bublitz 2024, p. 788.
[169] Ligthart 2024.
[170] Vermeulen & Battjes 2018, pp. 387, 384; Harris et al. 2023, p. 243.
[171] Bublitz 2020a, p. 396.
[172] Biber & Capasso 2022, p. 511.
[173] Which would in turn depend on how one operationalizes harm in this context.

competing interests, rather than to defining the right's scope. We come back to this in section 3.3.2.

In conclusion, we believe that neither the requirement of "direct" interference nor that of physical and/or psychological "harm" is compelling for delineating the scope of the right to mental integrity. Since the normative significance of these requirements is largely unclear, and as the current human right to mental integrity seems conceptually broader, we think that categorically excluding all indirect and harmless mental alterations from the right's scope is unwarranted.

But what if we reject both harm and directness as essential requirements for infringing the right to mental integrity? Wouldn't this extend the right's scope too much, to almost every direct and indirect mental influence by others, including a broad range of everyday, undoubtedly permissible social interactions that affect other people's minds, for example, by causing anxiety, disappointment or anger?[174] To prevent the right from being too broad, some kind of threshold should apply. This brings us to a third possible construction of the right.

3.3.1.3 Freedom from Significant Mental Interference

Douglas and Forsberg understand a legal right to mental integrity as "a right against (certain kinds of) non-consensual interference with the mind".[175] Analogous to the right to bodily integrity, they consider it plausible that some types of non-consensual mental influence will not infringe the right to mental integrity, because the effects are *not significant* enough:

> If I wave my hand near your arm, causing the hairs on your arm to quiver, I have not infringed your right to bodily integrity, even if I do this without your consent; the effect of the influence is not significant enough. Similarly, there may be mental influences that fail to infringe the right to mental integrity because their mental impact is too insignificant.[176]

Exactly how significant an influence must be to infringe the right, Douglas and Forsberg set aside for further investigation. Elsewhere, Douglas suggests that a mental interference might be too trivial to infringe the right in virtue of "falling below some threshold of magnitude".[177] In the same vein, Bublitz has proposed, also in analogy with bodily integrity, to define interferences with mental integrity as "actions that detrimentally affect the mind, i.e., mental states, processes, functions, and abilities, above a threshold of seriousness".[178] This includes the infliction of pain

174 Cf. Ligthart et al. 2023a, p. 6; Zohny et al. 2023, p. 4; Bublitz 2024, p. 788; Zuk 2024, p. 3.

175 Douglas & Forsberg 2021, p. 182. See also Ligthart et al. 2023a, p. 6; Douglas 2024.

176 Douglas & Forsberg 2021, p. 186.

177 Douglas 2024, p. 6, adding in footnote 16 that "we might suppose that this will depend on how many mental states or parts are interfered with, on the centrality and/or importance of those mental states or parts, and on the magnitude of any interferences with them".

178 Bublitz 2024, p. 788.

and mental injury, causing detriment to mental health and other undesirable, non-trivial changes to the mind. Regarding neurotechnology, Bublitz writes that the right to mental integrity comprises neurointerventions that cause "non-trivial detrimental mental effects". More specifically, the right would apply to "[s]ubstantive alterations of mental functioning, capacities, or important mental states",[179] including "non-consensual 'improvements' of mental functioning, such as coercive treatments in forensic or psychiatric settings, or coercive cognitive enhancement".[180]

The scope of such a right against *significant* mental interference is plausibly broader compared to a right against *direct harmful* mental interference (discussed above). Meanwhile, requiring a certain *threshold of seriousness or significance* could prevent the right from being too expansive. For instance, in both Douglas' and Bublitz' interpretations, inducing trivial mental effects does not qualify as a rights infringement.[181]

Constructing the right to mental integrity as a right against mental interference above a certain level of seriousness, seems to align well with how the ECtHR understands the right to personal integrity under Article 8 ECHR. As previously discussed, generally, Article 8 ECHR applies when the effects of an interference on the person's physical or mental integrity are "sufficiently adverse".[182] Where exactly this "sufficiently adverse" threshold is placed is largely unclear yet.[183] However, as discussed in section 3.2, for interferences with bodily integrity, the threshold appears not very demanding.

This may feed the objection that constructing the right to mental integrity as a right against "significant" mental interference – that is, interferences above a threshold of seriousness – is unpersuasive, because the threshold is (I) unclear and ambiguous and (II) bears the risk of being too low, possibly encompassing all kinds of significant, yet undoubtedly permissible, everyday mental influences inherent in social interaction.[184] Let us explain why we think that, from a legal perspective, this objection is not compelling.

First, using unspecified and open norms and thresholds is a typical feature of the law – human rights law in particular. For instance, regarding the protection of "private life" within the meaning of Article 8 ECHR, the ECtHR holds that "[t]he concept of 'private life' is a broad term not susceptible to exhaustive definition".[185] Likewise, regarding the prohibition of "torture", "inhuman" and "degrading" treatment of Article 7 ICCPR, the Human Rights Committee does not see the need for specifying these terms by drawing up a list of prohibited acts or by establishing sharp

[179] Cf. Douglas 2024, footnote 16 (considering a moral right to mental integrity).

[180] Bublitz 2024, p. 788.

[181] Bublitz 2024; Douglas 2024. As Bublitz writes, "all neurointerventions with *non-trivial* effects fall under the [right's] scope" (p. 7, emphasis added).

[182] ECtHR 6 February 2001, 44599/98 (*Bensaid/UK*), par. 46.

[183] Harris et al. 2023, p. 525.

[184] Ratoff 2024, p. 264; Blumenthal-Barby & Ubel 2024. Cf. Ryberg 2020, pp. 84–92.

[185] E.g., ECtHR (GC) 25 September 2018, 76639/11 (*Denisov/Ukraine*), § 95.

distinctions between the different forms of prohibited treatment.[186] Such open and unspecified concepts are not at all problematic for interpreting, applying and developing human rights on a case-by-case basis. On the contrary: they enable the dynamic and evolutive interpretation and formation of freedoms and rights that is typical of human rights law.

The same applies *mutatis mutandis* to the use of loosely defined thresholds for determining rights infringements, such as the threshold of "sufficiently adverse" effects for infringing the right to personal integrity under Article 8 ECHR and the "minimum level of severity" threshold of the prohibition of ill-treatment under Article 3 ECHR. Because these thresholds are formulated in general terms, they can adapt to ongoing developments in society. For example, regarding Article 3 ECHR, Harris et al. observe that over time, in practice, "the 'threshold' has been lowered to cover certain intermediate forms of ill-treatment (. . .) that would not have been in the minds of the Convention drafters".[187] Hence, objecting to the use of a *general* threshold for delimiting the right to mental integrity on grounds of vagueness and lack of specificity makes, in our view, little sense from a legal perspective.

Still, one could argue that such a general and unspecified threshold may lead to an overinterpretation of the right's scope – applying the right to an extremely broad range of both exceptional and everyday non-trivial mental influences, including those stemming from the news, advertisement, education and interpersonal relations and conversations. Our response to such an argument would be as follows.

First, we challenge the idea that a broad scope of the right to mental integrity would imply that all kinds of everyday non-trivial mental influences infringe the right. Only *non-consensual* interferences will do so. Much of the mental influences we expose ourselves to every day, including the news, advertisement and conversations with others, are influences of which we are generally aware and hence to which we are *capable* of consenting – unlike influences that operate below the level of our awareness. In fact, many of these everyday influences are ones to which we do indeed consent, either implicitly or explicitly. In choosing to read the news or to continue listening to others' reasons and arguments, for instance, we at least implicitly consent to being influenced by the information, views and ideas to which we are exposed. It is thus implausible to hold that all, or even most, of the everyday non-trivial interferences with our minds to which we are exposed would infringe the right to mental integrity (broadly conceived); though, of course, some such interferences *might* infringe the right– for example, if we are repeatedly exposed to others' persuasive efforts despite having requested or indicated that we do not wish to be, or if we are repeatedly exposed to pop-up ads to which we did not consent.

[186] CCPR General Comment No. 20, par. 4.
[187] Harris et al. 2023, p. 244.

Moreover, even if we assume that the threshold of a "significant" or "serious" mental interference would indeed be low and could therefore imply a broad scope of the right to mental integrity, we still do not think that this would lead to an overinclusive prohibition of all kinds of prima facie permissible acts and mental influences. A broad *scope* of the qualified right to mental integrity need not necessarily imply overprotection by the right. In the law, the scope of fundamental rights, including human rights, is typically broad. For example, Article 8 ECHR protects a person's sphere of privacy and personal autonomy, the scope of which "has expanded substantially over the years as the Court has interpreted the notion of private life to cover a broad range of interests".[188] Likewise, in domestic legal systems, constitutional rights are often formulated in broad and general terms, protecting many different aspects of people's private and public lives. For example, the right to freely develop one's personality laid down in Article 2(1) of the German Basic Law even includes the right to feed pigeons in the park and to go riding in the woods.[189] However, a broad scope of fundamental rights does not mean that every interference with the protected interest will *violate* the right and be therefore prohibited. Recall that most human rights, including the rights to privacy and respect for private life (Articles 17 ICCPR, 8 ECHR), are *qualified* rights. They permit limitations when necessary for and proportionate to protecting certain public interests or the right and freedoms of others.

In sum, to us, it seems implausible that a broad scope of the right to mental integrity would ipso facto imply overprotection by categorically prohibiting a broad range of mental influencing inherent to social interaction.[190] First, because much of these mental influences will not infringe the right due to (implicit) consent, and second, because infringements will often be justified based on a balancing of competing rights and interests.

What could the implications of the right to mental integrity, constructed as a right against *non-consensual significant* mental interference, be for the neurorehabilitation of convicted persons? Plausibly, most forms of non-consensual brain stimulation for reducing recidivism risks will infringe the right to mental integrity on this understanding. The mental effects of these interventions are typically non-trivial. Studies indicate that electrical stimulation of certain brain areas with tDCS can have significant effects on a convicted person's emphatic abilities, aggressive traits, and decision-making, such as risk-taking.[191] Non-consensually inducing such mental changes plausibly infringes the right against non-consensual significant mental interference. However, as mentioned, this does not say much yet about the *permissibility* of such interventions. The answer to this question depends largely on the

188 De Vries 2018.
189 Möller 2012, p. 4.
190 Provided that the right to mental integrity is a qualified right.
191 Sergiou et al. 2022; Knehans et al. 2022; Kuhn et al. 2024.

permissible limitations of the right, that is, on the ultimate balancing of competing interests allowed for by the right.[192] We explore this issue in the next section.

3.3.2 *Permissible Limitations*

Inducing mental changes in others is not exceptional in our everyday social lives. We do so all the time – in some social domains more than others. One could think of the compulsory education of children, the provision of psychopharmaceuticals to psychiatric patients, and the reformation and rehabilitation of convicted persons. When not consented to, many such mental influences plausibly infringe a right against significant mental interference. However, presumably, not all of them are legally (or morally) impermissible. There could be good reasons for legally allowing the bringing about of mental changes in persons for different purposes in different contexts. Again, one could think of educating children, treating forensic psychiatric patients and rehabilitating convicted persons. But how should the law distinguish permissible from impermissible interferences with mental integrity? As Bublitz writes, "[t]he key challenge for the construction of the right to mental integrity lies in developing a taxonomy that sorts the many examples of everyday and undoubtedly permissible social interactions adversely affecting minds of others (causing disappointment, anger, anxiety, etc.) from the supposedly impermissible ones. The legal criteria for this distinction have not been established".[193]

Developing such a taxonomy would exceed the scope of this book. Meanwhile, as the issue of permissible versus impermissible limitations of the right to mental integrity is essential to the permissibility of neurorehabilitation, we wish to briefly explore the following question here: How should judges determine whether an infringement of the right to mental integrity – understood as a right against nonconsensual significant mental interference – would be justified, or whether it would rather violate this right?[194]

Whether an infringement of the right to mental integrity is also a *violation* largely depends on an ultimate balancing of the competing interests at stake, which, in turn, will largely depend on the facts and circumstances of the individual case. In the preceding section, we concluded that neither the direct-indirect distinction nor the infliction of physical and/or psychological harm appear decisive factors for determining the *scope* of the human right to mental integrity. However, we think these factors would be relevant to the question of justification – and, consequently, the possible violation of the right. Let us recall that interferences with a person's body

192 See also Bublitz 2024, p. 788.

193 Bublitz 2024, p. 788. Cf. Nowak & Schabas 2019, p. 503.

194 In analogy with the right to bodily integrity, we here assume that a human right to mental integrity is typically a qualified right, which aligns with the qualified protection offered to mental integrity by Article 8 ECHR and 17 ICCPR. Cf. Ryberg 2020, p. 92; Mendlow 2018; Craig 2016. Meanwhile, some types of significant mental inference may also trigger absolute protection by the prohibition of ill-treatment or the right to freedom of thought.

and mind can infringe the right to personal integrity to different degrees, with different severities. The more *severe* the infringement, the more substantial the reasons must be to justify such an infringement.[195] For example, regarding *bodily* integrity, non-consensually inserting a needle in a person's body will less severely infringe the right compared to non-consensually performing surgery, the latter requiring stronger reasons to be justified. The same plausibly applies to *mental* integrity.[196]

This is where the direct-indirect distinction and the level of harm become relevant. If the primary aim of a right to mental integrity is to protect *autonomy* over mental states and processes, then it is plausible that the less mental *control* an intervention leaves to the affected person, the more severe the infringement of the right to mental integrity is. If we assume that, generally, direct interventions leave less control over mental states than indirect interventions, this will imply that, in general, stronger reasons are needed to justify infringements through direct interventions compared to indirect interventions. From that point of view, Bublitz may be right in saying that interventions that undermine or bypass mental control are "particularly troublesome" – they may be more difficult to justify.

The same applies *mutatis mutandis* to the issue of psychological harm. When an infringement of the right to mental integrity also entails some kind of (severe) psychological harm, such as stress or depression as a side effect of medication or brain stimulation, it is reasonable to suppose that this will contribute to the severity of the rights infringement, therefore requiring more substantial reasons for justification. Moreover, if the level of harm attains a certain severity threshold, absolute protection from the prohibition of ill-treatment could be engaged (see section 3.2).

What could all this mean for the use of non-consensual neurointerventions in criminal justice? These interventions are of direct nature, such as tDCS, TMS and psychopharmaceuticals. Hence, the mental changes they induce may leave little (if any) room for mental control by the person involved, and as such, they may interfere with the person's mental autonomy to a significant degree. Therefore, they will likely be considered to severely infringe the right to mental integrity, thus requiring weighty reasons to be justified. The need for such substantial reasons may further increase when the intervention entails harmful psychological side effects. If any such reasons exist, the prevention of severe crimes – such as abuse, rape and murder – is a likely candidate.

Although we think the above analysis makes sense in principle, it is unclear how strict the requirements for justification will be in practice. Recall that the context of criminal punishment and crime prevention allows for a wide range of severe and less severe interferences with both bodily and mental integrity (e.g., strip searches

[195] Christoffersen 2009, p. 208; Gerards 2023, p. 355.
[196] De Vries 2018, p. 691.

in prison,[197] collection of blood samples,[198] antilibidinal interventions to sex offenders[199]). In general, regarding potential violations of Article 8 ECHR – which includes the right to mental integrity – in the context of imprisonment, the ECtHR holds that

> normal restrictions and limitations consequent on prison life and discipline during lawful detention are not matters which would constitute a violation of Article 8 either because they are considered not to constitute an interference with the detainee's private and family life (. . .) or because any such interference would be justified.[200]

This is an important point, which may be used to substantiate at least two different arguments, both in another direction.

First, one could argue that imprisonment, in and of itself, often severely affects the incarcerated person's well-being and psychological functioning and may have serious impact on a variety of mental phenomena that are protected by the right to mental integrity, such as feelings, emotions, traits and desires. As touched upon earlier in this and the previous chapter, incarceration is notoriously known for its potential negative effects on the persons' psychological well-being, for example, by the traumatic experiences or mental harm incarceration can cause. Furthermore, research suggests that imprisonment has significant adverse effects on brain areas associated with self-control. Recent studies reported that neuropsychological capacities in incarcerated persons declined after three to four months in prison.[201] Meijers et al. hypothesize that the cause of the decline may be, at least in part, the *impoverished* prison environment, which is supported by the findings in animal studies (and some studies in humans) on the influence of the environment on brain and behaviour.[202] Recall, furthermore, that a recent study on the public attitudes towards incarceration and neurointerventions found that the participants considered neurointerventions "to be a weaker form of mind control than incarcerations and would lead to more change for the better".[203]

Against this background, one could argue that, if the effects on the mind caused by "normal restrictions and limitations" consequent on lawful incarceration normally do not raise any issues regarding the right to mental integrity, it is unpersuasive to oppose non-consensual neurorehabilitation by appealing to the right to mental integrity – provided that the mental effects are either of similar gravity or less severe compared to incarceration.[204]

197 ECtHR 7 October 2022, 49529/12 (*Syrianos/Grèce*), par. 79; UN Counter-terrorism implementation task force, *Basic Human Rights Reference Guide: The Stopping and Searching of Persons in the Context of Countering Terrorism*, OHCHR 2014.

198 ECtHR 15 May 2018, 41079/16 (*Caruana/Malta*).

199 Forsberg 2021.

200 ECtHR 16 May 2002, 39474/98 (*D.G./Ireland*), par. 105.

201 Meijers et al. 2018; Umbach, Raine & Leonard 2018; Meijers, Harte & Scherder 2023. See also Ligthart et al. 2019; Coppola 2019.

202 Meijers, Harte & Scherder 2023.

203 Denson, Griffiths & Smith 2024, p. 7.

204 Cf. Ryberg 2020, p. 73; Douglas 2018.

On the other hand, it can be argued that the mental changes entailed by imprisonment differ from those induced through neurointerventions in a way that is normatively significant, and, therefore, that neurointerventions may violate the right to mental integrity while imprisonment would normally not. For example, Birks and Buyx argue that although both neurointerventions and incarceration may involve equal interference with the person's mental states, harming the person to the same extent in the same respect, "it does not follow that the harm-doing is morally equivalent. There could be a difference in terms of *intention* between some of the harm-doings caused".[205] If intentional harm is harder to justify than unintentional but merely foreseen harm, Birks and Buyx argue, "then this could account for the view that neurointerventions are morally objectionable in one respect that incarceration is not".[206] Put differently: mental alterations that are a result of *unintended side effects* (e.g., of incarceration) are morally less objectionable than *intended* mental changes of similar intensity, such as those caused by neurointerventions that *aim* to induce mental change. In the same vein,[207] Shaw suggests that "intended effects and side effects may lie on a spectrum, and the closer the mental-integrity-undermining effects of a punishment or neurointervention fall toward the intended end of the spectrum, the harder the punishment or neurointervention may be to justify".[208]

Intuitively, the idea that unintended interference with mental integrity is less objectionable than intended interference may sound appealing.[209] However, in our view, the moral or – for the present purpose – legal significance of this distinction strongly depends on conceptualisation of (the right to) mental integrity that one follows. Birks and Buyx understand the "interest in mental integrity" as "a person's interest in not having at least some of his mental states *intentionally* altered by others in certain ways".[210] Likewise, Shaw proposes that the moral right to mental integrity "can be infringed by *intentionally* interfering with a person's mental states through nonrational means".[211]

Indeed, if the right to mental integrity is understood as a right against some forms of *intentional* mental interference, the "level of intentionality" is plausibly relevant for determining the severity of the rights infringement, which in turn affects its potential justification. This could mean that *knowingly* causing mental alterations by sending someone to prison less severely infringes the right to mental integrity than *purposely* inducing mental change of similar intensity, for example, by brain stimulation. However, if one adopts an understanding of the right to mental integrity that

205 Birks & Buyx 2018, p. 134 (emphasis added).
206 Birks & Buyx 2018, p. 134.
207 Though without arguing that neurointerventions are more objectionable than incarceration.
208 Shaw 2022.
209 Philosophers have long debated whether there is a morally significant difference between intentionally versus foreseeably causing harm. For a candidate view that holds that there is not, see Kagan 1991, Chapter 4. For a defence of this distinction, see Moschella 2023.
210 Birks & Buyx 2018, p. 136 (emphasis added).
211 Shaw 2022, p. 1418 (emphasis added).

does not include the requirement of intentionality, such as the "right against significant mental interference" we discussed in the previous section, the normative significance of the distinction between intentional versus side effects is at least questionable, also because, typically, to be justified, infringements of the right to mental integrity *need to be* intentional: they must pursue a 'legitimate aim' and be proportionate to that aim, such as the prevention of crime or the protection of the health of others. Moreover, including an "intentionality-requirement" into the scope of the right, may well result in reduced human rights protection against (neuro)interventions that have serious side effects on people's minds, just because those effects were not intended.

3.4 CONCLUDING REMARKS

International and European human rights offer robust protection to the integrity of persons. This includes the protection of bodily and mental integrity through different human rights, including the right to privacy, the right to security of person, the freedom of thought and the prohibition of ill-treatment. The non-consensual administration of invasive forms of brain stimulation that require (neuro)surgery, such as DBS, will severely interfere with a person's bodily integrity. They may even violate the prohibition of ill-treatment and the right to security of person. Meanwhile, regarding non-invasive forms of brain stimulation, such as tDCS and TMS, the bodily interference will often be minimal. Still, the mental alterations these interventions induce can be significant. In theory, such a mental interference may infringe the absolute right to freedom of thought in some cases in at least some cases. A central question in this regard is whether the targeted mental phenomena reasonably qualify as a "thought" in the meaning of this right. We argued that the typical targets of neurointerventions will probably be phenomena such as empathy, tendencies and behavioural control, which are more related to emotion and behaviour responses and less likely to be considered "thoughts".

Most non-consensual neurointerventions will likely infringe the qualified right to mental integrity, inherent in Articles 17 ICCPR and 8 ECHR. Legally, the meaning and scope of this right are currently unclear. Therefore, we looked at both legal and philosophical literature to tentatively construct the right as "a right against significant mental interference". Whether an infringement of this right is justified or constitutes a violation depends on an ultimate balancing of competing private and public interests, to which the notion of proportionality is central. For that balancing, we showed that the direct nature of neurointerventions is legally significant, as direct interventions can be considered to bypass mental control and therefore to infringe the right to mental integrity more severely, requiring weightier reasons for their justification. The same plausibly applies to neurointerventions that entail (severe) psychological harm, for example, as a consequence of unintended side effects.

4

The Right to Mental Privacy

On Privacy, Freedom of Expression and Freedom of Thought

4.1 INTRODUCTION

Thus far, we have largely considered technologies that are capable of *changing* persons' mental states. However, today, a range of technologies are also being developed that can *gain insight into* the mental realms of others.[1] One example is the measurement of brain activity, which has enabled researchers to make inferences about individual mental states and faculties. In particular, fMRI and EEG can measure brain activity in a way that allows for inferences about what a person remembers, recognises, thinks or feels. EEG has been used, for example, to identify concealed memories about a criminal offence;[2] and fMRI has been used to reveal sexual orientation,[3] political ideology[4] or a person's craving for cocaine.[5] Recently, various research groups used neurotechnology together with emerging forms of artificial intelligence (AI) to decode mental content from brain activity, with some interesting first results.[6] According to Brownsword, with the development of these kinds of "brain-reading" technologies, "researchers have a window into the brains and, possibly, into a deeper understanding of the mental lives of their participants".[7]

In view of these developments, the private sphere of our inner minds may no longer be as inaccessible to others in the way it used to be, raising questions about how the law should protect *mental privacy*.[8] Various interpretations of a right to

[1] Farahany 2023.
[2] Rosenfeld 2018.
[3] Safron et al. 2017.
[4] Yang et al. 2022.
[5] Kober et al. 2016.
[6] Bellier et al. 2023; Tang et al. 2023.
[7] Brownsword 2012, p. 223.
[8] This point has been made by, among others, Farahany 2012a; Richmond, Reeds & Edwards 2012; Shen 2013; Ienca & Andorno 2017; Goering 2021; Ienca 2021; Ligthart et al. 2023a. Consider also, however, that the prior inaccessibility of the mind may be somewhat overemphasised, given humans' extensive, natural mind-reading capabilities (see Meynen 2018). The point might thus more precisely be that these developments render the inner mind even more accessible than it once was.

mental privacy have been used in the literature.[9] Here, we understand this right in a broad sense, as a right not to reveal unexpressed mental phenomena such as mental states and content.[10]

Concerns about mental privacy raised by neurotechnology exceed the domain of medicine and scientific research, as the technology promises to be usable within other contexts too, including education, at work, in the military and criminal justice.[11] Presumably, these different contexts ask for tailored approaches to protect mental privacy. As before, our focus here is on criminal justice: more specifically, on neurotechnological "brain-reading" to predict future dangerousness – often referred to as "neuroprediction"[12] – within the context of rehabilitation.

Contemporary debates on the right to mental privacy vis-à-vis neurotechnology often focus on the *scope* of human rights. Scholars consider whether the protection of mental privacy is covered by the established framework of human rights law or whether it requires the recognition of a standalone and specific human right to mental privacy.[13] Meanwhile, as we saw in the preceding chapters, effective human rights protection of the mind not only depends on the scope of human rights, but also on their permissible *limitations*. In this chapter, we consider both the scope and permissible limitations of the right to mental privacy, with specific attention to the question of whether the protection of mental privacy has an absolute dimension in established human rights law.

The outline of this chapter is as follows. In section 4.2, we offer an overview of the human rights protection of mental privacy by three established human rights: (1) the right to privacy, (2) the right to freedom of expression, and (3) the right to freedom of thought. In section 4.3, we consider the interplay between these rights in their protection of mental privacy and explore a threshold criterion for engaging absolute protection by the right to freedom of thought. Along the way, we discuss the implications of our analysis for the non-consensual neuroprediction in criminal justice. Section 4.4 draws conclusions.

4.2 THE PROTECTION OF MENTAL PRIVACY IN HUMAN RIGHTS LAW

In response to recent calls to recognise a specific human right to mental privacy,[14] different scholars have argued that such a right is already protected within the existing framework of human rights law.[15] In particular, they point to the protective

9 See, e.g., Ienca 2021, p. 5; Wajnerman Paz 2021; Goering et al. 2021; Ligthart 2025a.
10 Ligthart 2025a.
11 Ligthart 2022; Farahany 2023.
12 Nadelhoffer et al. 2012; Aharoni et al. 2013; Tortora et al. 2020.
13 Ienca & Andorno 2017; Yuste, Genser & Hermann 2021; Ligthart et al. 2021; Bublitz 2022.
14 Ienca & Andorno 2017; www.neurorightsfoundation.org.
15 Ligthart et al. 2021; Alegre 2022; Bublitz 2022, 2024; Hertz 2023; Istace 2023; Susser & Cabrera 2023.

scope of (i) the right to privacy, (ii) the right to freedom of expression, and (iii) the right to freedom of thought – all three enshrined in human rights treaties across the globe. By adopting the 'living instrument approach' to human rights – which implies that human rights should be interpreted dynamically, in view of present-day conditions, including technological developments – it has been argued that these existing rights are well equipped to offer adequate protection against the non-consensual disclosure of mental states and content (be that either by forced testimony, non-consensual brain-reading, or the hacking of a person's BCI).[16] This living instrument approach was initially developed within the case law of the ECtHR,[17] but has now also been referred to by the UN Human Rights Committee (CCPR) when interpreting and applying the ICCPR.[18]

In this section, we consider how mental privacy is protected by the three human rights mentioned above – the right to privacy, the right to freedom of expression and the right to freedom of thought. We will show that it is evident that mental privacy is protected within the established framework of human rights law. However, much is still unclear about the right's permissible limitations.[19] Is mental privacy typically a qualified right, of which infringements can sometimes be justified, like for preventing crime? Or has it, on top of that, an absolute layer, that is, a dimension of mental privacy that can never be overridden in any circumstances?[20] And if the right to mental privacy has such an absolute layer, which infringements would then be covered by this absolute dimension? The issue of permissible limitations is central to section 4.3.

4.2.1 *The Right to Privacy*

The right to privacy has a robust foundation in human rights law. It is for instance recognised in the Universal Declaration of Human Rights (Article 12), the International Covenant on Civil and Political Rights (Article 17) and the European Convention on Human Rights (Article 8) – with the latter (as earlier indicated) referring to the right to "respect for private life".

What is meant by a right to privacy? According to the UN Human Rights Council, privacy can be considered "as the presumption that individuals should have an area of autonomous development, interaction and liberty, a 'private sphere' with or without interaction with others, free from State intervention and from excessive

16 In the context of criminal procedure, the privilege against self-incrimination has the potential to offer additional protection to (some aspects of) mental privacy. For extensive analyses on the implications of the privilege against self-incrimination vis-à-vis non-consensual brain-reading, see Farahany 2012b; Shen 2013; Ligthart 2022.

17 Harris et al. 2023, pp. 7–8.

18 CCPR 13 August 2003, 829/1998 (*Judge/Canada*).

19 Cf. Bublitz 2024; Ligthart & Van de Pol 2025.

20 Cf. Ienca & Andorno 2017, p. 15.

unsolicited intervention by other uninvited individuals".[21] Several moral rationales have been advanced as underpinning this right to privacy.[22] Many scholars emphasise the instrumental value of privacy for enabling freedom and autonomy, with some arguing (more strongly) that without the protection of private life, individual freedom and autonomy would be impossible.[23] Other scholars suggest that privacy has non-instrumental value, or value in-and-of-itself, such that in its absence people would fail to flourish.[24] And still others argue that a right to privacy is justified for respect-based reasons – that is, that refraining from intruding on a person's privacy is necessary to respect that individual as a person or being "with sensibilities, ends, and aspirations of their own".[25]

The right to privacy is relevant for our present analysis because obligations to reveal private mental phenomena – for example, using non-consensual brain-reading – are likely to infringe the right to privacy. The right to privacy is, after all, both widely applicable and broad in scope – both in the case of Article 17 ICCPR and Article 8 ECHR. It applies to state agents who might interfere with a person's privacy. It also requires that states adopt legislative and other measures to give effect to the protection of privacy.[26] And the right's breadth means that it should protect against a wide spectrum of privacy interference, including by modern means.

Looking first to the international context, Article 17 ICCPR "is a short but versatile provision, capable of answering a broad diversity of unlawful or arbitrary incursions into privacy (…) which could not have been specifically foreseen by its drafters".[27] For example, Article 17 ICCPR applies to AI systems that process personal data for algorithmic decision-making.[28] It also covers the protection of metadata, as such data, when analysed and aggregated, "may give an insight into an individual's behaviour, social relationship, private preference and identity".[29] Furthermore, the UN High Commissioner for Human Rights, when discussing the right to privacy, refers to data-driven technologies that "increasingly enable States and business enterprises to obtain fine-grained information about people's lives, make inferences about their physical and mental characteristics and create detailed personality profiles".[30] The High Commissioner considers informational privacy to be particularly important in the age of modern technology and digital

21 UNHRC, The right to privacy in the digital age, A/HRC/39/29, 3 August 2018, par. 5.

22 See, for example, Inness 1992; Corlett 2002; Marmor 2015.

23 See, for example, Bates 1964, p. 432; Corlett 2002, p. 336; Alfino & Mayes 2003, pp. 6, 12.

24 Moore argues, for example, that since we have a "near universal need for seclusion or separation at different times" from others, the ability to "control access to oneself (…) and to [one's] personal information is an essential part of human flourishing"; see Moore 2010, p. 33.

25 Benn 1984, p. 227.

26 CCPR General Comment No. 16, par. 1.

27 Taylor 2020, p. 458.

28 Special Rapporteur on the right to privacy, 25 January 2021, A/HRC/46/37.

29 OHCHR, The right to privacy in the digital age, A/HRC/39/29, 3 August 2018, par. 5.

30 OHCHR, The right to privacy in the digital age, A/HRC/39/29, 3 August 2018, pars. 5, 15.

environments.[31] The High Commissioner also holds that the right to privacy of Article 17 ICCPR is not only impacted by the *examination* and *use* of personal data by humans or algorithms. Even the mere *generation* and *collection* of data relating to a person's identity, family or life will affect the right, "as through those steps an individual loses some control over information that could put his or her privacy at risk".[32]

In the European context, the ECtHR emphasises that "private life" is a broad concept that does not lend itself to exhaustive definition.[33] It is clear though that the right to private life covers the protection of "personal data". Referring to Article 2 of the Data Protection Convention 1981, the ECtHR defines personal data as "any information that relates to an identified or identifiable individual".[34] According to Article 3 of the EU Law Enforcement Directive (2016/680), "personal data" means "any information relating to an identified or identifiable natural person ('data subject'); (...) such as a name, an identification number, location data, an online identifier or to one or more factors specific to the *physical*, *physiological*, genetic, *mental*, economic, cultural or social identity of that natural person".[35]

The ECtHR considers the protection of personal data of fundamental importance to the enjoyment of the right to respect for private life and holds that Article 8 ECHR comprises "the right to a form of informational self-determination, allowing individuals to rely on their right to privacy as regards data which, albeit neutral, are collected, processed and disseminated".[36] When considering whether personal information relates to someone's "private life" in the meaning of Article 8 ECHR, and whether the collection, storage or use of that information infringes this right, the ECtHR has due regard to: (1) the nature of the records, (2) the results that may be obtained, (3) the specific context in which the information has been recorded and retained and (4) the way in which these records are used and processed.[37]

Examples of infringements of Article 8 ECHR in the context of criminal justice include taking and retaining a photograph on arrest, yielding fingerprints and cellular samples for DNA analysis, and the collection of personal information via a GPS tracking system.[38] Plausibly, the right to privacy also applies to the employment of other emerging technologies that yield personal data, including

[31] OHCHR, The right to privacy in the digital age, A/HRC/39/29, 3 August 2018, par. 5.

[32] OHCHR, The right to privacy in the digital age, A/HRC/39/29, 3 August 2018, pars. 5, 7.

[33] ECtHR (GC) 25 September 2018, 76639/11 (*Denisov/Ukraine*), par. 95 (see also section 3.3).

[34] ECHR (GC) 8 November 2016, 18030/11 (*Magyar Helsinki Bizottság/Hungary*), par. 192.

[35] Emphasis added. On this directive see Kosta & Boehm 2024. On brain data and the GDPR, see Rainey et al. 2020; Ienca & Malgieri 2022.

[36] ECHR (GC) 27 June 2017, 931/13 (*Satakunnan Markkinapörssi Oy and Satamedia Oy/Finland*), par. 137.

[37] ECHR 13 February 2020, 45245/15 (*Gaughran/UK*), par. 70; ECHR (GC) 4 December 2008, 30562/04 and 30566/04 (*S. & Marper/UK*), par. 67.

[38] ECHR 13 February 2020, 45245/15 (*Gaughran/UK*), pars. 70, 63; ECHR 14 April 2020, 75229/10 (*Dragan Petrović/Serbia*), pars. 69, 79; ECHR 2 September 2010, 35623/05 (*Uzun/Germany*); ECHR 14 April 2020, 75229/10 (*Dragan Petrović/Serbia*), pars. 69, 79.

neurotechnological brain-reading such as with fMRI and EEG.[39] Such brain-reading could moreover produce *sensitive* personal data, allowing the drawing of inferences about, for example, emotions, sexual orientation and/or mental health.

Given its broad scope, there is reason to suppose that the right to privacy as guaranteed by Articles 17 ICCPR and 8 ECHR *also implies* a right to mental privacy. It is reasonable to suppose, first, that the ethical values thought to ground a right to privacy – that is, the values of freedom and autonomy, human flourishing, and respect for persons – are crucially advanced by the protection of mental privacy. Think of how a lack of mental privacy would likely limit the freedom and "natural flow" of people's ideas (and hence actions),[40] and of how some degree of *mental* seclusion and separation is plausibly necessary for beings like ourselves to function and flourish.[41] Second, legally, it is indeed plausible that a right to mental privacy is ipso facto covered by the general right to privacy. As Bublitz argues, it seems evident that the latter established right covers the former: "[s]everal international instruments protect a general right to privacy or private life. According to the standards of legal interpretation, this abstract right implies more context or domain-specific variations. In other words, mental privacy is implied by the more general right to privacy".[42]

Many lawyers will confirm and endorse this view. For example, already in their seminal article on the right to privacy published in 1890, Warren and Brandeis observed that "the common law secures to each individual the right of determining, originally, to what extent his thoughts, sentiments, and emotions shall be communicated to others".[43] This legal protection, they argued, is merely an instance of the general right to be let alone – the right to privacy – which could be invoked to protect against "invasion either by the too enterprising press, the photographer, or the possessor of any other modern device for recording or reproducing scenes and sounds".[44] Over a century later, the UN Special Rapporteur on the Right to Privacy (Article 17 ICCPR) warned "that constantly developing technologies pose important challenges for the protection of privacy: these technologies may reveal the most intimate behaviour, wishes, preferences and indeed the very thoughts of individuals in ways that previously were not possible".[45] As the UN Special Rapporteur on Freedom of Religion or Belief highlights, in the United States,

[39] Ligthart 2022; Bublitz 2024.

[40] This phrasing is from Sher 2021, p. 92, though Sher is talking about how internalised prohibitions on thought would plausibly limit mental freedom. Virginia Woolf remarked, somewhat similarly, that "A lock on the door means the power to think for oneself", see Woolf 2001, and also McCarthy-Jones 2019.

[41] Brownlee comments on how "we all need routine moments of silence and solitude as a balm for the soul" and this seems applicable to the mental realm specifically, see Brownlee 2020, p. 96. Brownlee points to the creative leaps that we make when we labour (and have space) alone, and we could make a similar point about the value of thinking (and being allowed to think) alone, without scrutiny.

[42] Bublitz 2022, p. 7. See also Bublitz 2024.

[43] Warren & Brandeis 1890, p. 198.

[44] Warren & Brandeis 1890, pp. 205–206. See also Bublitz 2022, p. 7.

[45] UN Special Rapporteur on the right to privacy, 15 October 2018, A/HRC/37/62.

"courts recognise that an individual right to privacy encompasses mental privacy".[46] Likewise, in the European legal context, it has been argued that the right to respect for private life pursuant to Article 8 ECHR covers, among many other things, the protection of mental privacy.[47] These observations seem to confirm that a right not to reveal thoughts, emotions, sentiments, preferences, wishes, or other private mental phenomena – a right to mental privacy – is covered by the general right to privacy.[48]

Non-consensual neuroprediction arguably *infringes* the right to privacy,[49] notwithstanding that the right is unlikely to *prohibit* neuroprediction across the board. Recall that infringements of the right to privacy can be justified under both Article 17 ICCPR and 8 ECHR if they have an non-arbitrary basis in domestic law and are necessary for and proportionate to a legitimate purpose, such as the prevention of crime and disorder.[50] Given that permissible privacy infringements have included, among many other things, secret surveillance and DNA testing for the purpose of preventing crime and protecting the rights of others,[51] and legally obliging witnesses to reveal their knowledge and memories about a criminal offence in court,[52] the right to (mental) privacy is unlikely to prohibit, in principle, *all* non-consensual applications of neuropredictive technologies that reveal private information about brain and mental states for the purpose of preventing crime.[53] We return to this in section 4.3.

4.2.2 *The Right to Freedom of Expression*

The secrecy of our mental states and content also receives protection from the right to freedom of expression, guaranteed by Articles 19 ICCPR and 10 ECHR.[54] The relevance of this right to the protection of mental privacy lies in its negative aspect, guaranteeing the freedom *not* to express oneself. This negative freedom is something we have an interest in possessing. We have an interest in having a "reasonable measure of control" over the ways in which we express and present ourselves to

46 UN Special Rapporteur on the Freedom of religion or belief, 5 October 2021, A/76/380, par. 26, referring to Long Beach City Employees Assn. v. City of Long Beach (1986); Stanley v. Georgia (1969).

47 Ligthart et al. 2021; Ligthart 2025a.

48 Cf. Bublitz 2022, p. 7, who notes that: "Proponents of a novel, standalone right to mental privacy need to show why this reading is false; why privacy of the mind is, in principle, different to, say, the privacy of the bedroom. Without this, it seems they are merely different domains of application of a broader idea, the right to be let alone."

49 Ligthart 2022.

50 We highlighted this in Chapters 2 and 3. See also Lavrysen 2018; Taylor 2020, pp. 459–471.

51 Taylor 2020, pp. 476–479; Harris et al. 2023, pp. 538–539, 542–545.

52 In the ECHR context, privacy complaints on this issue have been interpreted as concerning the freedom of (non-)expression: ECHR 23 October 2018, 26892/12 (*Wanner/Germany*). See next section.

53 Ligthart 2022.

54 Ligthart 2022, p. 253; Istace 2024.

others[55] – consider how expressing ourselves might sometimes open us up to social scrutiny and potential social harm.

The freedom not to express oneself was clearly emphasised by the European Commission on Human Rights (EComHR) in the case of *Strohal/Austria*, where the EComHR argued that "the right to freedom of expression by implication also guarantees a 'negative right' not to be compelled to express oneself, i.e., to remain silent".[56] The Grand Chamber of the ECtHR "does not rule out that a negative right to freedom of expression is protected under Article 10 of the Convention, but finds that this issue should be properly addressed in the circumstances of a given case".[57] Recently, the ECtHR confirmed that the right to freedom of expression has a negative aspect: "A holistic protection of the freedom of expression necessarily encompasses both the right to express ideas and the right to remain silent; otherwise, the right cannot be practical or effective."[58] Compelling the applicants to express a message with which they disagreed infringed the right's negative aspect in this case. In the same vein, the General Comment to Article 19 ICCPR states: "Freedom to express one's opinion necessarily includes freedom not to express one's opinion."[59]

This is, in our view, a logical implication of the *freedom* to express oneself, which entails that the expression of opinions, ideas and other information is freely chosen – that one can freely choose between expressing and not expressing oneself. A right not to express opinions, ideas, feelings, knowledge and other kinds of information corresponds, in our view, almost seamlessly to a right to mental privacy – at least, if one understands this right as a right not to reveal unexpressed mental phenomena such as mental states and content.

Apart from few exceptions,[60] the content of an expression is irrelevant to the applicability of the right to freedom of expression.[61] Referring to the work of the CCPR, Taylor writes that the freedom of expression protects the dissemination of content "which many, in some cases most, may find unwelcome or repugnant (spanning pornography, offensive art, anti-Semitic messages or messages in support of terrorism)".[62] Likewise, according to the ECtHR, the right to freedom of expression is "applicable not only to 'information' or 'ideas' that are favourably received or regarded as inoffensive or as a matter of indifference, but also to those that offend, shock or disturb".[63] As such, the scope of the right to freedom of expression is

55 Marmor 2015, p. 7. Note that Marmor is speaking of the moral value of privacy more generally here, but the point clearly also has relevance for the more specific freedom not to express oneself.
56 EComHR 7 April 1994, 20871/92 (*Strohal/Austria*). See also EComHR 1 March 1993, 17488/90 (*Goodwin/UK*), par. 48; EComHR 13 October 1992, 16002/90 (*K./Austria*), par. 45.
57 ECHR (GC) 3 April 2012, 41723/06 (*Gillberg/Sweden*), par. 86. Cf. ECHR 23 October 2018, 26892/12 (*Wanner/Germany*), pars. 39–42.
58 ECtHR, 22 October 2024, 39446/16, 106 and others (*Kobaliya and Others/Russia*), par. 84.
59 CCPR General Comment No. 34, par. 10.
60 See e.g. Van Rijn 2018, p. 772.
61 Taylor 2020, p. 538.
62 Taylor 2020, p. 544.
63 ECHR (GC) 7 February 2012, 39954/08 (*Axel Springer AG/Germany*), par. 78.

considered "extremely broad".[64] The logical implication of this is that the negative freedom not to express oneself is broad too.

Interestingly, the right to freedom of expression protects not only the *substance* of information but also a diverse range of *forms and means* by which information is expressed, transmitted and received.[65] For example, among many other things, the ECtHR has applied the right to speech, poetry, painting, radio, film, handcuffing oneself to a barrier during protest, disrupting foxhunting by blowing a hunting horn and performing a puppet show satirical of politicians.[66] The General Comment on Article 19 ICCPR mentions spoken, written and sign language, non-verbal expression such as through images, objects of art and dress, and legal submissions.[67]

So, both Articles 19 ICCPR and 10 ECHR guarantee a broad right to freedom of expression. They protect opinions, ideas, facts, value statements and other information of almost *any content*, transmitted through practically *any means*, which may, in theory, also concern neurotechnological means, such as fMRI, EEG and BCI. Crucially, they also protect the freedom *not* to express; and given this, the right to freedom of expression likely protects against the obligation to disclose private information, such as mental phenomena, through neuroprediction.[68]

Similar to the right to privacy, the right to freedom of expression pursuant to Article 10 ECHR will not *prohibit*, in principle, the non-consensual use of neuropredictive tools, as the right may be subjected to "formalities, conditions, restrictions or penalties" that have a legal basis and are necessary within a democratic society for the legitimate interest of, among other things, preventing disorder and crime.[69]

Note, however, that Article 19 ICCPR distinguishes between, respectively, the right to *hold opinions* without interference and the freedom to *express information and ideas of all kinds*. Whereas the latter freedom to express information (including opinions) may be limited, for example for the protection of public order, the former may not: the right to freely hold opinions is an absolute right, not susceptible to

64 Rainey, McCormick & Ovey 2021, p. 488.

65 CCPR General Comment No. 34, par. 12; ECHR (GC) 15 December 2005, 73797/01 (*Kyprianou/Cyprus*), par. 174; Harris et al. 2023, p. 599.

66 ECtHR (GC) 15 December 2005, 73797/01 (*Kyprianou/Cyprus*) (speech); ECtHR (GC) 8 July 1999, 23168/94 (*Karataş/Turkey*) (poetry); ECtHR 24 May 1988, appl.no. 10737/84 (*Müller and others/Switzerland*) (painting); ECtHR 28 March 1990, 10890/84 (*Groppera Radio AG and Others/Switzerland*) (radio); ECtHR 20 September 1994, (*Otto-Preminger-Institut/Austria*) (film); ECtHR 3 May 2022, 18079/15 (*Bumbeş/ Romania*) (handcuffing); ECtHR 25 November 1999, (*Hashman and Harrup/UK*) (blowing a hunting horn); ECtHR 20 October 2009, 41665/07 (*Alves da Silva/Portuga*) (puppet show).

67 CCPR General Comment No. 34, par. 12.

68 Ligthart 2022, p. 139; Ligthart et al. 2023a, p. 12. Note, that the right not to be compelled to *express* oneself suggests that for its applicability, a person should be compelled to *act* in a way that qualifies as *expressing themselves*. Therefore, the right is unlikely to apply to neuropredictive tools that do not involve any kind of engagement of the person that could possibly qualify as "expressing" information, such as an MRI-scan showing that one has tumour in the frontal lobe (Ligthart 2022, p. 145).

69 Cf. ECtHR 23 October 2018, 26892/12 (*Wanner/Germany*).

restriction or limitation,[70] and this right "includes [the] freedom *not* to express one's opinion".[71] Hence, strictly speaking, the protection of mental privacy, in the form of privacy of *opinion*, is absolute under Article 19 ICCPR. Regarding neuroprediction in criminal justice, the relevance of this absolute component of Article 19 ICCPR will probably be limited. Neuropredictive applications in this domain are likely to reveal information about phenomena such as self-control and emotional processing, and thus hardly qualify as revealing the person's *opinion* about something. Infringement of the absolute right to freedom of opinion is, therefore, unlikely. Article 19 ICCPR thus does not necessarily prohibit *all* non-consensual usage of neuroprediction – provided that such usage does not qualify as compelling persons to express "opinions".

4.2.3 *The Right to Freedom of Thought*

The right to freedom of thought, conscience and religion is guaranteed by Articles 18 ICCPR and 9 ECHR, and is often espoused as being central to the enjoyment of other basic rights and liberties, as well as being crucial for democracy.[72] The right is often considered to consist of an internal and external dimension, offering protection within the so-called *forum internum* and *forum externum*.[73] The internal dimension of the right is often considered to be absolute, not permitting "any limitations whatsoever".[74] It covers the freedom to have, change and adopt a religion, conviction and thought. In the external dimension, the right guarantees the qualified freedom to *manifest* religion and belief. The manifestation of *thought*, however, is not protected by the right to freedom of thought pursuant to Articles 18 ICCPR and 9 ECHR. These Articles only protect *unmanifested* thought. The manifestation of thoughts, such as through speech and expression, is protected by the right to freedom of expression.[75]

In the internal, absolute dimension, the right to freedom of thought is generally considered to guarantee three substantive freedoms: (1) that no one is compelled to reveal their thoughts, (2) that one's thoughts are not impermissibly altered and (3) that no one will be sanctioned for their thoughts.[76] The UN Special Rapporteur on Freedom of Religion or Belief holds that the first freedom implies that *mental privacy* is a "core attribute" of freedom of thought and also includes, arguably,

70 CCPR General Comment No.34, par. 5, 9; Taylor 2020, p. 543.

71 Our emphasis. Taylor 2020, p. 542. See also CCPR General Comment No.34, pars. 9–10.

72 Swaine 2018; McCarthy-Jones 2019.

73 Roberts 2020; Bublitz 2021.

74 CCPR General Comment No. 22, par. 3; UN Special Rapporteur on the Freedom of religion or belief, 5 October 2021, A/76/380; Vermeulen & Roosmalen 2018. But the absolute nature has recently been challenged: Ligthart 2025c.

75 Evans 1997, p. 285; Loucaides 2012, pp. 84–85.

76 Vermeulen & Roosmalen 2018; Bublitz 2021; UN Special Rapporteur on the Freedom of religion or belief, 5 October 2021, A/76/380.

a right to remain silent.[77] According to the Rapporteur, the freedom not to be compelled to reveal one's thoughts is currently under threat by, inter alia, neurotechnologies that allow the drawing of inferences about a variety of unexpressed mental states.[78] Likewise, considering the potential of neurotechnological lie detection and memory detection in criminal justice, Bublitz finds it "hard to imagine a better paradigmatic case against which freedom of thought should provide protection".[79]

However, the scope of the mental privacy protection afforded by the right to freedom of thought depends, considerably, on how one interprets "thoughts" in the context of this right. As discussed in Chapter 3, some have argued for a broad interpretation, such that the right protects *any* mental state with content and thinking as a mental process (robust-scope view).[80] For example, O'Callaghan et al. have argued that thought in the meaning of Articles 18 ICCPR and 9 ECHR "can be understood as encompassing all forms of unmanifested mental activity, including 'deliberation, imagination, belief, reflection, reasoning, cogitation, remembering, wishing, sensing, questioning, and desiring'".[81] On such an understanding, the freedom not to reveal private "thoughts" comes down to a broad right to mental privacy – that is, a right not to reveal *any* unexpressed mental state and content. As also discussed in Chapter 3, for the interpretation of the right to freedom of thought pursuant to Article 18 ICCPR, such a robust interpretation receives some support,[82] also from the UN Special Rapporteur on Freedom of Religion or Belief.[83]

Adopting such a broad scope would have profound effects on the human rights protection of mental privacy: if we assume a broad understanding of "thought", the privacy protection offered by the right to freedom of thought will considerably overlap with both the right to privacy and the right to freedom of expression. All three rights will then imply a right *not* to reveal unexpressed personal mental states and content. This poses a theoretical difficulty, as the protection of mental privacy by the right to freedom of thought is considered *absolute*, as opposed to the *qualified* protection offered by the right to privacy and, in the European context, the freedom of non-expression. This raises the question: How should the law distinguish between the applicability of either absolute or qualified mental privacy protection?[84] The answer to this question will be crucial for the permissibility of interferences with

77 UN Special Rapporteur on the Freedom of religion or belief, 5 October 2021, A/76/380, par. 26. Also: Alegre 2022, p. 27. For a critical analysis of the report, see Ligthart et al. 2022; O'Callaghan et al. 2023.

78 UN Special Rapporteur on the Freedom of religion or belief, 5 October 2021, A/76/380, pars. 26, 69, 76, 94.

79 Bublitz 2014, p. 8. See also McCarthy-Jones 2019; Hertz 2023. Cf. Ligthart 2022.

80 McCarthy-Jones 2019; Alegre 2022; Bublitz 2025; Hertz 2025.

81 O'Callaghan et al. 2024, p. 7.

82 As opposed to the interpretation of Article 9 ECHR: Chapter 3, section 3.2.

83 UN Special Rapporteur on the Freedom of religion or belief, 5 October 2021, A/76/380.

84 Ligthart 2025a; Ligthart & Van de Pol 2025.

mental privacy, including through non-consensual neuroprediction in criminal justice. We explore this question in the next section.

4.3 TOWARDS A THRESHOLD FOR THE RIGHT TO FREEDOM OF THOUGHT?

For the remainder of this chapter, let us assume a broad scope of the right to freedom of thought along the lines of the robust-scope view.[85] Let us also assume that, therefore, mental privacy is protected by both the absolute right to freedom of thought and the qualified rights to privacy and to freedom of expression. We then have the following question: How should judges determine which interferences with mental privacy would engage either absolute or qualified protection? How should they determine when the absolute right to freedom of thought applies to a specific case of privacy interference, such as the neuroprediction of convicted persons?[86]

At present, neither the law, jurisprudence, literature nor the report on freedom of thought by the UN Special Rapporteur provides clarification about this issue. However, in recent work, different scholars have suggested developing a *severity threshold* to determine whether a mental interference, such as revealing private mental phenomena with neurotechnology, would infringe and therefore violate the absolute right to freedom of thought.[87] For example, Bublitz proposes to adopt the "seriousness" of the privacy interference as a guiding principle for determining whether revealing (information about) unexpressed thought infringes the right.[88] He suggests a threshold for infringement that requires "interferences of some intensity or gravity", the assessment of which may draw on a range of factors, including the importance of the content of the thought, the nature of the interference and the intrusiveness of the means by which a thought is detected.[89]

Developing such a threshold for the applicability of a specific human right is not uncommon in human rights law.[90] It may indeed be a suitable approach for distinguishing absolute from qualified protection of mental privacy – that is, for distinguishing between the application of either the right to freedom of thought or the right to privacy/freedom of non-expression.[91] Meanwhile, it raises the question of which "interferences" can be considered "serious" enough to infringe the absolute right to freedom of thought.[92] There are different ways to explore and examine this question, including the use of thought experiments and involving ethical considerations and psychological or neuroscientific views on the intensity of different types of

85 Bublitz 2025.
86 Cf. Bublitz 2025, p. 20.
87 Ligthart et al. 2022; Ligthart & Van de Pol 2025; Bublitz 2025; O'Callaghan & Shiner 2025, p. 13; Hertz 2025.
88 Bublitz 2025, p. 19.
89 Bublitz 2025, p. 18.
90 Gerards 2013, p. 102. See also Chapter 3, section 3.3.1.
91 See also Ligthart et al. 2022.
92 Ligthart 2025b.

interference with thought.[93] Furthermore, the law itself may provide some helpful guidance.

As Christoffersen writes, "[t]he relationship between relative and absolute rights will often be one of *lex generalis/lex specialis*: the relative provisions provide a general and wider measure of protection at a lower level, whereas the absolute provisions generate more specific and narrower protection at a higher level".[94] Consider, for example, the protection of bodily and mental integrity under the ECHR.[95] The qualified right to respect for private life in Article 8 ECHR provides broad protection of bodily and, possibly, also mental integrity in a large variety of instances.[96] On top of that, the prohibition of ill-treatment of Article 3 ECHR provides further absolute – though much narrower – protection of bodily and mental integrity, that is, protection against a category of grave and harmful interferences.

The ECtHR has developed a legal mechanism to distinguish absolute from qualified protection of bodily and mental integrity under Article 3 and 8 ECHR. In order to determine the applicability of the absolute prohibition of ill-treatment – over and above the qualified right to respect for private life – the ECtHR employs a severity threshold: Article 3 ECHR only applies to treatment attaining a "minimum level of severity". Although the prohibition of ill-treatment is absolute, the severity threshold is typically relative and depends on all circumstances of the individual case.[97] These include certain *characteristics of the treatment* (like its physical and mental effects and the manner and method of its execution), the *context* in which the treatment was imposed (such as in prison or in an atmosphere of heightened tension and emotions), *characteristics of the victim* (like one's sex, age and state of health) and the *purpose* for which the treatment was inflicted together with the intention and motivation behind it.[98]

The ECtHR considers these factors relevant for distinguishing absolute from qualified protection of bodily and mental integrity. We suggest that it is worth exploring whether these factors *also* prove useful for distinguishing absolute from qualified protection of mental privacy,[99] though we acknowledge the differences between integrity and privacy rights. In sections 4.3.1, 4.3.2 and 4.3.3 we consider the potential relevance of (1) characteristics of the interference, (2) the context of the interference and (3) the characteristics of the victim for distinguishing absolute from qualified protection of mental privacy. We do not consider the potential relevance of the *purpose* or *intention* of an interference – the fourth factor mentioned above. Including such a factor would ultimately amount to including a proportionality test,

93 Cf. Bublitz 2025.
94 Christoffersen 2009, p. 156.
95 See Chapter 3.
96 Nowak 2012; Michalowski 2020, p. 408.
97 ECtHR (GC) 26 October 2000, 30210/96 (*Kudła/Poland*), par. 91.
98 ECtHR (GC) 15 December 2016, 16483/12 (*Khlaifia and Others/Italy*), par. 160; ECtHR 1 June 2010, 22978/05 (*Gäfgen/Germany*), par. 88.
99 Ligthart & Van de Pol 2025.

adding a qualification to the absolute protection of mental privacy.[100] The question, then, becomes whether a certain intervention, in a certain context, given the characteristics of the victim, is proportionate in light of the purpose or intention of the intervention. However, what we aim to delineate here is the type of cases that would receive *absolute* protection from the right to freedom of thought, that is, *regardless* of the importance of the purpose of the interference.

Before proceeding, we wish to clarify that, in line with the current status of the law, we assume that the right to freedom of thought is an absolute human right. We are aware of recent suggestions to formulate strict exceptions or inherent limitations to the right,[101] and we think these suggestions deserve serious consideration.[102] We also recognise that many theorists doubt that *truly absolute* rights exist at the level of fundamental morality. As Brownlee puts it, "when the numbers [or stakes] get large enough, we all tend to become consequentialists".[103] However, in this explorative section we follow the dominant view in human rights law and accept that there is value in recognising a limited number of human rights as absolute *at the level of law* (e.g., the prohibition of torture, the prohibition of slavery, and some aspects of the freedom of thought, conscience and religion). The question of how to distinguish absolute from qualified protection of mental privacy therefore arises.

4.3.1 *Characteristics of the Privacy Interference: Means and Targeted Mental Phenomena*

A general characteristic of an interference with mental privacy that may be relevant for distinguishing the applicability of the absolute right to freedom of thought from the qualified right to privacy or freedom of expression, relates to the *method* of revealing personal mental states. Of course, this can be interpreted in different ways, however, as we will explain, we consider this aspect in terms of "control" – more specifically the level of *control* the employed method leaves to the person whose mental states are being revealed. Regarding interventions that aim to *change* or *modulate* a person's mental states (like neurointerventions), Bublitz has argued that the level of self-control a person retains should be relevant to the applicability of the absolute right to freedom of thought, as infringements of the *freedom* of thought typically disrespect a person's *control* over their own thoughts and thinking. According to Bublitz: "This is a necessary, but not a sufficient condition, and it forms part of a test of infringement: Does an intervention respect the other as a free

100 Cf. Vermeulen & Battjes 2018, p. 384; Harris et al. 2023, pp. 272–273. See on this issue under Article 3 ECHR also Addo & Grief 1998; Mayerfield 2008; Greer 2015; Mavronicola 2021.

101 Loucaides 2012; McCarthy-Jones 2019; Bublitz 2021; Ligthart 2025c.

102 Cf. Ligthart et al. 2022; Ligthart 2025c.

103 Brownlee 2019, p.114.

and self-controlled thinker; or does it undermine or bypass control? The latter infringes freedom of thought, the former may not."[104]

A similar line of reasoning may be explored regarding the privacy dimension of the right to freedom of thought.[105] One of the dominant approaches to information privacy conceives of privacy as a right to *control* personal information.[106] For example, as Fried argued, "privacy is not simply an absence of information about us in the minds of others; rather it is the *control* we have over information about ourselves".[107] The emphasis on controlling personal information is also reflected in the law. For instance, under Article 8 ECHR, the ECtHR has recognised a right to "informational *self-determination*".[108] Furthermore, recital 7 of the European GDPR states firmly that "natural persons should have *control* of their own personal data". The value of controlling personal information, including mental states, seems also relevant to mental privacy under the right to freedom of thought. As the drafters of Article 9 ECHR put it, the right to freedom of thought, conscience and religion intends to protect "not only from 'confessions' imposed for reasons of State, but also from those abominable methods of police enquiry or judicial process which rob the suspect or accused person of *control* of his intellectual faculties and of his conscience".[109]

It appears generally accepted that within the *forum internum* the right to freedom of thought is absolute. Hence, absolute human rights protection of mental privacy, one could argue, may at least be warranted regarding means that disclose thoughts directly from the *forum internum*, that is, means that do not involve any form of expression and conscious control whatsoever, and to which consent is not obtained. An example of such means could be the hacking of a person's BCI, which seems to destroy the core essence of mental privacy, that is, the person's *ability to control* the disclosure and dissemination of private mental content.[110] Bublitz has argued in the same direction, proposing that the "main condition prompting freedom of thought protection is the revelation of *unexpressed* thoughts", which means that "the

104 Bublitz 2021, p. 82. See also Bublitz 2020b and, for discussion, Focquaert & Schermer 2015; Douglas 2018; Levy 2020.

105 Bublitz 2025; Ligthart & Van de Pol 2025; Ligthart 2025a.

106 Allen 2000; Schwartz 2000, p. 820.

107 Fried 1968, p. 482 (original emphasis).

108 ECHR (GC) 27 June 2017, 931/13 (*Satakunnan Markkinapörssi Oy and Satamedia Oy/Finland*), par. 137.

109 EComHR, *Preparatory work on Article 9 of the European Convention on human rights*, Strasbourg, 16th August 1959, pp. 3–4 (emphasis added).

110 Contrast obligations to reveal through *self-controlled* means of expression one's religious adherence, by taking a religious oath in court, by filling in a wage-tax form, or by providing personal information to receive an identity card, which the ECtHR considered to concern the *qualified* freedom to *manifest* religion and belief: ECtHR 3 June 2010, 42837/06, 3237/07, 3269/07, 35793/07 and 6099/08 (*Dimitras and others/Greece*); ECtHR 21 February 2008, 19516/06 (*Alexandridis/Greece*); ECtHR 17 February 2011, 12884/03 (*Wasmuth/Germany*); ECtHR 2 February 2010, 21924/05 (*Sinan Işik/Turkey*). ECtHR 20 June 2020, 52484/18 (*Stavropoulos and others/Greece*), par. 44. Also: ECtHR 15 June 2010, 7710/02 (*Grzelak/Poland*), par. 87.

rightholder has not manifested them through voluntary actions such as speech".[111] He submits that neuroimaging "does not work *through* the person as a subject – by coercing or compelling her – but bypasses her as a subject to extract unexpressed thought. This breach of the inner sphere may suffice to reach the required level of seriousness".[112]

Following this line of thought, the non-consensual use of neuroimaging for the purpose of risk assessment in criminal justice may, in some instances, be considered to infringe the absolute right to freedom of thought – that is, when they do not involve any form of expression and conscious control whatsoever. However, since identifying relevant mental phenomena, such as certain intentions or inclinations, with neurotechnology will usually require at least some engagement from the person themselves (e.g., performing a task, observing stimuli, not manipulating the assessment), it is questionable whether their non-consensual use can regularly be considered to completely bypass or undermine the person's mental control.

Another relevant characteristic of mental privacy interference that could contribute to determining the "seriousness" of the interference relates to the precise *mental phenomenon* that is targeted and revealed. The significance of a person's interests in not revealing information about certain types of mental states and content may be important.[113] For example, there may be good reasons to assume that the significance of the interest in not revealing one's political or religious ideas could justify absolute protection from the freedom of thought.[114] The significance of the person's interest in not revealing one's sexual preferences may be another example. Meanwhile, the personal interest in having one's mental privacy respected may be weaker in relation to more trivial information about mental phenomena, of which absolute human rights protection would be less persuasive. One could think of a person's memory about a specific event, like the lovely sunset one experienced in Italy last summer,[115] a person's intention to grab a cup of tea during the coffee break or one's opinion about a new Netflix series.

Whereas many would probably agree that the secrecy of political opinions deserves stronger privacy protection than the secrecy of a preference for tea or coffee,[116] much of the area in between is grey. What about emotions: whether one feels happy or sad? What about an opinion about a colleague? A memory about

111 Bublitz 2025, p. 21 (original emphasis). See also O'Callaghan & Shiner 2021, p. 135: "only when thoughts are unmanifested they should be deserving of absolute protection."

112 Bublitz 2025, p. 21 (original emphasis).

113 Cf. Bublitz 2025.

114 Cf. ECtHR February 2010, 21924/05 (*Sinan Işik/Turkey*), par. 42; ECtHR 8 July 2008, 9103/04 (*Georgian Labour Party/Georgia*), par. 120.

115 Interestingly, the ECtHR approaches legal duties of witnesses to disclose their memories of a particular event, like a criminal offence, under the *qualified* right to freedom of expression rather than under the *absolute* right to freedom of thought: ECtHR October 2018, 26892/12 (*Wanner/Germany*).

116 Note that connecting the level of privacy protection to the sensitivity of personal data is common in the law. See, e.g., Special Rapporteur on the right to privacy, 20 July 2022, A/77/196, pars. 6–8.

a criminal offence? Or a wild fantasy of becoming famous one day? Is the personal interest in keeping information about these mental states secluded from others significant enough to engage absolute mental privacy protection? It is hard to answer this question in isolation from other relevant considerations – perhaps most notably, the *context* within which one is obliged to reveal information about them. For instance, in the future, neuropredictive tools may well reveal information about different types of mental phenomena, ranging from emotional responses and reduced self-control to sexual orientation and information indicative of mental disorders. Whereas, in general, the significance of the personal interest in not revealing these types of information plausibly differs between them, their disclosure and use in the context of criminal justice for risk assessment may have similar adverse effects on the interest of personal liberty. For example, all such information could potentially contribute to the assessment of a certain expected risk of recidivism and, therefore, leading to the rejection of a parole request. Let us turn to considering the relevance of the context of a mental privacy interference in more detail in the next section.

4.3.2 *Context of the Privacy Interference*

The significance of the personal interest in not disclosing mental states – which may be a relevant consideration for granting absolute protection, as discussed in the previous section – plausibly depends on the context within which one is obliged to do so. In some contexts, being forced to revealing one's true views and ideas may be unpleasant but is unlikely to harm vital personal interests. Meanwhile, in other contexts, the revelation of private ideas, thoughts and feelings may have significant detrimental effects, ranging from not being offered a job, to the deprivation of liberty, and even death.

Consider, for instance, how the risk of being harmed by expressing one's homosexual feelings and desires depends significantly on the country (legal system) in which they are disclosed. Or consider the obligation to provide information about one's emotions and intentions in the context of requesting a gun license, which could result in the rejection of one's request, compared to being obliged to disclose emotions and intentions in the context of a criminal prosecution, which could result in a conviction. Whereas the former seems not to face any principled objections, and many would feel it should be permissible, the latter is in principle prohibited in most legal systems by the right to silence and the privilege against self-incrimination,[117] which, according to some, primarily aims to protect the accused's mental privacy.[118] As such, the context wherein one reveals information about specific mental phenomena appears to affect the personal interest in (not) doing so. Perhaps, this could

[117] See also Articles 14(3)(g) ICCPR and 6 ECHR.

[118] Dann 1970; Arenella 1982. See Dressler, Michaels & Simmons 2021, p. 446; Farahany 2012b with further references. Cf. Gerstein 1970; Galligan 1988.

inform our normative analysis of whether, when and which mental states deserve either absolute or qualified protection from human rights.

These intuitions about different informational norms applying in different (social) contexts are reminiscent of Nissenbaum's philosophical account on information privacy. In her book *Privacy in Context*, Nissenbaum argues that privacy concerns should not be limited solely to concerns about control over and access to personal data. Rather, privacy is also about context-dependent social norms that govern the "appropriate flow of information" in different settings and relationships, ranging from family, friends and the workplace to schools, health care and law enforcement. Nissenbaum calls this conception of privacy "contextual integrity",[119] which, in practice, means that different rules and norms apply about confidentiality, access to and control over personal data across different contexts, such as the context of friendship, doctor-patient relationships and criminal justice.[120]

Although the dominant account in law conceives of privacy as *control* over personal information, the ECtHR does consider the *context* of an interference with personal data relevant under Article 8 ECHR. In determining whether an interference with personal data infringes the right to respect for private life, "the Court will have due regard to the specific context in which the information at issue has been recorded and retained".[121] Perhaps, a context-based understanding of privacy may also inform our legal thinking about attributing either absolute or qualified protection to interferences with mental privacy. This may be particularly relevant to the evaluation of mental privacy interference in the context of criminal justice, such as through neuroprediction, since the personal interests at stake in this context are often significant, such as the limitation of personal liberty and a possible decline of well-being as a result of extending the duration of incarceration (due to one's being at "high risk" of reoffending).

4.3.3 *Characteristics of the Victim: Vulnerability*

When assessing, under Article 3 ECHR, whether a specific treatment attains a minimum level of severity and thus engages absolute protection of bodily and mental integrity from the prohibition of ill-treatment, the ECtHR takes account of a variety of personal characteristics of the victim, such as their sex, age and state of

119 Nissenbaum 2010, pp. 231–232.

120 Nissenbaum stresses that her framework of contextual integrity is, primarily, a justificatory framework for establishing whether emerging technologies, systems and practices that affect the flow of personal information are morally legitimate. It is not meant as a theory for a legal right to privacy nor a definition of privacy as a legal concept. Nonetheless, Nissenbaum believes her account on information privacy can serve as a foundation for law and regulation by providing a standard against which legal rights and regulation can be tested, as there seems no inherent problem with context-specific legal regulation: Nissenbaum 2010, p. 236. See also De Groot, Tesink & Meynen 2024.

121 ECtHR 13 February 2020, 45245/15 (*Gaughran/UK*), par. 70. See also ECtHR (GC) 4 December 2008, 30562/04 and 30566/04 (*S. & Marper/UK*), par. 67; ECtHR 25 September 2001, appl.no. 44787/98 (*P.G. and J.H./UK*), par. 57; De Vries 2018, p. 673.

health. In the case of *Khlaifia and Others/Italy*, the Grand Chamber phrases and, arguably, broadens this factor by appealing in more general terms to the victim's *vulnerability*: "In order to determine whether the threshold of severity has been reached, the Court also takes other factors into consideration, in particular (…) [w] hether the victim is in a vulnerable situation, which is normally the case for persons deprived of their liberty."[122]

Various groups of people have been identified as being particularly vulnerable in the ECtHR's case law, including children, people with mental disabilities and persons deprived of their liberty.[123] These groups are considered vulnerable because they are more susceptible to harm than others.[124] By recognising them as vulnerable, the ECtHR acknowledges their challenges and specific needs and underlines the duty of states to provide enhanced protection of people belonging to these groups.[125]

Could a person's vulnerability also be relevant to the question of whether an interference with mental privacy should engage either absolute or qualified protection from human rights? Some people may be more vulnerable to (severe) interference with their mental privacy than others. Think, for example, of those who are illiterate, using a BCI for non-medical purposes such as in gaming, who might be less able to understand, oversee and, therefore, resist the potential threats to mental privacy posed by emerging neurotechnology. Other vulnerable persons may include minors, elderly, people with mental disabilities[126] and convicted persons deprived of their liberty who are 'offered' neurotechnology.[127]

Much has been written about different types and conceptions of "vulnerability" and how it could be relevant to the law. Here, we wish to briefly point to the work of Robert Goodin, who argues that governments, private companies and natural persons bear a special responsibility for protecting those who are particularly vulnerable.[128] Goodin conceives of vulnerability as a relational concept. People are vulnerable to the actions of others – that is, to the infliction of harm on them by others. This kind of relational vulnerability creates a special responsibility of those to whom others are particularly vulnerable: "If A's interests are vulnerable to B's actions and choices, B has a special responsibility to protect A's interest; the strength of this responsibility depends strictly upon the degree to which B can affect A's interests."[129] This special responsibility applies primarily to the

122 ECtHR 15 December 2016, 16483/12 (*Khlaifia and Others/Italy*), par. 160.
123 Peroni & Timmer 2013; Harris et al. 2023, p. 243.
124 Peroni & Timmer 2013.
125 Timmer 2013; Limanté 2022, p. 30. Cf. ECtHR 15 December 2016, 16483/12 (*Khlaifia and Others/ Italy*), par. 161.
126 We are aware of the literature criticizing this so-called "labelling approach" to vulnerable groups and persons. Engaging in this debate on how to conceptualize and use "vulnerability" for normative analyses would, however, exceed the scope of this book. See for this, e.g., Fineman 2008; Luna 2009; Rogers, Mackenzie & Dodds 2012.
127 Cf. Ligthart, Dore-Horgan & Meynen 2023.
128 Goodin 1985. On vulnerability, see also Rogers, Mackenzie & Dodds 2012.
129 Goodin 1985, p. 118.

protection of so-called "vital interests" or "primary goods", such as food, shelter, physical and mental health, self-respect and civil liberties (which includes the civil liberty of mental privacy).[130]

Goodin argues that a person's vulnerability or dependency does not really cause moral concern in and of itself. However, it "necessarily creates opportunities for the strong to *exploit* the weakness of those who are vulnerable and dependent", and this is what causes moral concern and requires taking special responsibility to protect the vulnerable.[131] Exploitation is often defined as taking *unfair* advantage of other people, which implies a normative judgement about those who exploit.[132] Perhaps, this could be relevant to the law too, as a person's vulnerable status may not only increase their risk of being *harmed* (i.e., having their mental privacy interfered with) but also add an additional *wrong* when others, such as government officials, take *unfair* advantage of a person's vulnerable status by yielding, processing and/or disclosing intimate information about people's private mental states and content.

Possibly, this additional wrong could be relevant to determining whether an interference with mental privacy should engage either absolute or qualified human rights protection.[133] As Goodin argues, in no case should people's vulnerabilities "be so severe and asymmetrical that one party has exclusive, discretionary control over resources that the other needs to protect his vital interests".[134] He calls this the principle of "preventing exploitable vulnerabilities". If we apply this principle to the case of protecting mental privacy, absolute prohibition of discretionary control by others over revealing mental content of (certain) vulnerable persons may be appropriate.[135] Whether and how this principle of "preventing exploitable vulnerabilities" could indeed be relevant to the application of the absolute right to freedom of thought, and whether it would fit within the ICCPR and ECHR frameworks, merits further elaboration.

Regarding the neuroprediction of convicted persons, different vulnerabilities could, potentially, be relevant. First, the vulnerable position arising from incarceration – that is, the incarcerated person's "vulnerability at the hands of the authorities, who exercise complete control over her throughout her detention".[136] Second, research shows that incarcerated persons have high rates

[130] Goodin 1985, p. 111.

[131] Goodin 1985, pp. 193–194 (emphasis added).

[132] Zwolinski, Ferguson & Wertheimer 2022, par. 2.2.

[133] Cf. the absolute Article 4 ECHR, for the application of which the exploitative character of a particular treatment is a central element: Jovanovic 2020.

[134] Goodin 1985, p. 206.

[135] Cf. the debate on thought "manipulation", where the exploitation of vulnerabilities is sometimes referred to as a relevant factor for infringing the absolute right to freedom of thought: Teo 2024; Keese & Leiser 2025; UN Special Rapporteur on the Freedom of religion or belief, 5 October 2021, A/76/380, par. 35.

[136] ECtHR 13 May 2008, 52515/99 (*Juhnke/Turkey*), par. 76.

of psychiatric disorders,[137] which could add to a person's vulnerability.[138] Third, one could argue that, with the rise of neurotechnologies, every person is inherently vulnerable to the exploitation of the lack of control we have over the neural correlates of mental states. As Bublitz argues, "many neuroimaging methods exploit the fact that people lack control over the physiological correlates of thought".[139] Whether, and, if so, to what extent, these different forms of vulnerability should indeed be relevant to the application of the absolute right to freedom of thought is an open question in need of further research.

4.3.4 *Brief Recap*

In this section, we explored how the law could distinguish between the *qualified* protection of mental privacy, provided by the right to privacy and right to freedom of expression, and the *absolute* protection offered by the right to freedom of thought. This will be highly relevant for the permissibility of mental privacy interferences, which are likely to occur in neurorehabilitation. Analogous to the "minimal level of severity" threshold for the applicability of Article 3 ECHR, we explored the possibility of developing a severity threshold for infringing the privacy dimension of the absolute right to freedom of thought. For the construction of such a threshold, we suggested four potentially relevant factors: (1) the method of revealing mental phenomena, focusing on the level of the subject's control; (2) the significance of the personal interest in not revealing specific mental phenomena; (3) the context of the privacy interference; and (4) the person's vulnerability.

4.4 CONCLUDING REMARKS

The personal interest in mental privacy receives considerable protection from the ICCPR and ECHR. This protection is anchored across three different human rights: the right to privacy, the right to freedom of expression and the right to freedom of thought – the latter being considered an absolute right. Some forms of non-consensual neuroprediction in criminal justice plausible interfere with mental privacy and, therefore, potentially infringe the right to privacy and the freedom of non-expression. Regarding the right to freedom of thought, our analysis showed that the right's relevance largely depends on how one interprets "thought". On a broad understanding, which receives some support regarding Article 18 ICCPR (as opposed to Article 9 ECHR), some forms of neuroprediction might be capable of revealing protected "thoughts". One could think of brain data allowing to draw inferences about sexual orientation, or about an intention to commit a criminal offence.

137 Fazel et al. 2016.
138 Ligthart, Dore-Horgan & Meynen 2023.
139 Bublitz 2025, p. 21.

In this chapter, we also explored how the law could distinguish between the *absolute* protection of mental privacy offered by the right to freedom of thought, and the qualified protection provided by the right to privacy and right to freedom of expression. This issue will be crucial for the permissibility of mental privacy interference, such as through neuroprediction. We considered the possibility of developing a severity threshold for infringing the privacy dimension of the absolute right to freedom of thought. For the construction of such a threshold, we identified four potentially relevant factors: (1) the method of revealing mental phenomena, (2) the significance of the personal interest in not revealing certain mental phenomena, (3) the context of the privacy interference and (4) the person's vulnerability.

PART II

The Positive Dimension

Arguments for Offering Neurorehabilitation

5

The Right to Mental Self-Determination

An Autonomy-Based Right to Be Offered Neurorehabilitation?

5.1 INTRODUCTION

We tend to think that we are prima facie morally entitled to determine the course of our own lives to some degree, and to make our own decisions about matters that are personal to us. Dworkin speaks of our "right to make decisions about the character of [our] lives".[1] Feinberg suggests that we plausibly have a personal domain over which we are "sovereign" and hence where we "alone" have the final say about "what is to happen".[2] And Akhlaghi defends the idea that we have a *pro tanto* or defeasible moral right to "autonomous self-making" – viz. a *pro tanto* moral right to autonomously decide to make certain "transformative choices" that will influence how our lives will go and who we will become.[3]

These differing claims all circle around the thought that we have a moral right to, what we might call, "self-determination" or "self-authorship". They support the thought that we have a *pro tanto* moral right to make and pursue certain personal and/or self-regarding decisions for ourselves such that we ought not to be prevented in doing so by third parties – at least insofar as these decisions and actions are indeed self-regarding or personal and do not (threaten to) violate the rights of, or otherwise harm, others.

A *legal* right to self-determination is inherent in our system of human rights and explicitly recognised under Article 8 of the European Convention on Human Rights (ECHR), which "embraces, among other things, a right to self-determination".[4] Furthermore, Article 8 ECHR has been interpreted by the ECtHR as encompassing the protection of "personal development" and "personal autonomy"[5] – two concepts

1 Dworkin 1986, p. 6.

2 Feinberg 1989, pp. 52, 54.

3 Akhlaghi 2023, p. 9.

4 ECtHR (GC) 27 August 2015, 46470/11 (*Parrillo/Italy*), par. 153. Our system of human rights as a whole is underscored by the principle that, as former judge of the ECtHR Martens once put it, a person "should be free to shape himself and his fate": Dissenting opinion of Judge Martens in ECtHR 27 September 1990, 10843/84 (*Cossey/The United Kingdom*).

5 ECtHR 29 April 2002, 2346/02 (*Pretty/the United Kingdom*; ECtHR 4 December 2003, 39272/98 (*M.C./Bulgaria*); ECtHR (GC) 7 April 2007, 6339/05 (*Evans/the United Kingdom*).

closely resembling, and which have been understood to roughly equate to, the self-determination described above.

This chapter examines the case for a legal right to *mental* self-determination, highlighting the legal and moral rationales that support such a right, before interrogating what such a right might imply for the case of neurorehabilitation. More specifically, we are interested in the *positive dimension* of such a right to mental self-determination. That is, the right to voluntarily alter and exercise control over our mental states, for example, with the help of neurotechnologies, psychoactive drugs or psychological techniques, without being thwarted in these efforts by third parties. Such a right is sometimes alternatively referred to as a right to cognitive liberty.[6]

The question of whether we have a right to mental self-determination has become increasingly pertinent as new and emerging tools for altering our mental experiences develop. We can now avail of psychological techniques such as cognitive behavioural therapy or mindfulness strategies should we wish to alter our patterns of thinking.[7] Various pharmaceuticals can, or may soon, aid us in supplanting our negative emotions, anxious thoughts or traumatic memories.[8] And in future years, we may be able to avoid experiencing certain mental states with the aid of closed-loop brain technology – devices that can not only detect patterns in neural activity but also respond to them by stimulating the brain. Such devices may halt particular patterns of activity before they can manifest themselves.[9] The options available to us for exercising mental self-determination are thus increasing.

The question of whether we have a legal right to mental self-determination, including by accessing neurotechnologies or psychological techniques, therefore arises.[10] And the answer to this question has relevance for our analysis of whether convicted persons have a rights-based claim to neurorehabilitation – that is, for the question of whether human rights protection of persons' powers of mental self-determination at least sometimes supports a rights-based claim to access neurorehabilitation (and if so, when).

The plan for this chapter is as follows. In section 5.2, we examine the legal and moral arguments that have been, or might be, advanced in support of persons' legal right to self-determine or exert control over their mental states, including by accessing neurotechnologies. We then interrogate whether and when this putative right to

6 See Boire 2000; Sententia 2004; Ienca & Andorno 2017; Farahany 2023.

7 Reinecke et al. 2013.

8 See, for example, Starcevic 2012; Forstmann et al. 2020; Ebrahimi et al. 2020; Giustino, Fitzgerald & Maren 2016.

9 Kellmeyer et al. 2016. Neurofeedback training – where a person attempts to train themselves to gain voluntary control over their thoughts or feelings with the aid of real-time feedback from brain activity – might also offer similar possibilities; see Hampson, Ruiz & Ushiba 2020.

10 For debate on whether there is a need for such a right, see Bublitz & Merkel 2014; Ienca & Andorno 2017; Michalowski 2020; Bublitz 2020a; Hertz 2023; Farahany 2023. See Ligthart et al. 2023a for a review of the neurorights debate.

mental self-determination might imply a state duty to *offer* or *provide* neurorehabilitation in section 5.3.

Three brief clarifications before we begin. First, in this chapter, as in elsewhere in the book, our interest is in examining the case for a legal right (henceforth, just right) to mental self-determination, but we explore both legal and moral rationales for such a right. By a legal rationale, we mean the sort of rationale that establishes the existence of a right by drawing on existing law. By a moral rationale we mean a rationale that appeals to moral reasons or principles in defending the case for embracing and accommodating a given right.[11] Second, when discussing the human rights protection of private life, we use the phrases "respect for private life" and "respect for privacy" interchangeably. Third, in this chapter, we focus on the *positive* right to exert control over one's thoughts, including with the aid of neurotechnologies, but note that, in the literature, the right to mental self-determination has been invoked to denote both this positive right, and the negative right against third party interference with a person's mental states – which we understand as the right to mental integrity.[12]

5.2 LEGAL AND MORAL RATIONALES FOR A HUMAN RIGHT TO MENTAL SELF-DETERMINATION

5.2.1 *Introduction*

There are a number of routes by which we could defend the existence – or argue the case for embracing – a right to mental self-determination, four of which we shall consider below. The first three routes advance legal rationales for a right to mental self-determination, respectively, (1) by claiming that such a right implicitly suffuses liberal legal and political orders, or could be derived specifically (2) from the right to freedom of thought or (3) from the more general right to self-determination, as protected in the right to respect for private life pursuant to Article 8 ECHR and Article 17 ICCPR. The fourth route advances a moral argument for accommodating a right to mental self-determination within our systems of human rights. This route involves arguing, firstly, that we have moral reasons for thinking that states have a defeasible moral duty not to thwart people's attempts to alter and exercise control over their own mental states, including with the aid of neuro- and other technologies. This route then makes a case for the desirability of enforcing this moral duty by accommodating a right to mental self-determination within our systems of human rights.

We shall unpack these routes in turn but, note, that only two of them specify how persons' powers of mental self-determination might find *concrete* protection in

[11] See Douglas & Forsberg 2021, p. 185, for further discussion of this distinction between legal and moral rationales.

[12] See Chapter 3 of this book.

human rights law – the routes that see the right to mental self-determination as either a derivative right of the right to respect for private life or a derivative right of the right to freedom of thought. In the discussion that follows, we work on the assumption that the rationales discussed are capable of supporting, either that a legal right to mental self-determination already exists, or that it can be accommodated in existing law. We assume this while acknowledging that some scholars have appealed to one or more of these rationales when defending a need to recognise a self-standing right to mental self-determination.[13]

5.2.2 A *Right to Mental Self-Determination as Implicit in Law*

Turning now to the first rationale, the idea is that a right to mental self-determination is implicit in liberal legal and political orders. Bublitz makes this kind of argument, in a seminal paper co-authored with Merkel, and then again in later work.[14] Bublitz's reasoning is as follows. His first claim is that liberal legal orders are premised on the idea that persons are freely-deciding beings and the principal authors of the preferences on which their decisions and actions are based. He justifies this claim by highlighting how the law holds people accountable for their actions and "antecedent mental states" *as if* they are freely deciding.[15] His second claim is that legal orders premised on the idea of freely deciding persons must legally protect persons' powers of mental self-determination if they are to avoid "internal incoherences".[16] The point is that a legal order that treats people as though they are freely deciding or mentally self-determining when they lack legal powers to be so would be an incoherent one. And insofar as our legal orders are not incoherent, Bublitz argues we must have legal powers in the form of a right to mental self-determination. Importantly, Bublitz emphasises, this is not a matter of our legal orders having to *grant* us a right to mental self-determination. Rather, our legal orders are simply "bound by reasons of inner consistency to (...) *embrace*" a right to mental self-determination,[17] owing to the fact that mental self-determination is "among the basic assumptions on which liberal legal orders are built".[18]

The idea that a right to mental self-determination is somehow implicit in the law is also suggested by Farahany,[19] Sententia,[20] and Boire[21] – though these authors do not appeal to reasons of internal consistency when making their claims. Instead, they

[13] Ienca & Andorno 2017; Farahany 2023.
[14] Bublitz 2013; Bublitz &Merkel 2014.
[15] Bublitz 2013, p. 242.
[16] Bublitz 2020a, p. 399.
[17] Bublitz 2015, p. 1322, emphasis added.
[18] Bublitz & Merkel 2014, p. 62.
[19] Farahany 2023.
[20] Sententia 2004.
[21] Boire 2000.

appeal to the idea that a right to mental self-determination is necessary for the enjoyment of all other rights and freedoms the law protects. Farahany insists that:

> a careful reading of the Universal Declaration of Human Rights (UDHR) suggests that an individual right to self-determination is a necessary precondition for all the individuals rights in enumerates, including the right to be equal in dignity (Article 1 of the UDHR); to be free from discrimination (Article 7); to privacy (Article 12); freedom of expression (Article 19); and the right to one's own personality (Article 22, which secures to an "individual economic, social and cultural rights indispensable for his dignity and the free development of his personality").[22]

Farahany further claims that the importance of mental self-determination for the realisation of all of our other rights and freedoms has been noted by the U.S. Supreme Court, albeit not in these exact words. She points, for example, to the Supreme Court's comment in *Ashcroft* v. *Free Speech Coal.*, that "the right to think is the beginning of freedom", and to their comment in *Palko* v. *Connecticut* that "freedom of thought (...) is the matrix, the indispensable condition, of nearly every other form of freedom".[23] And she insists that the right to self-determination includes, among other things, a right to *mental* self-determination or "the right to choose how we will change our own brain and mental experiences".[24]

Farahany's claim that mental self-determination is "essential to all other legal rights" and for "securing our most cherished freedoms" also surfaces in the work of Sententia and Boire.[25] Sententia describes a right to mental self-determination as "fundamental" and "the necessary substrate for just about every other freedom".[26] Boire likewise pronounces mental self-determination as "the quintessence of freedom" – as something that must be afforded legal protection if notions of freedom, so central to our legal and political orders, are "to mean anything".[27]

These observations parallel a qualification made by the France representative René Cassin during the drafting of the Universal Declaration of Human Rights. Speaking about the right to freedom of thought specifically, Cassin suggested this right was "the basis and the origin of all other rights".[28] The UN Special Rapporteur on Freedom of Religion or Belief likewise emphasised, in their recent report to the UN General Assembly, "the essentiality of 'freedom of thought' for the dignity,

[22] Farahany 2023, p. 76.

[23] Farahany 2019, p. 99, footnote 117. See *Ashcroft* v. *Free Speech Coal.*, 535 U.S. 234, 253 (2002) and *Palko* v. *Connecticut*, 302 U.S. 319, 326–27 (1937), for the original references.

[24] Farahany 2023, p. 118.

[25] Farahany 2019, p. 75, 101.

[26] Sententia 2004, p. 227.

[27] Boire 2000, p. 8.

[28] E/CN.4/SR.60, p. 10.

agency and existence of the human being".[29] And while the protection of persons' powers of mental self-determination may be broader than the protection of freedom of thought (as noted in section 5.2.3), conceptual affinities between freedom of thought and mental self-determination as we have defined it clearly exist. This renders the above comments relevant for a defence of the claim that a right to mental self-determination is implicit in law, owing to its importance for individual freedom.

5.2.3 *A Right to Mental Self-Determination as Protected by the Right to Freedom of Thought*

A second, though related, route by which we might defend the existence of persons' right to mental self-determination is by seeing it as a derivative right of the right to freedom of thought pursuant to Article 18 ICCPR and Article 9 ECHR.[30]

Although we acknowledge the relevance of the right to freedom of thought for the protection of mental self-determination, we do not focus on this particular way to carve out space for a right to mental self-determination for two reasons. First, because we think it more straightforward to understand persons' right to mental self-determination as inherent in the more general right to self-determination (section 5.2.4). And second, because we do not wish to limit our analysis to the protection of self-determination over 'thoughts' alone. Rather, we are aiming to identify the contours of a more holistic right that may also apply to the self-determination of mental phenomena that are not plausibly covered by the right to freedom of thought, including feelings, behavioural control and empathic abilities – which are (also) potential targets of neurorehabilitation.[31]

Furthermore, deriving a right to mental self-determination from the right to freedom of thought faces another complexity, as the latter is often considered to be an absolute right. However, it seems that if mental self-determination *is* to find protection within the law, then it should take the form of non-absolute protection. Bublitz and Merkel say something similar when defending a right to mental self-determination.[32] Accepting that the right to freedom of thought protects against "severe" interferences with contents of opinion, thinking processes and patterns of thought, they claim that "there ought to be another, presumably non-absolute right protecting the mind".[33] Deriving a right to mental self-determination from the right to freedom of thought may render the right absolute, meaning that persons could

[29] UN Special Rapporteur on the Freedom of religion or belief, 5 October 2021, A/76/380, par. 1. See also O'Callaghan et al. 2023.

[30] Cf. Bublitz 2015.

[31] See also Chapter 3, section 3.2.4.

[32] Bublitz & Merkel 2014.

[33] Bublitz & Merkel 2014, p. 64.

never be legally prevented from altering or exerting control over their thoughts, including with the aid of neuro- and other technologies, under any circumstances. And affording mental self-determination this kind of legal protection seems to be too strong, while potentially giving rise to some counter-intuitive implications. It could mean, for instance, that states may *never* block a person's access to mental self-determination-enhancing neurotechnologies, even when accessing such technologies risks occasioning great harm to that person and/or others.[34] This seems to be an undesirable implication, and hence provides another reason not to harness the right to freedom of thought as the vehicle by which to afford a right to mental self-determination concrete legal protection.

5.2.4 *A Right to Mental Self-Determination as Protected by the Right to Privacy*

A third way a right to mental self-determination might be defended involves arguing that such a right is derivable from – and hence protected by – the right to respect for private life, as enshrined in Article 17 ICCPR and Article 8 ECHR.[35] This possibility has been noted by Michalowski in her suggestion that "a prima facie right to use mind-changing tools (. . .) is an argument that can potentially be made under Article 8(1)" ECHR.[36] We expand on this possibility in the paragraphs that follow, first by drawing on the case law that interprets the relevant legal provisions as protecting a general right to self-determination. We then argue that persons' right to self-determination contains or implies a right to mental self-determination. This line of argument finds support in some remarks made by the relevant treaty bodies.

The idea that persons' right to respect for private life protects a general right to self-determination has received most attention in the European context. Recall that the ECtHR in *Parillo/Italy* explicitly recognised that the concept of "private life" within the meaning of Article 8 ECHR embraces a "right to self-determination".[37] Relatedly, as indicated in previous chapters, the ECtHR's case law on Article 8 ECHR interprets "private life" broadly, interpreting it as covering, for instance, the physical and psychological integrity of the person,[38] "multiple aspects of the person's

34 See Dore-Horgan & Douglas 2025, for discussion of these kinds of counter-intuitive implications with respect to persons' putative moral right to acquire greater control over our thoughts. Consider also that absolute protection of mental self-determination might render laws that prohibit certain recreational drug use (laws that exist in many jurisdictions) to be in *violation* of human rights – something that many might consider counter-intuitive.

35 Note, Article 17 ICCPR does not refer to "*respect*" for private life, but instead simply refers to the prohibition of "arbitrary" or "unlawful" interference with persons' privacy.

36 Michalowski 2020.

37 ECtHR (GC) 27 August 2015, 46470/11 (*Parrillo/Italy*), par. 153.

38 ECtHR 26 March 1985, 8978/80 *(X and Y/the Netherlands)*, par. 22; ECtHR 25 March 1993, 13134/87 *(Costello-Roberts/the United Kingdom)*, par. 36; ECtHR (GC) 29 April 2002, 2346/02 *(Pretty/the United Kingdom)*, par. 61.

physical, social and ethnic identity",[39] and persons' freedom to lead a "private social life".[40] The protection of private life under Article 8 ECHR has also been interpreted as implying a right to personal autonomy and personality development – two concepts that, as said, closely resemble self-determination as we have defined it. Personal autonomy, just like self-determination, "evokes the image of a person in charge of" and "part author" of their own lives – at least on one understanding of personal autonomy.[41] Personal or personality development is plausibly also a large component of what it means to self-determine the course of one's life and to become the person one wants to be.

Some cases prior to *Parillo/Italy* made room for a right to self-determination by emphasising how a right to personality development is protected under Article 8 ECHR. In an early case of the European Commission of Human Rights (EComHR), the Commission, though rejecting the applicant's claim that the freedom to keep a dog was protected under the "private life" of Article 8 ECHR, observed that "the right to respect for private life comprises, to a certain degree, the right to establish and to develop relationships with other human beings, especially in the emotional field for the development and the fulfilment of one's own personality".[42] This position was reiterated in *Bruggermann and Scheuten/Federal Republic of Germany*, where the Commission ruled that although not every state action that limits an "individual's possibility of developing his personality (...) constitute[s] an interference with private life in the sense of Article 8 of the Convention", Article 8 guarantees the individual "a sphere within which he can freely pursue the development and fulfilment of this personality".[43] These early cases thus carved out a space for a right to self-determination by emphasising how private life encompasses personality development, at least to a certain degree.

Other cases of the ECtHR likewise made room for a right to self-determination by emphasising how *personal autonomy* is protected under Article 8 ECHR. In these cases, the ECtHR has gradually moved from talking about personal autonomy as merely an important notion or principle underlying the interpretation of Article 8 to talking about personal autonomy as a *right* of persons. The reference to personal autonomy in *Pretty/the United Kingdom* – a case concerning assisted suicide – is an example of the former.[44] Here, the Court asserted that while "no previous case has established as such any right to self-determination as being contained in Article 8 of

39 ECtHR 4 September 2004, 53176/99 *(Mikulić/Croatia)*, par. 53; ECtHR 4 December 2008, 30562/04 and 30566/04 *(S. and Marper/the United Kingdom)*, par. 66.

40 ECtHR (GC) 5 September 2017, 61496/08 *(Bărbulescu/Romania)*, par. 70.

41 Waldron 2005, pp. 307, 315. Here, Waldron draws on Raz 1986.

42 EComHR 18 May 1976, 6825/74 *(X/Iceland)*.

43 EComHR 12 July 1977, 6959/75 *(Bruggermann and Scheuten/Federal Republic of Germany)* pars. 56, 55. This case concerned the question of whether restrictions on the termination of an unwanted pregnancy constituted an interference with the right of respect to private life, and the conclusion was that they did not.

44 ECtHR 29 April 2002, 2346/02 *(Pretty/the United Kingdom)*.

the Convention, the Court considers that the notion of personal autonomy is an important principle underlying the interpretation of its guarantees".[45] It is exactly this consideration to which the Grand Chamber referred in *Parrillo/Italy* when holding that a right to self-determination is covered by the right to respect for private life in Article 8 ECHR.[46]

References to a *right* to personal autonomy then began in the case of *M.C./Bulgaria* – a case concerning the positive duties arising under Articles 3 and 8 ECHR with respect to effective legal protection against rape – when Judge Tulkens proclaimed that "rape infringes not only the right to personal integrity (...) but also the right to autonomy as a component of the right to respect for private life".[47] Subsequent judgments of the ECtHR reaffirmed this relationship between the right to respect for private life and the right to personal autonomy.[48] For instance, the ECtHR in *Evans/the United Kingdom* observed that private life "encompass[es], *inter alia*, aspects of an individual's physical and social identity, including the right to personal autonomy [and] personal development".[49] At the same time, some other judgments of the Court specifically proposed a connection between the rights protected under Article 8 ECHR and persons' self-determination.[50] For example, the ECtHR in *Connors/the United Kingdom* stipulated that Article 8 concerns, among other things, "rights of central importance to the individual's identity [and] self-determination".[51]

Similar developments have happened internationally and in the inter-American context with regard to the interpretation of Article 17 ICCPR and Article 11 American Convention on Human Rights (ACHR). The Inter-American Court of Human Rights has identified a similar range of rights inherent in the protection of privacy (guaranteed by Article 11 ACHR), as have been identified as covered by the right to the respect of private life in the European context. To quote from the Inter-American Court's espousal of the point in *Artavia Murillo* v. *Costa Rica* (a case concerning in-vitro fertilisation):

> The protection of private life encompasses a series of factors associated with the dignity of the individual, including, for example, the ability to develop his or her own personality and aspirations, to determine his or her own identity and to define his or her own personal relationships (...) [It] encompasses aspects of physical and social identity, including the right to personal autonomy, personal development (...) The effective exercise of the right to private life is decisive for the possibility of

45 ECtHR 29 April 2002, 2346/02 *(Pretty/the United Kingdom)*, par. 61.

46 ECtHR (GC) 27 August 2015, 46470/11 (*Parrillo/Italy*), par. 153.

47 ECtHR 4 December 2003, 39272/98 *(M.C./Bulgaria)*, concurring opinion of Judge Tulkens.

48 See ECtHR (GC) 7 April 2007, 6339/05 *(Evans/the United Kingdom)*, par. 71; ECtHR 7 May 2009, 3451/05, *(Kalacheva /Russia)*, par. 27.

49 ECtHR (GC) 7 April 2007, 6339/05 *(Evans/the United Kingdom)*, par. 71.

50 ECtHR 27 May 2004, 66746/01 (*Connors/the United Kingdom*), par. 82; ECtHR 21 June 2011, 48833/07 *(Orlić/Croatia)*, par. 63; ECtHR 6 Dec 2011, 7097/10 *(Gladysheva/Russia)*, par. 93.

51 ECtHR 27 May 2004, 66746/01 (*Connors/the United Kingdom*), par. 82.

> exercising personal autonomy on the future course of relevant events for a person's quality of life (...) and [it] is an essential condition for the free development of the personality.[52]

The Inter-American Court elsewhere links the right to respect for private life to "a person's right to self-determination and to freely choose the options and circumstances that give meaning to his or her existence, in accordance with his or her own choices and convictions".[53] And the UN Human Rights Committee's development of Article 17 ICCPR – while not specifically relying on the concepts of self-determination or personal autonomy – nonetheless suggests, in an opinion appended to the Committee's views in *Hertzberg et al./Finland*, that the right to privacy pursuant to Article 17 ICCPR protects "the right to *be* different and live accordingly".[54] This perhaps suggests a right to personal autonomy or self-determination. As Nowak/Schabas write in their commentary on Article 17 ICCPR, "privacy covers that area of individual autonomy in which human beings strive to achieve self-realization by way of actions that do not interfere with the liberty of others. This liberty of action inherent in private self-determination may be exercised alone or together with others".[55]

All of the above illustrates that the right to respect for private life – a right most extensively developed in the case law pertaining to Article 8 ECHR – has been interpreted as protecting a right to personal autonomy, self-determination or something similar to these concepts. Precisely what the right to self-determination amounts to – that is, its precise substance or the specific kinds of interests it covers – is still very much a matter of debate for the courts. Clearly, and to quote from Gross, "not every curtailment of autonomy is a compromise of privacy".[56] We must therefore ascertain the *kinds* of incursions on autonomy or self-determination that could raise an issue under the right to respect for private life, before we can comment on whether the right to personal autonomy/self-determination implies a right to specifically *mental* self-determination.

Some remarks of the ECtHR prove instructive here. In particular, the observation that the right to self-determination protects the most "intimate" aspects of how

52 *Artavia Murillo ("In Vitro Fertilization") v. Costa Rica*, Inter- Am. Ct. H.R. (ser. C) No. 257, (28 November 2012), par. 143. The Court here held that "personal decisions" to produce biological children by in-vitro fertilisation were protected under the ACHR and ordered Costa Rica to authorise and subsidise IVF services; see De Jesus 2014, for discussion.

53 *Atala Riffo and Daughters* v. *Chile*, Inter- Am. Ct. H.R. (ser. C) No. 254, (24 February 2012), par. 36. The Court in this case held that the Republic of Chile violated the petitioner's right to privacy (Article 11 ACHR) and their right to protection of the family (Article 17 ACHR) by inquiring into her sexual orientation and by denying her custody of daughters on the basis of her sexual orientation.

54 *Hertzberg et al./Finland*, CCPR/C/15/D/61/1979, 2 April 1982 (emphasis added).

55 Nowak & Schabas 2019, p. 472.

56 Gross 1971, p. 181.

we conduct our lives.[57] The idea that intimacy considerations demarcate just which exercises of personal autonomy or self-determination qualify for protection under the right to privacy is also espoused by a number of philosophical and legal scholars, and by the U.S. Supreme Court in its assessment of the U.S. Constitution's protection of privacy. Both Gerety and Inness assert respectively that "intimacy is the chief restricting concept"[58] and "the common denominator"[59] of privacy. The U.S. Supreme Court likewise characterises privacy as an "interest in independence in making certain kinds of important decisions"[60] – those that deal with matters "involving the most intimate and personal choices a person may make in a lifetime"[61] which include "decisions relating to marriage (...); procreation (...); contraception (...); family relationships (...); and childrearing and education".[62]

Evidently, the kinds of matters that count as "the most intimate and personal" is still a further question, and the above comment of the U.S. Supreme Court – referencing marriage, procreation, family and so on – names but a few candidates. The ECtHR has clearly disqualified some acts from the category of intimate and personal. In the case of *Friend and Countryside Alliance and others/the United Kingdom*, for instance, it ruled that a ban on hunting "was too far removed from the personal autonomy of the applicants (...) for the hunting bans to amount to an interference with the rights under Article 8".[63] This remained the case notwithstanding that the applicants derived "an obvious sense of enjoyment and public fulfilment" from participating in hunting.[64]

Other activities have been suggested to be sufficiently personal or intimate as to qualify for protection under the right to self-determination. Activities and choices pertaining to bodily matters, for one, seem to have acquired such a status, so long as these activities and choices are (i) *purely* self-regarding and do not involve non-consensual bodily interference with others; and (ii) do not risk rights violations or human error and abuse, if protected in law. So, for instance, the ECtHR has observed that personal autonomy under Article 8 ECHR protects "the right to make choices about one's own body" including

57 See, for example, ECtHR 27 August 2015, 46470/11 (*Parrillo/Italy*), par. 159; ECtHR 22 July 2003, 24209/94 (*Y.F./Turkey*), par. 33; ECtHR (GC) 29 June 2007, 15472/02 (*Folgerø and Others/Norway*), par. 98.

58 Gerety 1977, p. 263.

59 Inness 1992, p.56.

60 *Whalen* v. *Roe*, 429 U.S. 589 (1977), 599. https://supreme.justia.com/cases/federal/us/429/589/.

61 *Planned Parenthood of Southeastern Pa.* v. *Casey* (91–744), 505 U.S. 833 (1992), 851.

62 *Carey* v. *Population Services Int'l*, 431 U.S. 678 (1977), 685.

63 ECtHR 24 November 2009, 16072/06 and 27809/08 (*Friend and Countryside Alliance and others/the United Kingdom*), par. 33.

64 ECtHR 24 November 2009, 16072/06 and 27809/08 (*Friend and Countryside Alliance and others/the United Kingdom*), par. 33.

choices pertaining to sexual relations which are among "the most intimate in the private sphere" – so long as the other parties involved in these sexual relations validly consent to them.[65]

The ECtHR has likewise observed, in the case of *Pretty/the United Kingdom*, that the principle of personal autonomy enshrined in Article 8(1) ECHR includes a "right to make choices about one's own body".[66] It did this while also noting the caveat mentioned earlier: that an interference with the exercise of an Article 8 ECHR right could be compatible with Article 8(2) ECHR if (i) it is in accordance with the law, (ii) pursues a legitimate aim and (iii) is necessary in a democratic society for that aim.[67] The Court in *Pretty* considered whether a blanket ban on assisted suicide violated the applicant's right to respect for private life. The conclusion was that, while the personal autonomy of the applicant was at stake in this case, the United Kingdom's blanket ban on assisted suicide was not disproportionate to protect the rights and freedoms of others – and hence did not involve a violation of Article 8 ECHR – because "clear risks of abuse" would exist if such a provision were relaxed.[68] The upshot of this reasoning thus seems to be that bodily choices are protected under the right to respect for private life up to a certain point – so long as they do not violate or risk future violations of the rights and freedoms of others.[69]

Further observations of the ECtHR go beyond characterising the intimacies of personal autonomy or self-determination solely in bodily terms. Some remarks indicate a broader understanding of these intimacies – as those choices and aspects of our lives where, to use Rubenfeld's words, "our identity or self-definition is at stake".[70] The ECtHR has observed that matters pertaining to the development and expression of one's gender identity come under the ambit of private life and hence self-determination.[71] Decisions to take steps to become

65 ECtHR 17 February 2005, 42758/98 and 45558/99 (*K.A. and A.D./Belgium*). This case raised the issue of the extent to which acts of sadomasochism ought to be protected by the right to respect for private life, with the Court ruling that no violation of Article 8 ECHR took place in convicting persons for engaging in non-consensual sadomasochistic practices. See also ECtHR 19 February 1997, 21627/93, 21628/93 and 21974/93 (*Laskey and Others/the United Kingdom*), where the ECtHR observed that "not every sexual activity carried out behind closed doors necessarily falls within the scope of Article 8" (par. 36) and that governments were entitled to adopt measures under criminal law to protect people against torture-like sexual acts (pars. 39–40).

66 ECtHR 29 April 2002, 2346/02 (*Pretty/the United Kingdom*), par. 66.

67 ECtHR 29 April 2002, 2346/02 (*Pretty/the United Kingdom*), pars. 66, 68.

68 ECtHR 29 April 2002, 2346/02 (*Pretty/the United Kingdom*), pars. 66, 74.

69 See also Nowak & Schabas 2019, pp. 472–473.

70 Rubenfeld 1989, p. 737. Rubenfeld here is referring to and critiquing the "personhood theory of privacy" as it is espoused by the U.S. Supreme Court (by "personhood theory", we mean the idea that privacy protects against state interference with decisions that are essential to personhood). It is clear, however, that the ECtHR also seems to work with a "personhood theory of privacy". See Solove 2002 for discussion of different conceptions or theories of privacy.

71 ECtHR (GC) 11 July 2002, 28957/95 (*Christine Goodwin/the United Kingdom*). Following this case, the Court spoke of gender identity being "one of the most intimate areas of a person's private life"; see

a genetic parent[72] or to endeavour to discover one's genetic origins[73] also come under Article 8 ECHR's ambit. Furthermore, the ECtHR held that a person's "ability to exercise a conscious and considered choice regarding the fate of her embryos concerns an intimate aspect of her personal life and accordingly relates to her right to self-determination".[74]

Regardless of whether the right to self-determination is understood solely in terms of bodily autonomy, or in terms of self-authorship or identity-creation more generally, the prospects for deriving a right to *mental* self-determination from it seem promising. From one vantage, taking steps to exert control over what is in or on one's mind *is* an exercise of bodily autonomy – or more precisely, it is an exercise of bodily autonomy insofar as we assume that the body (brain) and mind are intimately related. From another vantage, a person's mental life seems as crucial to that person's identity as something can get. The mind, just like the body, is often considered to be very closely linked to a person's self. Bublitz and Merkel assert, for instance, that "what is even more constitutive of a subject than her body is her mind".[75] And on some views of the nature of the self, the mind, or some portion of it, *is* the self. Descartes famously identified the mind with the self,[76] and indeed some physicalists, in identifying the mind with the brain, also see the mind/brain as akin to the self.[77]

But even if the mind is not *coextensive* with the self, it is plausible that a certain, minimal degree of control over one's mental life is necessary for a person to play some role in determining and developing their own personality, identity or self.[78] How, after all, could an individual make authentic choices about the kind of person they wish to be unless they possess at least some ability to exert control over their choices and the thoughts or mental states from which these choices stem? We can imagine a person who, for instance, due to severe mental illness or supreme environmental stressors,[79] cannot focus their mental states in the direction they

ECtHR (GC) 12 June 2003, 35968/97 (*Van Kück/Germany*) par. 56; and ECtHR (GC) 8 January 2009, 29002/06 (*Sclumpf/Switzerland*), pars. 100–111.

72 ECtHR 7 March 2006, 6339/05 *(Evans/the United Kingdom)*, par. 57; and ECtHR (GC) 10 April 2007, 6339/05 *(Evans/the United Kingdom)*, par. 71.

73 ECtHR 4 February 2002, 53176/99 *(Mikulic/Croatia)*; ECtHR (GC) 13 February 2003, 42326/98 *(Odièvre/France)*.

74 ECtHR (GC) 27 August 2015, 46470/11 (*Parrillo/Italy*), par. 159.

75 Bublitz & Merkel 2014, p. 62.

76 More precisely, Descartes suggests that the self can *either* be taken to be a mind or a human being; see Chamberlain 2020 for discussion. Nonetheless, Descartes insists that the self or subject cannot exist in the absence of thinking.

77 For example, Churchland 2011.

78 Recall that the Inter-American Court of Human Rights considers that the right to respect for private life encompasses the protection of "the ability to develop his or her own personality and aspirations, to determine his or her own identity"; see *Artavia Murillo ("In Vitro Fertilization")* v. *Costa Rica*, Preliminary Objections, Merits, Reparations, and Costs, Judgment, Inter- Am. Ct. H.R. (ser. C) No. 257 (28 November 2012), par. 143.

79 That cause, for example, severe pain or fear.

wish, cannot reject or seek to divert their attention away from unwanted mental states, and cannot change their mental states even when this is something they desire. In this situation, it seems obvious that the relevant person cannot even partly author their own decisions at this point in time. Consider, more specifically, how a person who struggles to control their urge to lash out aggressively has *less* control or authorship over their personality, identity or life than they might otherwise have done, notwithstanding that they can still exert control over other aspects of their personality – for example, whether they are compassionate or generous.

The case law of the ECtHR does not specify a link between the development of personality or identity and mental self-determination. This Court does, however, link the development of personality to one's mental life, or more precisely, to one's mental stability. As indicated in Chapter 2, in their judgments in *Bensaid/the United Kingdom* and in *Odièvre/France*, the ECtHR stipulated that "the preservation of *mental stability* is (. . .) an indispensable precondition to effective enjoyment of the right to respect for private life" or the right to identity and personal development contained therein.[80] Granted, mental stability is not synonymous with mental self-determination (indeed, it is more suggestive of mental *health*).[81] But maintaining mental stability plausibly requires some degree of mental control or mental self-determination. Consider how reduced executive control or executive dysfunction is associated with certain mental health conditions.[82] Consider, too, how emotional control is often considered important for the maintenance of mental stability or mental health.[83]

The above observations about the relationship between body and mind, mind and self, and mental stability and mental control, all indicate that there is scope to derive a right to *mental* self-determination from the already elaborated right to self-determination or personal autonomy. Moreover, the fact that the right to bodily autonomy has been observed (in at least one piece of case law[84]) to protect a person's prerogative to use assisted reproduction technologies suggests that the right to mental self-determination *could*, likewise, be interpreted as protecting

80 ECtHR 6 February 2001, 44599/98 (*Bensaid/United Kingdom*), par. 47; ECtHR (GC) 13 February 2003, 42326/98 (*Odièvre/France*), par. 29 (emphasis added).

81 For our discussion of the right to mental health and its relevance, or otherwise, for neurorehabilitation, see Chapter 6 of this book.

82 Parola et al. 2020; Cotrena et al. 2020; Halse et al. 2022; Esmaili et al. 2023.

83 Gross & Muñoz 1995; Kraiss et al. 2020; Menefee et al. 2022; Fernandes, Wright, Essau 2023.

84 *Artavia Murillo ("In Vitro Fertilization") v. Costa Rica*, Inter- Am. Ct. H.R. (ser. C) No. 257, (28 November 2012). In ECtHR 28 August 2012, 54270/10 *(Costa and Pavan/Italy)*, where the details of the case were quite different, the ECtHR did not exactly conclude that Article 8 ECHR protected a prerogative to access assisted reproduction technologies. The Court in this case did, however, rule that preventing the applicants from recourse to medical-assisted procreation when they carried a genetic defect while simultaneously permitting abortion in cases where the foetus was suffering from the relevant illness violated Article 8 ECHR.

a prerogative to use mental control-enhancing neurotechnologies in certain circumstances.

It may be that the right to mental self-determination will not be interpreted as protecting this prerogative on occasions when (i) a country's domestic law prohibits access to relevant technologies, and (ii) in the opinion of the relevant courts, allowing access to mental control-enhancing neurotechnologies creates a clear risk of abuse. Recall how the ECtHR emphasised in *Pretty/the United Kingdom* that interference with the exercise of an Article 8 ECHR right could be compatible with Article 8(2) ECHR if the interference is in accordance with domestic law and necessary and proportionate for fulfilling the aims laid out in Article 8(2).[85] Therefore, insofar as the two mentioned conditions are not fulfilled, a right to mental self-determination, inherent in the right to private life, *could* lend support to a rights-based claim to freely make use of self-enhancing neurotechnology.

5.2.5 *A Moral Argument for a Right to Mental Self-Determination*

A fourth way we might justify a right to mental self-determination is by demonstrating, first, that we have a *pro tanto* (i.e., defeasible) moral right to mental self-determination and, second, that it may be desirable to practically implement and enforce this right through law. As to the first of these claims, one of us has recently defended the related claim that we have a moral right to *acquire control* over our thoughts, with this putative right being understood as a *pro tanto* right that others not interfere with our attempts to acquire the wherewithal for such control, including by accessing psychological techniques or neurotechnologies.[86] The arguments harnessed to make this related claim can, we think, be repurposed as arguments for a *pro tanto* moral right to self-determination and we shall repurpose them accordingly here. Recall that we understand a right to mental self-determination as a right that others not interfere with our attempts to *alter and exercise control* over our thoughts including with the help of neurotechnologies, psychoactive drugs or psychological techniques. Consider then how this putative right is closely related to, but not wholly coextensive with, the putative moral right to acquire the wherewithal for mental control.

Whether we have a moral right to mental self-determination depends, at least in part, on whether we have an interest in being mentally self-determining. That we have such an interest seems plausible. Farahany claims we have such an interest when asserting that mental self-determination is "a fundamental interest essential to individual and social flourishing"[87] and that "respecting people's right to self-determination (…) will (…) enable human flourishing".[88] The credibility of this

[85] ECtHR 29 April 2002, 2346/02 (*Pretty/the United Kingdom*), par. 68.
[86] Dore-Horgan & Douglas 2025.
[87] Farahany 2019, p. 109.
[88] Farahany 2023, p. 80.

claim becomes evident, moreover, when we consider how the power to alter and exercise control over our thoughts likely has value for us on many prominent theories of well-being.[89]

Mental state theories, for instance, consider mental self-determination to have instrumental value insofar as our mentally self-determining acts produce positive mental states[90] – something that is at least sometimes likely, given that persons are typically motivated to achieve such states.[91] Desire-satisfaction or preferentist theories likewise attribute value to mental self-determination: this time insofar as, and to the extent that, having powers of mental self-determination is something we desire (non-instrumental value), and insofar as we exercise our powers of mental self-determination to produce mental states that we desire to have (instrumental value).[92] Lastly, objective list theories frequently assign non-instrumental value to self-determination more generally or to closely related powers such as autonomy.[93] Indeed, one particular objective list theory explicitly equates well-being with powers of self-determination.[94] And *mental* self-determination, as suggested in the previous section, can reasonably be considered a facet of self-determination more generally.

Our interest in having powers of mental self-determination is, however, not enough to justify our possessing a moral right to it. There are many things we have an interest in securing – for example, wealth and others' esteem – to which we do not have a moral right, notwithstanding that our interest in having these things may sometimes be powerful. Thus, for persons to have a moral right to mental self-determination, it must also be the case that our interest in having mental self-determination is accompanied by some other justifying reason for the right – that is, by some reason that explains why third parties have a *pro tanto* duty to respect this particular interest, as against other interests of ours.

One candidate reason appeals to the idea that our mental life is "our business" or ours alone to control,[95] and motivates this idea by making an analogy with how we typically envisage our relationship with, and our powers over, our bodies. Douglas and Forsberg appeal to this analogy when arguing that one commonly advanced justification for a *legal* right to bodily integrity – namely, that our body is something over which we are "sovereign" just as states are sovereign over their

89 The discussion that follows borrows heavily from Dore-Horgan & Douglas 2025. See Parfit 1984, appendix C, for a tripartite classification of theories of well-being.

90 By instrumental value, we mean that something has value as a means to some end. By non-instrumental value, we mean that something has value apart from its utility for other ends.

91 Haybron 2016.

92 Heathwood 2016.

93 See, for example, Nussbaum 2000; and Griffin 1986.

94 Ryan & Deci 2017.

95 Clearly, third parties can alter our mental states by, for example, simply engaging us in conversation, endeavouring to persuade us or bringing certain objects or ideas into our awareness. But the idea that we alone should have the power to exert *control* over our mental states is implicit in discussions of the presumptive wrongfulness of "brainwashing", thought control or coercive persuasion (see, for example, Antón 2020).

territory – provides like support for a defeasible legal right to mental integrity.[96] They point to how the philosophical and legal literature is replete with claims that we have sovereignty over our bodies and hence have a presumptive right that others not interfere with our self-regarding bodily choices.[97] This idea is also prevalent in our folk intuitions and everyday practice. Think of how we typically judge that people should be afforded the freedom to obtain a facelift, a tattoo or a piercing from a willing expert if they so wish. Think, too, of how we usually consider a person's reproductive and medical choices are theirs to make, at least presumptively.[98] Douglas and Forsberg suggest, then, that insofar as we accept we have a degree of sovereignty over our self-regarding bodily choices, justificatory consistency requires that we also accept we have like sovereignty over our minds. To quote from them directly:

> Though discussions of (. . .) personal sovereignty more frequently draw out implications for the body than for the mind, it seems clear that appeals to self-ownership or personal sovereignty will also support rights over the mind, since the mind clearly also either is, is part of, or is closely connected to, the self. Indeed, most currently dominant accounts of the self give the mind a more central role than the body in the self.[99]

Building on Douglas and Forsberg's points, our argument here is that if we *have* a limited degree of sovereignty over our minds, we have a second reason for thinking that persons have a *pro tanto* moral duty to refrain from interfering with our acts of mental self-determination, aside from the interest-based reason advanced above. This second reason presents a route by which to justify just *why* our interest in mental self-determination is an interest that third parties are presumptively obliged to respect. Our preliminary case for a moral right to mental self-determination therefore rests on two claims: (1) the claim that we have a (presumably strong) interest in having powers of mental self-determination and (2) the claim that we are the legitimate sovereigns over our mind.

Arguing for a moral right to mental self-determination is all well and good, but as earlier indicated, our interest is in exploring how the putative moral right to mental self-determination might be harnessed in the service of defending a corresponding legal right. The existence of a moral right does not straightforwardly imply a legal right or the need to recognise one, even allowing that human rights in general are often thought to mirror underlying moral rights. For a moral right to merit practical implementation and enforcement in law, a further argumentative step is required – one that justifies why the law should be concerned about such a right.

96 Douglas & Forsberg 2021.
97 Ripstein 2006; Archard 2008.
98 There are, of course, some controversial cases here, hence the qualification of "presumptively".
99 Douglas & Forsberg 2021, p. 191.

One relevant reason that might be offered in the case of the right to mental self-determination appeals to the idea that a corresponding legal right is necessary because of the potentially increasing ease with which persons' efforts at mental self-determination might be frustrated. Why think that persons' efforts at mental self-determination might sometimes be readily frustrated, and in the future, perhaps more so? Well, because advances in pharmaceuticals, psychological techniques and neurotechnologies mean that persons increasingly have the possibility to make use of a *wider range* of *external tools* to aid their efforts at altering and controlling their mental states. These externalised acts of mental self-determination will invariably be easier to frustrate than "within-the-head-exercises" of mental self-determination. Many exercises of mental self-determination, after all, enjoy a level of "natural" protection by virtue of the fact that they take place in our brains, shielded from the outside world by the skull.[100] Our externalised efforts at mental self-determination do not enjoy this same kind of natural protection. If the state wishes to frustrate your efforts to alter your mental states with the aid of a good book, cognitive behavioural therapy, a psychedelic drug or a brain stimulation technique, it is simply a matter of denying you recourse, or frustrating your access, to these tools (perhaps sometimes through criminalisation),[101] rather than interfering with your existing brain states. And insofar as it is possible to frustrate access to these tools (which it clearly is), we have a candidate reason as to why the putative moral right to mental self-determination is something the law should be concerned about protecting. The ever-expanding range of tools at our disposal for facilitating mental self-determination arguably makes this concern even more exigent.

Saying that a moral right to mental self-determination exists and ought to be legally protected, however, is not the same as saying that we need to create a self-standing right to mental self-determination. Some scholars have argued for the need to recognise such a self-standing right.[102] But as earlier indicated, we are open to, and have defended, the possibility that a right to mental self-determination can be derived from the existing right to respect for private life as covered by, for example, Article 8 ECHR. Our invoking of a moral argument for a legal right to mental self-determination is therefore not intended to support calls for a new, self-standing right to mental self-determination. Rather, we are simply highlighting that there is (at least) one plausible moral argument that favours embracing and accommodating a legal right to mental self-determination, while allowing that this accommodation could be done in a variety of ways, including by seeing this right as a derivative right of the right to respect for private life.[103]

100 Dore-Horgan & Douglas 2025.

101 Consider how the use of psychedelic drugs is prohibited in many jurisdictions; see Chesak 2024.

102 Ienca & Andorno 2017; Farahany 2023.

103 As earlier indicated, others might, alternatively, see it as coming under the ambit of the right to freedom of thought.

5.3 A STATE DUTY TO PROVIDE NEUROREHABILITATION?

Our discussion thus far has focused on three routes by which we might defend and carve out space for a right to mental self-determination. We must now consider whether this right grounds a state duty to *offer* or *provide* "mental self-determination-enabling" neurotechnologies to relevant convicted persons. Clearly, no understanding of such a duty has been articulated or developed in the relevant jurisprudence to date. Much remains open for interpretation. Moreover, on *initial* examination, one might surmise that persons' right to respect for private life does not necessarily entail a state duty to provide neurotechnologies to any given population.

We say this because privacy rights are typically characterised in negative terms – a characterisation that is largely reiterated in the associated case law and general comments. Article 17 ICCPR refers *only* to persons' right to legal protection from "arbitrary or unlawful *interference*" with their privacy.[104] The UN Human Rights Committee reiterates that "Article 17 [ICCPR] provides for the right of every person to be protected against arbitrary or unlawful interference with his privacy."[105] The primarily negative character of the rights protected under Article 8 ECHR is also emphasised by the ECtHR. The ECtHR has stated that the *primary* object of Article 8 ECHR "is essentially that of protecting the individual against arbitrary *interference* by the public authorities".[106] Indeed, in the case of *Chapman/the United Kingdom*, the ECtHR effectively denied that Article 8 ECHR grounds a state duty to provide measures that might help persons *realise* or *enjoy* the rights contained therein.[107] Referring to Article 8's protection of the right to respect for home, the ECtHR in *Chapman* stated that "Article 8 does not (...) give a right to be provided with a home" and "whether the State provides funds to enable everyone to have a home is a matter for political not judicial decision".[108]

Similar reasoning could thus be applied to the interpretation of Article 8 ECHR with regard to the (putative) right to mental self-determination. That is, the ECtHR could interpret the right to respect for private life pursuant to Article 8 ECHR as *not* entailing a state duty to fund or otherwise make available resources (including neurotechnologies) that enable mental self-determination. Similar interpretations could also be advanced by the UN Human Rights Committee with respect to the right to privacy enshrined in Article 17 ICCPR. And if persons' right to mental self-determination were solely to find grounding in the right to respect for private life, and if the right to respect for private life were so interpreted, then this would mean that the right to mental self-determination fails to generate positive duties for states

104 Our emphasis.
105 CCPR General Comment No. 16, par. 1.
106 ECtHR 9 October 1979, 6289/73 (*Airey/Ireland*).
107 ECtHR 18 January 2001, 27238/95 (*Chapman/the United Kingdom*).
108 ECtHR 18 January 2001, 27238/95 (*Chapman/the United Kingdom*), par. 99.

with respect to the provision of neurorehabilitation – an outcome that would undermine the relevance of the foregoing discussion.

Yet, this is not the end of the story. A state duty to fund or make available resources that enable mental self-determination arises under the right to privacy in certain circumstances. It is generally accepted in the legal literature, after all, that states have duties with respect to *fulfilling* human rights, at least to a degree – where "fulfil" denotes taking positive steps to help rights-bearers fully realise these rights.[109] There is also a robust body of ECtHR case law illustrating that the rights and freedoms enshrined in the ECHR, including Article 8 ECHR, produce a wide variety of positive obligations in certain circumstances.[110] We expand on these developments, and on their relevance for the case of neurorehabilitation, in the paragraphs that follow.

Consider first how states' duties with respect to human rights contain or include a duty to "fulfil" these rights. This idea is advanced by the UN's Committee on Economic Social and Cultural Rights (CESCR) in their comment that "*all* human rights impose (...) three types or levels of obligations on state parties: the obligations to respect, protect and fulfil".[111] Expanding on what "fulfil" means, the CESCR states that

> the obligation to *fulfil* can be disaggregated into the obligations to facilitate, promote and provide. The obligation to facilitate requires the State to take positive measures to assist individuals and communities to enjoy the right. The obligation to promote obliges the State party to take steps to ensure that there is appropriate education [with respect to the right in question]. state parties are also obliged to fulfil (provide) the right when individuals or groups are unable, for reasons beyond their control, to realise that right themselves by the means at their disposal.[112]

Discharging these disaggregate obligations, moreover, requires that states "adopt appropriate legislative, administrative, budgetary, judicial, promotional and other measures towards the full realisation of the right", the CESCR contends.[113]

Now, clearly, given that these comments come from the CESCR, positive actions of this kind are required in the case of *economic*, *social* and *cultural* rights. Yet, the CESCR also invokes the idea that positive actions are (presumptively) required more widely – that is, in the case of civil and political rights – in its use of the phrase "*all* human rights".[114] A number of scholars suggest that obligations of fulfilment apply to all human rights, too. For example, Scott and Macklem suggest that over the

109 See Ahmed & de Jesús Butler 2006.

110 Stoyanova 2023; Gerards 2023, p. 174, with further references.

111 CESCR General Comment No. 14, par 33 (emphasis added). Also: CESCR General Comment No. 13, par. 46; CESCR General Comment No. 12, par. 15.

112 CESCR General Comment No. 15, par. 25 (original emphasis).

113 CESCR General Comment No. 14, par. 33.

114 CESCR General Comment No. 14, par. 33; CESCR General Comment No. 13, par. 46; CESCR General Comment No. 12, par. 15 (emphasis added).

decades, "the United Nations has invested considerable energy in developing the idea of a multilayered obligations structure that may potentially be generated for any right whether it be a civil liberty or a social right".[115] That *all* human rights imply (at least some) obligations of fulfilment thus indicates that the right to respect for private life could contain a duty to provide mental self-determination-enabling tools and technologies, at least in certain circumstances.

The ECtHR also recognises that positive obligations arise under the ECHR. The ECtHR's comments in the case of *Sengtes/the Netherlands* are an illustrative example in this regard.[116] The applicant in this case suffered from a degenerative muscle disease and complained that the state's denial of his request to be provided with a robotic arm constituted a breach of Article 8 ECHR, given that *if* provided with a robotic arm, his "severely curtailed level of self-determination would be increased".[117] The Court observed in this case:

> While the essential object of Article 8 is to protect the individual against arbitrary interference by the public authorities, it does not merely compel the State to abstain from such interference: in addition to this negative undertaking, there may be positive obligations inherent in effective respect for private or family life.[118]

The ECtHR in *Sengtes* further observed that Article 8 ECHR may impose such positive obligations on the state when a "direct and immediate link" exists between the measures sought by an applicant and their private life.[119] The Court assumed the existence of such a link in *Sengtes* but nonetheless declared the complaint inadmissible because the Dutch state had provided the applicant with an electric wheelchair with an adapted joystick. The ECtHR further claimed that national authorities were best positioned to assess precisely which measures they could provide and allocate given "their familiarity with the demands made on the health care system as well as with the funds available".[120] Still, this case illustrates that Article 8 ECHR sometimes entails a state duty to provide certain measures or resources when "the State's failure to adopt [such] measures interferes with that individual's right to personal development".[121]

Importantly, the ECtHR emphasises that "it is incumbent on the individual concerned to demonstrate the existence of a special link between the situation complained of and the particular needs of his or her private life".[122] The ECtHR

115 Scott & Mecklam 1992. See also Ahmed & de Jesús Butler 2006 for this line of thought.

116 ECtHR 8 July 2003, 27677/02 (*Sengtes/the Netherlands*). Note, though, that the ECtHR has identified a positive obligation to protect privacy as arising under Article 8 ECHR since ECtHR 13 June 1979, 6833/74 (*Marckx/Belgium*). See also ECtHR 24 February 1998, 21439/93 (*Botta/Italy*).

117 ECtHR 8 July 2003, 27677/02 (*Sengtes/the Netherlands*). p. 5.

118 ECtHR 8 July 2003, 27677/02 (*Sengtes/the Netherlands*). p. 5, 6. See also ECtHR 9 October 1979, 6289/73 (*Airey/Ireland*).

119 ECtHR 8 July 2003, 27677/02 (*Sengtes/the Netherlands*), p. 5.

120 ECtHR 8 July 2003, 27677/02 (*Sengtes/the Netherlands*), pp. 5–7.

121 ECtHR 8 July 2003, 27677/02 (*Sengtes/the Netherlands*), pp. 5–6.

122 ECtHR 8 July 2003, 27677/02 (*Sengtes/the Netherlands*), pp. 5–7.

also notes that as far as positive obligations under Article 8 ECHR are concerned, what is required will vary from case to case owing to "the diversity of the practices followed and the situations obtaining in the Contracting States".[123] Determining the content of Article 8's positive obligations will depend on several factors, including "the importance of the interest at stake and whether 'fundamental values' or 'essential aspects' of private life are at stake".[124] Another candidate factor – suggested by Feldman and perhaps relevant for the specific case of neurorehabilitation – is whether a particular aspect of a person's private life impacts their "capacity to give effect to their moral choices" or to live their life "in accordance with [their] ethical standards".[125]

The relevance of these observations to the case of neurorehabilitation is clear. They highlight how states may have a (defeasible) duty under Article 8 ECHR to make mental control-enhancing neurotechnologies available to convicted persons, when these individuals have mental states that significantly limit their ability to live the kind of life that they want and/or one which accords with their moral precepts. Whether or how frequently such a limitation exists for those who might be candidates for neurorehabilitation is, of course, an empirical matter. We do not know how commonly the mental states of convicted persons prevent them from living the life that they want, nor how frequently state assistance in the form of neurorehabilitation might be necessary to help convicted persons give effect to their choices.

Nonetheless, it is reasonable to suppose that there are some convicted persons whose unwanted thoughts render it extremely difficult for them to think and act as they want. Some persons convicted of sexual crimes, for example, experience persistent and unwanted sexual urges that presumably make it difficult for them to live a crime-free life. Some convicted of violent crimes might also find that their sudden urge to lash out renders it difficult for them to live a life of their own choosing. In these situations, a failure to make neurorehabilitation available – as and when effective neurorehabilitation *is* available – may raise an issue under Article 8 ECHR. Additionally, if the state holds those who offend *accountable* for actions that stem from mental states over which they have little control and which prevent them from living the kind of life they want, then the case for providing access to relevant neurorehabilitation seems even stronger. Recall Bublitz's point that legal orders premised on the idea of freely deciding persons must legally protect persons' powers of mental self-determination if they are to avoid "internal incoherences" in holding people accountable for their actions.[126]

[123] ECtHR 12 May 1985, 9214/80, 9473/81, 9474/81 (*Abdulaziz, Cabales and Balkandali*), par. 67.

[124] ECtHR (GC) 16 December 2010, 25579/05 (*A, B and C/Ireland*), par. 248. See, furthermore, Gerards 2023, p. 176 et seq.

[125] Feldman 1997, p. 270.

[126] Bublitz 2020a, p. 399.

5.4 CONCLUDING REMARKS

This chapter has examined the legal and moral rationales that seem to support a legal right to mental self-determination, including by accessing neurotechnologies. It further interrogated what the right to mental self-determination might imply for the neurorehabilitation of those who offend – specifically, whether it might imply a state duty to offer or provide neurorehabilitation in certain circumstances. We concluded that the right to mental self-determination – as a component of the right to respect for private life – may generate a duty on the part of states to offer or provide "mental self-determination-enabling" neurotechnologies in certain select circumstances. These circumstances are, we suggest, when there is a clear link between availing of these neurotechnologies and being able to live the kind of life that one chooses. More precisely, states may have an obligation if there are disruptive mental phenomena that hamper living a life free from crime and punishment. Such circumstances plausibly have relevance for at least some candidate cases of neurorehabilitation.

6

The Right to Mental Health

A Socio-economic Right over the Mind?

6.1 INTRODUCTION

As discussed in Chapter 1, the primary focus of this book is on the potential of neurotechnology to support the rehabilitation of convicted persons by improving *risk assessment* and *risk management* – rather than on its potential for diagnosing and treating mental or brain disorders. Still, in some cases, neurorehabilitation might well become conducive or even crucial to the improvement of mental health in forensic populations. Brain stimulation to attenuate aggressive impulses might serve to reduce the mental distress experienced by some persons subject to these impulses. Furthermore, aggression can be a symptom of a recognised mental illness, such as a psychotic disorder, or may be a core feature of a disorder, as in intermittent explosive disorder. Diminishing aggression using neurotechnology could in such cases be relevant to the person's mental health, which appears to be an interest protected by human rights law. For example, Article 12 of the International Covenant on Economic, Social and Cultural Rights (ICESCR) recognises a "right to the highest attainable standard of physical and mental health".

The right to health is sometimes referred to in discussions on human rights vis-à-vis emerging neurotechnologies. For example, Bublitz has highlighted the possibility of human rights comprising positive obligations to provide "access to therapeutic neurotechnologies restoring bodily or mental integrity", which "may often overlap with the right to health (Article 12 ICESCR)".[1] Likewise, in a recent report on neurotechnology and human rights, the Advisory Committee of the Human Rights Council considers the implications of Article 12 ICESCR, holding that when "safe, effective, secure and human-rights compliant neurotechnology products do exist, access becomes a key element of the right to health. States should then grant access, without discrimination".[2]

[1] Bublitz 2024, p. 796.

[2] Advisory Committee, UNHRC, Impact, opportunities and challenges of neurotechnology with regard to the promotion and protection of all human rights, A/HRC/AC/31/CRP.1 (8 August 2024), par. 32.

In this chapter, we explore whether a right to health could produce an argument in favour of offering neurorehabilitation to some populations of convicted persons. Note, that throughout, we assume that health and the right to health, necessarily encompass *mental* health. Hence, we take the legal and ethical literature relating to health and the right to health to pertain to mental health. This assumption is not a controversial one. Even though mental health is sometimes overlooked as a component of health,[3] many contemporary attempts to define health encompass both physical and psychological elements.[4] For example, according to the preamble of the Constitution of the World Health Organisation (WHO): "Health is a state of complete physical, mental and social well-being." The relevance of mental health is also stressed in the annual reports of the UN Special Rapporteur on the right to the highest attainable standard of health, emphasising that "there is no health without mental health".[5] Hence, in what follows, we understand the right to mental health as a specified right inherent in the right to health.

When considering a right to mental health in the criminal justice context, it is important to realise that a high prevalence of mental illness has consistently been reported within prison populations – including psychosis, depression and personality disorders.[6] As Gable and Gostin write, "[i]n many countries around the world prisons have become the de facto mental health systems".[7] Furthermore, factors related to psychiatric co-morbidity are among the risk factors for suicide attempts in prison.[8] Additionally, a considerable number of those who offend end up not in prison but in forensic psychiatric institutions. Clearly, these people also need to be taken into account to get an accurate picture of the relevance of mental illness to the criminal justice system.

Criminal justice is thus not just *a* setting relevant to the right to mental health, but rather one of the most important contexts to which the right applies.[9] Yet, the criminal justice system's primary aim is not to treat the mental health issues of those who offend but rather to enact justice, typically by *punishing* those who offend (e.g., through imprisonment) and also by *protecting* society against the future harm these individuals may cause (e.g., by detaining them in prison or forensic psychiatric institutions). Mental health needs of those who offend are not the priority of

3 UN Special Rapporteur on the right of everyone to the enjoyment of the highest attainable standard of physical and mental health, 2 April 2015, A/HRC/29/33, pars. 74–75.

4 See, for example, Starfield 2001; Card 2017.

5 UN Special Rapporteur on the right of everyone to the enjoyment of the highest attainable standard of physical and mental health, 2 April 2015, A/HRC/29/33, par. 76. See also UN Special Rapporteur on the right of everyone to the enjoyment of the highest attainable standard of physical and mental health, 12 April 2019, A/HRC/41/34.

6 Fazel et al. 2016.

7 Gable & Gostin 2009.

8 Favril, Shaw & Fazel 2022.

9 Cf. Report of the UN Special Rapporteur on the right of everyone to the enjoyment of the highest attainable standard of physical and mental health, 18 April 2018, A/HRC/38/36.

criminal justice, or at least not the direct priority.[10] And this observation gives us reason to assume that the mental health needs of those who offend will not always be met within criminal justice settings and contexts. There is thus a strong need to consider the legal protection of the mental health of these individuals.

This chapter proceeds as follows. Section 6.2 considers the foundation of the right to mental health, both from a legal and a moral perspective. In section 6.3, we discuss different understandings of "mental health" in relation to the right's scope, followed by an exploration of the right's implications for the neurorehabilitation of convicted persons in section 6.4. In section 6.5 we draw conclusions.

6.2 LEGAL AND MORAL BASES OF A RIGHT TO MENTAL HEALTH

6.2.1 *Legal Bases*

According to Article 12 ICESCR, the state parties to the Covenant "recognize the right of everyone to the enjoyment of the highest attainable standard of physical and mental health".[11] In the General Comment to this provision, the UN Committee on Economic, Social and Cultural Rights (CESCR) clarifies that the right to health is not to be understood as a right to *be* healthy but rather as a right to the enjoyment of a variety of *facilities, goods, services and conditions* necessary for the realisation of the highest attainable standard of health.[12]

The right includes both freedoms (such as the right to control one's own health) and entitlements (such as the right to a system of health protection and equal opportunity to enjoy the highest attainable standard of health).[13] States are under an obligation to respect the right to health by, inter alia, "refraining from denying or limiting equal access for all persons, including prisoners or detainees (...) to preventive, curative and palliative health service".[14] Within their available resources, state parties should provide, without discrimination, available, accessible and acceptable health facilities, goods and services, which are scientifically and medically appropriate and of good quality.[15]

Unlike the rights and freedoms discussed in the preceding chapters (e.g., the right to privacy, freedom of thought, self-determination), the right to health is a socio-economic right, rather than a civil or political right. Although both categories of rights were adopted together within the Universal Declaration of Human Rights

[10] An individual's mental health needs may become a priority if treating them becomes necessary to protect society.

[11] Cf. Article 10 of the Additional Protocol to the American Convention on Human Rights in the area of Economic, Social and Cultural Rights.

[12] CESCR General Comment No. 14, pars. 8–9.

[13] CESCR General Comment No. 14, par. 8.

[14] CESCR General Comment No. 14, par. 34.

[15] CESCR General Comment No. 14, par. 12. See also Riedel (2020, pp. 107–123). And regarding mental health UN Special Rapporteur on the right of everyone to the enjoyment of the highest attainable standard of physical and mental health, 28 March 2017, A/HRC/35/21, pars. 54–62.

(UDHR),[16] the international community subsequently decided that both categories are legally different and impose different obligations on states.[17] This ultimately resulted in two separate binding human rights treaties: the International Covenant on Civil and Political Rights (ICCPR) and the International Covenant on Economic, Social and Cultural Rights (ICESCR).

The obligations imposed on states by these treaties differ in the following ways. Article 2(1) ICCPR requires state parties "to respect and to ensure to all individuals" all civil and political rights enshrined within the ICCPR. By contrast, Article 2(1) ICESCR "only" requires state parties "to take steps, individually and through international assistance and co-operation, especially economic and technical, to the maximum of its available resources, with a view to achieving progressively the full realization of the rights recognized in the present Covenant".

Leijten explains that "[w]hereas the ICCPR rights are phrased as individual, subjective rights, ICESCR rights merely require states to *take steps* towards the fulfilment of socio-economic guarantees, subject to the requirement of *progressive realization* and in the light of the *available resources*".[18] The "progressive realisation" standard acknowledges that "the full realization of all economic, social and cultural rights will generally not be able to be achieved in a short period of time".[19] Still, states should "move as expeditiously and effectively as possible towards that goal"[20] – to the maximum of their available resources, including financial, natural and scientific resources.[21] According to Nowak, the difference between these obligations and those deriving from civil and political rights "could not have been more drastic".[22] As he explains:

> Civil and political rights have to be immediately respected and ensured, and every failure of a state party to respect and ensure them can be qualified as a violation of the respective obligation (…). Economic, social and cultural rights, on the contrary, are considered as mere "programme rights". For states, it seems to be enough to take a few steps, such as asking for international development assistance, in order to prove that they have complied with their respective obligations.[23]

The European Convention on Human Rights (ECHR) typically refers to civil and political rights and does not guarantee, explicitly, a right to health.[24] However, the

16 See, for example, Article 25(1) UDHR: "Everyone has the right to a standard of living adequate for the health and well-being of himself and of his family, including food, clothing, housing and medical care and necessary social services."

17 Nowak 2020, p. 10.

18 Leijten 2017, p. 28 (emphasis added).

19 CESCR General Comment No. 3, par. 9.

20 CESCR General Comment No. 3, par. 9.

21 Skogly 2012.

22 Nowak 2020, p. 10.

23 Nowak 2020, p. 10. See also Leijten 2017, pp. 143–146.

24 Contrast Recital 11 of the European Social Charter, emphasising that "Everyone has the right to benefit from any measures enabling him to enjoy the highest possible standard of health attainable." However, complaints about the Social Charter can only be made collectively and final decisions do

European Court of Human Rights (ECtHR) holds that "[w]hilst the Convention sets forth what are essentially civil and political rights, many of them have implications of a social or economic nature".[25] In the ECtHR's view, there is "no water-tight division" separating socio-economic rights and the rights and freedoms guaranteed within the ECHR.[26]

Overlap between civil or political and socio-economic issues is observable in an expanding number of cases. As Leijten points out, a "vast number of health- and health care-related decisions and judgements can be found in the ECtHR's case law"[27] – particularly in relation to Articles 2, 3 and 8 ECHR.[28] According to the Grand Chamber, member states are under a "positive obligation, by virtue of the relevant provisions of the Convention, notably Articles 2 and 8, to take appropriate measures to protect the life and health of those within their jurisdiction".[29] Article 3 ECHR additionally requires that states ensure that the health and well-being of *imprisoned persons* in particular are adequately secured, inter alia, by providing them with the requisite medical assistance.[30] Similar reasoning is employed with respect to the ICCPR, where the Human Rights Committee indicates that the right to life (Article 6 ICCPR) and the right to humane treatment (Article 10 ICCPR) could "raise issues" with respect to the protection of health in detention.[31]

In sum, safeguarding people's physical and mental health has a clear basis in the established framework of human rights – either explicitly, as a socio-economic right, or implicitly, as a positive obligation inherent in civil and political rights.

6.2.2 *Moral Bases*

Various *moral* rationales also support protecting a right to mental health, three of which we detail here. A first (Rawlsian-inspired) moral basis for a right to mental health sees the right as important for protecting persons' moral right to *fair equality of opportunity*.[32] Daniels, for instance, contends that enjoying a certain threshold of physical and mental health is essential for persons to have a "normal opportunity

not have the same legal status as judgements of the ECtHR: Leijten 2017, p. 31. See also Article 35 of the EU Charter of Fundamental Rights.

25 ECtHR 9 October 1979, 6289/73 (*Airey/Ireland*), par. 26.

26 ECtHR 9 October 1979, 6289/73 (*Airey/Ireland*), par. 26.

27 Leijten 2017, pp. 42, 251.

28 Martini 2020.

29 ECtHR (GC) 8 April 2021, 47621/13 and 5 others (*Vavřička and Others/Czech Republic*), par. 282.

30 ECtHR 20 January 2009, 28300/06 (*Sławomir Musiał/Poland*), par. 87. See also the Guide on the case-law of the European Convention on Human Rights, *Prisoners' rights*, (31 August 2024), pars. 148–161.

31 *Cabal and Pasini* v. *Australia* CCPR/C/78/D/1020/2002, 7 August 2003, par. 7.7.

32 A moral right to fair equality of opportunity has been defended by Rawls 1999b [1977], and Buchanan 1984, among others.

range".[33] He further argues that our right to health is grounded in our moral claim to healthcare provision which – by "reducing the impact of disease and disability" – "protect[s] the range of opportunities open to us".[34]

A second moral basis for the right to mental health is provided by Nussbaum, and developed further by Ruger (though these scholars do not use the language of "rights" when discussing their claims).[35] Nussbaum and Ruger argue that securing the capability of health is necessary for justice – and not just because having a certain level of health is necessary to secure equality of opportunity (as Daniels suggests) but rather because securing health capabilities is intrinsically important for justice. Nussbaum argues that a just state ought to make certain human capabilities including "bodily health" available to its citizens, where capabilities are those "capacities, liberties, and opportunities that have value in any plan of life citizens may (...) choose".[36] The protection of *mental* health is arguably also implicit in Nussbaum's account. As Fourie points out, Nussbaum's reference to bodily health plausibly "include[s] the physical *and* mental health associated with a common-sense understanding of the biological functioning of the body".[37] Nussbaum's reference to emotions and the importance of "not having one's emotional development blighted by fear and anxiety" could also be interpreted as a reference to mental health.[38] Building on Nussbaum's work, Ruger suggests that the state should additionally protect some "complex" health capabilities, such as the "capability to take part in the life of the community", the "capability to engage in various forms of social interaction" and the "capability to enjoy recreational activities"[39] – all of which are clearly relevant for, and may be conducive to health and well-being, *both* physical and mental.[40]

33 Daniels 2008, p. 61. Notably, Daniels' account applies to physical as well as mental health.

34 Daniels 2008, p. 64.

35 A variation on this approach is advanced by Powers & Faden 2006. These scholars, however, consider that States have an obligation to pursue and promote their citizens' *health*, not just their *capability* to enjoy good health. Their focus on functioning is perhaps most understandable when it comes to the case of children, for whom Powers and Faden have a particular concern. This focus may have relevance for other (vulnerable) populations too – for example, for those who, due to certain mental illnesses or disorders, may fail to enjoy the autonomy so prized within Nussbaum's capabilities approach.

36 Nussbaum 2000, p. 148.

37 Fourie 2016, p. 193 (emphasis added).

38 Nussbaum 2000.

39 Ruger 2006, p. 42 (figure 1).

40 Ruger 2006 includes mental health in her account. For instance, in the concluding section of her paper, she writes: "To promote the good life, a capability and health account values longevity and freedom from disease. It emphasizes prevention and treatment, favoring those most deprived in health and at risk of health deprivation. It also emphasizes individual agency and supports efforts to improve health to equip individuals with the *mental* and physical ability required for agency" (emphasis added).

A third moral basis for a right to health is, what might be described as, a rule-consequentialist justification.[41] The idea here is that we recognise a right to health, not because persons have any individual moral claim to health care provision but because protecting citizens' health by means of a right to health care brings about the *best consequences for society* overall. We can readily envisage the many ways in which a legal right to health would be good for society. There are the well-being benefits that may accrue to persons if they themselves enjoy good health; the well-being benefits that may accrue to us when the health of those we care about is protected; and the second-order benefits of protecting health, such as the boost it might provide to economic growth, employment, societal productivity etc.[42] One good societal consequence in protecting *mental* health specifically is plausibly that doing so reduces the incidence of violent and/or aggressive outbursts that stem from mental ill-health – and also the mental distress such outbursts often cause, for both victims and perpetrators. As Green points out, there is a "clearcut association between (…) aggressive behaviors and mental and substance abuse disorders" and this represents one "way in which mental illness detracts from the common good".[43] A right to mental health might thus be desirable for several reasons, and not only because upholding such a right promises to benefit those suffering from ill-health.

Note that depending on which (or which combination) of moral bases for a right to mental health we favour, we may arrive at different conclusions about the right to mental health's protective *scope*. If persons have a moral claim to the *capability* of health, then the right to health may encompass not just a right to health services but also a right to other goods and conditions (e.g., to certain living and working conditions) necessary to realise health. This seems in line with the CESCR's observation that the right to health is a right to the enjoyment of a variety of facilities, goods, services and conditions that *promote* health (though Nussbaum speaks of merely being able to have "good health" as opposed to the CESCR's reference to the "highest attainable standard of health").

Alternatively, if we follow Daniels and see the right to health as grounded in persons' moral claim to fair equality of opportunity, then the right will be to the health-related "care that effectively (…) protects the range of opportunities that would otherwise be open to us".[44] Daniels himself thinks that this limits the scope of the right to health to solely those treatments that "effectively promote normal functioning" and which treat medically recognised diseases or disorders,[45] though,

[41] For discussion of the rule consequentialist moral basis for individual rights, see Talbott 2010. For discussion of problems with rule-consequentialist justifications for rights, see Freeman 2012.

[42] Francis et al. 2023. See also Green 2000.

[43] Green 2000, pp. 21–22. Meanwhile, the relationship between mental illness and violent behaviour should not be exaggerated; see also Bijlsma et al. 2019 for this point.

[44] Daniels 2008, p. 367.

[45] Daniels 2008, p. 367.

in our view, it is not obvious this is the case.[46] But working with a "fair equality of opportunity" justification clearly limits the right to health in other ways – for example, it limits the right to a more basic standard of health care than the "highest attainable standard" that Article 12 CESCR suggests. A rule-consequentialist justification, if favoured, also does this. Some kinds of healthcare services likely do not, as a general rule, produce more net welfare when provided – for example, interventions that are extremely costly and benefit few. We turn to consider the scope of the right to mental health in the next section.

6.3 WHAT IS MENTAL HEALTH? CONSIDERING THE SCOPE OF A RIGHT TO MENTAL HEALTH

What precisely is covered by the concept of "mental health"? At least on a folk understanding, the "mental" of mental health is typically understood to pertain to the emotional and/or psychological realm – that is, to a person's thinking, inclinations and feelings, which are often reflected in behaviour or behavioural patterns. That said, a clear-cut distinction between mental and physical health is difficult to draw: often both are connected. Many health conditions involve mental and physical symptoms and can have both mental and physical causes. Consider how a patient with hyperthyroidism may have osteoporosis and cardiac arrythmias as well as anxiety as symptoms.[47] Consider, too, how mental or psychological factors such as stress may increase a person's susceptibility to physical illness[48] and how genetic factors may increase a person's likelihood of developing a mental disorder.[49] In fact, a considerable part of the research on mental health has been biological (brain-oriented) in nature.[50] When talking about *mental* health, in this chapter, therefore, we work on the assumption that the reference to "mental" concerns emotional and psychological matters, while acknowledging that there are overlaps, and no clear cut-off point, between mental and physical health.

What, then, is mental *health*? We consider this question below, first, from a conceptual perspective, followed by the approach in human rights law.

6.3.1 *Positive and Negative Conceptions of Mental Health*

From a conceptual perspective, two general understandings of "health" can be distinguished.[51] The first, more restricted understanding, is that health refers to the

46 Consider how a person may lack fair equality of opportunity if they lack confidence in their abilities to pursue their life plans or if they have a low level of subjective well-being, even when their confidence is not pathologically low and when they do not meet the criteria for a diagnosis, e.g., of major depression.

47 Lee & Pearce 2023.

48 Kivimäki & Steptoe 2018.

49 Assary et al. 2018.

50 See, e.g., Andreasen 2001.

51 Wren-Lewis & Alexandrova 2021.

absence of medically recognised and described illnesses or disorders.[52] In the realm of mental health, examples of such disorders are major depression, psychosis and personality disorders – which fall within the scope of psychiatry as a medical discipline. The second, broader, understanding conceives of mental health in terms of mental *well-being*. This well-being-based concept is sometimes referred to as a "positive" conceptualisation of mental health, as opposed to the "negative" understanding of absence of disease.[53]

We consider both positions in more detail below and illustrate their normative relevance when considering neurorehabilitation in view of a right to "mental health". Our discussion is organised around three hypothetical scenarios, each of which involve brain stimulation that targets the neural correlates of a convicted person's aggressive outbursts. In these scenarios, the relevance of a mental disorder moves from central to peripheral to absent. In each of them we assume that the convicted person desires to have access to the neurotechnology, is fully informed about it and voluntarily chooses to submit to it. We also assume that the technology is safe and effective.

> *Scenario 1: "A mental disorder"*. Alex has been convicted of a violent crime and has received a diagnosis of intermittent explosive disorder, which is characterised by recurrent behavioural outbursts representing a failure to control aggressive impulses (DSM-5, code 312.34). These outbursts are core features of Alex's mental disorder. They risk dangerous and harmful behaviour and hamper Alex's successful rehabilitation. The outbursts can be targeted and attenuated with brain stimulation.
>
> *Scenario 2: "Causing distress"*. Sophie has been convicted of a violent crime but her aggressive outbursts do not meet the criteria for diagnosis of intermittent explosive disorder, nor for other mental disorders of which aggressive outbursts may be a component. Meanwhile, these aggressive outbursts cause Sophie mental distress and she is considerably troubled by these outbursts and does not wish to have them. These outbursts also risk dangerous and harmful behaviour and hamper Sophie's rehabilitation. They can be targeted and attenuated with brain stimulation.
>
> *Scenario 3: "Hindering social contribution"*. Lou has been convicted of a violent crime but their aggressive outbursts again do not meet the criteria for diagnosis of a mental disorder. These outbursts do not cause Lou mental distress in and of themselves. They do, however, hinder Lou's maintenance of a job and various social relationships and this is something Lou regrets. These outbursts directly hamper Lou's rehabilitation and can be targeted and attenuated with brain stimulation.

52 Boorse 1976, holding that "An organism is healthy at any moment in proportion as it is not diseased".
53 Wren-Lewis & Alexandrova 2021.

To what extent does the use of brain stimulation in these scenarios contribute to the person's mental health? The answer to this question depends on whether we are working with a positive or negative conceptualisation of mental health, as alluded to earlier in this section.

Consider first the "negative" understanding of mental health – as the absence of medically recognised mental disorders, leading us to the question: What is a mental disorder and when is it either present or absent? Many definitions of mental illness have been proposed and criticised, and precisely what a mental disorder consists in remains an area of intense scholarly debate.[54] The DSM-5 defines a mental disorder as

> a syndrome characterized by clinically significant disturbance in an individual's cognition, emotion regulation, or behavior that reflects a dysfunction in the psychological, biological, or developmental processes underlying mental functioning. Mental disorders are usually associated with significant distress or disability in social, occupational or other important activities. An expectable or culturally approved response to a common stressor or loss, such as the death of a loved one, is not a mental disorder. Socially deviant behavior (e.g., political, religious, or sexual) and conflicts that are primarily between the individual and society are not mental disorders unless the deviance or conflict results from a dysfunction in the individual, as described above.[55]

Interestingly, this general definition, though conceptually informative, does not play a direct role in mental healthcare diagnoses. Rather, diagnoses are made by healthcare professionals assessing whether a given patient meets the criteria for a *specific* disorder, such as depression, psychosis or bipolar disorder. These diagnostic criteria are intended to promote consistency across, and standardise, mental healthcare diagnoses. There is, however, always the possibility of differences in interpretation when consulting the criteria for a given disorder. Criteria sometimes change such that the boundaries of a given mental disorder can shift from time to time.[56] There are also different diagnostic classification systems – such as the DSM and International Statistical Classification of Diseases and Related Health Problems (ICD)[57] – with disparate (though considerably overlapping) criteria for specific

54 See, e.g., Bolton 2008 and Radden 2024.

55 American Psychiatric Association 2013, p. 20. Note that, according to the DSM, we should be careful not to assume that (deviant) behaviour leading to conflicts with society implies the presence of a mental disorder. The history of psychiatry shows that conflicts between citizens and states have occasionally resulted in people being labelled as "mentally ill" and sent to psychiatric hospitals to be "treated" for ill health. In fact, there appears to be a risk of abuse of psychiatry, such as in the former Soviet Union and East Germany, where dissidents were sometimes diagnosed with mental illness and involuntarily admitted to a mental hospital (Van Voren 2016). As Reich 2005 explains, more generally, mental illness may be a convenient tool to "solve" societal problems, such as those opposing a government or ideology.

56 Bolton 2008. For example (minor) changes in the criteria for Tourette's syndrome: Batterson et al. 2014, and more generally: First et al. 2022.

57 World Health Organisation. ICD-11: International Statistical Classification of Diseases and Related Health Problems. 2024.

disorders. In saying, then, that the negative understanding equates mental health to the absence of a specific diagnosable mental disorder, this understanding acknowledges that the boundaries of mental health can, and will, change over time, as the diagnostic criteria are constantly evolving. Our assumption for present purposes is that this negative understanding implies that a person has *mental health* when they do not meet the criteria for a specific disorder detailed in the current edition of the relevant diagnostic classification systems.

What does this negative understanding of mental health imply for the three scenarios described above? It implies, firstly, that Alex's receipt of brain stimulation in the first scenario contributes to his mental health. Alex meets the criteria for diagnosis of intermittent explosive disorder; the brain stimulation targets a core symptom or feature of this disorder; and, as we stipulated, the brain stimulation in this case can be expected to be effective.

The negative understanding of mental health implies, secondly, that the described brain stimulation does not advance mental health in Scenarios 2 (involving Sophie) and 3 (involving Lou). Both Sophie and Lou do not, after all, and as per our stipulation, meet the criteria for diagnosis of a mental disorder.

Consider next the "positive" conceptualisation of mental health, and let us look to the understanding advanced by the WHO, conceiving of mental health as

> a state of well-being in which the individual realises his or her own abilities, can cope with the normal stresses of life, can work productively and fruitfully, and is able to make a contribution to his or her community.[58]

On this understanding, mental health is "more than the absence of mental illness".[59] Rather, it is understood broadly. Recall how the WHO's preamble to their Constitution describes health more generally as "a state of *complete* physical, mental and social well-being".[60] As Wren-Lewis and Alexandrova emphasise, in the eyes of the WHO, for a person to realise mental health "it is not enough to be free of depression, anxiety, or schizophrenia, or any other diagnosable psychiatric condition; one also needs to be well enough to thrive and flourish in one's community".[61] Mental health is thus intimately connected to how a person functions and flourishes within their own community; and as such, the WHO understanding of mental health has affinities with Ruger's earlier-mentioned "complex health capabilities".[62]

58 WHO, *Promoting Mental Health: Concepts, Emerging Evidence, Practice*, 2005, p. 2. See also WHO, Fact sheet "Mental health", www.who.int (visited on 20 August 2024).

59 WHO, *Promoting Mental Health: Concepts, Emerging Evidence, Practice*, 2005, p. 2.

60 Emphasis added.

61 Wren-Lewis & Alexandrova 2021, p. 691.

62 Recall that Ruger identifies "the capability to take part in the life of the community", the "capability to engage in various forms of social interaction", and the "capability to enjoy recreational activities" as crucial health capabilities. Ruger 2006, p. 42 (figure 1).

On this positive understanding of mental health, targeting aggressive outbursts with brain stimulation is plausibly conducive to mental health in all three of the above scenarios of Alex, Sophie and Lou. Taking them in reverse order, targeting Lou's aggressive outbursts via brain stimulation may make it easier for Lou to hold down a job and to cultivate and maintain meaningful social relationships. These effects would clearly also allow Lou to make a greater contribution to their community, as per the WHO understanding of mental health above.[63] In the case of Sophie, brain stimulation that reduces her aggressive outbursts will relieve Sophie's considerable mental distress. And attenuating the very thing that challenges Sophie's peace of mind would bring her closer to "a state of complete physical, mental and social well-being," as the WHO describes, thus contributing to her mental health on this understanding. As far as the brain stimulation also facilitates Sophie's functioning and flourishing in the community, it would fall under the WHO's conceptualisation of health as "a state of well-being in which the individual (. . .) can work productively and fruitfully, and is able to make a contribution to his or her community".[64]

Looking lastly to the case of Alex, his aggressive outbursts, we stipulated, are a symptom of a recognised mental disorder – specifically, intermittent explosive disorder. Treating or managing this disorder via safe and effective brain stimulation clearly brings Alex closer to that "state of *complete* physical, mental and social well-being," the WHO describes. Thus, on this positive conceptualisation of health, the brain stimulation would be conducive to Alex's mental health.

Note that the WHO's definition of mental health has been criticised for being too demanding and unhelpful for the scientific measurement of health.[65] Smith describes it as "a ludicrous definition that would leave most of us unhealthy most of the time".[66] Wren-Lewis and Alexandrova voice similar concerns regarding the WHO's definition of *mental health*: "it is incredibly demanding: it describes a life in which individuals realize their full potential, as well as work productively and contribute to their community. Not many people meet such high standards".[67]

Wren-Lewis and Alexandrova propose conceptualising mental health in an alternative way, as having the capacities "to feel, think, and act in ways that enable us to value and engage in life".[68] This conceptualisation centres on "valuing" and

63 An improved ability to cultivate and maintain meaningful social relationships is also plausibly conducive to Lou's flourishing in life and in their community in other ways – e.g., insofar as having these relationships and/or avoiding regret promotes positive mental states (mental state theories of well-being); is something Lou desires or facilitates their satisfaction of other desires (preferentist theories); or is something that has value for Lou irrespective of whether it causally contributes to other things of value (objective list theories). For this tripartite classification of theories of well-being, also utilised in previous chapters, see Parfit 1984, appendix C.

64 Again, alleviating mental distress plausibly has instrumental and/or non-instrumental value on a range of theories of well-being, from mental state theories through to objective list accounts.

65 Van der Linden & Schermer 2022.

66 Smith 2008.

67 Wren-Lewis & Alexandrova 2021, p. 691.

68 Wren-Lewis & Alexandrova 2021, pp. 691, 696.

"engaging" in life, instead of focusing on "well-being". Still, the emphasis on cognitive, emotional and behavioural functioning – and the lack of reference to mental *disorders* specifically – may mean that Wren-Lewis and Alexandrova are also understanding mental health broadly, as a form of mental well-being. Moreover, if mental health consists in having the cognitive, emotional and behavioural capacities for valuing and engaging in life, then attenuating the aggressive outbursts of the above protagonists via brain stimulation appears conducive to their mental health on Wren-Lewis and Alexandrova's understanding too. Lou's aggressive outbursts are, after all, impeding their ability to engage with others socially and to hold down a job – two things that are likely important (though by no means the only) routes by which a person can engage with, and derive value from, life. The fact that Sophie's aggressive outbursts cause her to experience mental distress suggests that these actions do not allow her to derive value from and to engage in life in the manner that she wishes. And given that Alex's diagnosis of intermittent explosive disorder implies either that Alex is experiencing marked distress or has problems with occupational or interpersonal functioning, then Alex's ability to value and engage in life is plausibly undermined too, prior to brain stimulation.

Other examples of positive definitions could be given,[69] but we hope these suffice as an illustration of what such positive conceptualisations would generally entail. All in all, it appears that the scope of a *right to mental health* can be interpreted in at least two different ways: (1) as a right to treatment for (diagnosed) mental disorders, and (2) as a right to the protection and promotion of mental well-being or human flourishing, with an emphasis on social functioning.

6.3.2 *Mental Health in Human Rights Law*

Which understanding of mental health can be found in human rights law? Seemingly, a positive understanding, but not necessarily as broad an understanding as that which is advanced by the WHO.

At the international level, and referring to "the right to mental health and well-being",[70] the Special Rapporteur on the right to the highest attainable standard of physical and mental health indicates that Article 12 ICESCR protects "mental well-being"[71] – something that is clearly broader than the mere absence of medically recognised mental disorders. The Rapporteur also acknowledges – as we did above – that "[t]erminology in the sphere of mental health is a contested terrain", and that there is a need to accept "different terms according to how people define their own

69 See, for example, Galderisi et al. 2015.

70 UN Special Rapporteur on the right of everyone to the enjoyment of the highest attainable standard of physical and mental health, 12 April 2019, A/HRC/41/34, par. 1; UN Special Rapporteur on the right of everyone to the enjoyment of the highest attainable standard of physical and mental health, 28 March 2017, A/HRC/35/21, par. 1.

71 UN Special Rapporteur on the right of everyone to the enjoyment of the highest attainable standard of physical and mental health, 12 April 2019, A/HRC/41/34.

experiences of mental health".[72] This might be interpreted as indicating that the Rapporteur considers mental health to be broader than the diagnostic categories of psychiatric medicine, including, perhaps, persons' own experience of and perspectives on their mental health – though the Rapporteur's statement here is open to other interpretations. The Special Rapporteur's annual report of 2015, meanwhile, explicitly connects mental health with mental (or more precisely, emotional and social) well-being:

> The modern understanding of mental health includes good emotional and social well-being, healthy non-violent relations between individuals and groups, with mutual trust of, tolerance of and respect for the dignity of every person.[73]

We thus have good reason to believe that a positive understanding of mental health operates at the international level. It is also noteworthy that "non-violent relations" are mentioned here, suggesting relevance for the rehabilitation of those who have committed violent offences. Still, we cannot yet conclude that international human rights law works with *as broad* an understanding as that found within the WHO's definition of mental health – that is, to include "complete" mental well-being – notwithstanding that Article 12 ICESCR speaks of "the highest attainable standard of health". The highest attainable standard of health, after all, may still not consist in *complete* mental well-being.

As discussed, the ECHR does not guarantee a right to (mental) health as such. Rather, positive obligations to protect and foster people's mental health are implicit in the civil and political rights guaranteed by the Convention, such as the right to life and the right to bodily and mental integrity. In the criminal justice context, alleged violations of human rights relating to mental health often consist in convicted persons claiming to have received insufficient psychological or psychiatric treatment for a diagnosed mental disorder, like in prison.[74] For example, in a number of cases concerning the prohibition of ill-treatment, the ECtHR held that regarding "the treatment of prisoners with mental-health problems (...) Article 3 of the Convention requires States to ensure that the health and well-being of prisoners are adequately secured by, among other things, providing them with the requisite medical assistance".[75] There is thus reason to assume that the protection of mental health under the ECHR includes, or at least closely relates to, the protection of well-being.

72 UN Special Rapporteur on the right of everyone to the enjoyment of the highest attainable standard of physical and mental health, 12 April 2019, A/HRC/41/34, par. 10.

73 UN Special Rapporteur on the right of everyone to the enjoyment of the highest attainable standard of physical and mental health, 2 April 2015, A/HRC/29/33, par. 77.

74 See, for example, ECtHR (GC) 26 April 2016, 10511/10 (*Murray/The Netherlands*); ECtHR (GC) 31 January 2019, 18052/11 (*Rooman/Belgium*).

75 ECtHR (GC) 26 April 2016, 10511/10 (*Murray/The Netherlands*), par. 105. See also ECtHR 26 October 2000, 30210/96 (*Kudla/Poland*), par. 94; ECtHR 14 November 2002, 67263/01 (*Mouisel/France*), par. 40; ECtHR 26 October 2006, 59696/00 (*Khudobin/Russia*), par. 93.

Case law pertaining to the right to liberty pursuant to Article 5 ECHR seems to go a step further, by subsuming a person's "dangerousness" under the umbrella of mental health:

> Any detention of mentally ill persons must have a therapeutic purpose, aimed specifically, and in so far as possible, at curing or alleviating their mental-health condition, *including,* where appropriate, *bringing about a reduction in or control over their dangerousness.*[76]

This quote clearly suggests that, according to the ECtHR, reducing a person's dangerousness can be seen as (an element of) improving their mental health.

In a recent case, the ECtHR likewise considered that for the detention of a "person of unsound mind" to be lawful, it must take account of whether an "individualised treatment plan was put in place".[77] This should include attending to specific needs of the person's mental health, and should be "aimed specifically, in so far as possible, at curing or alleviating his condition, including, where appropriate, bringing about a *reduction in or control over the level of danger posed*, with a view to preparing him for possible future *reintegration into society*."[78]

These considerations seem to support a broader understanding of mental health than the absence of diagnosed mental disorders, which could include treatment for reducing a person's dangerousness too. This reduction is directly linked to the goal of reintegration into society. Still, from the available ECtHR case law, it is not obvious that the right to mental health is a right to those freedoms and entitlements that enable the state of "complete" well-being described by the WHO. There is, nonetheless, reason to believe that human rights law – both international and European – supports a positive obligation to safeguard mental well-being to at least some extent; and that European human rights law also includes a positive obligation, for reasons of mental health, to bring about a reduction in persons' dangerousness.[79] This suggests that all three scenarios above (concerning Alex, Sophie and Lou) might invoke concerns about mental health from a human rights perspective, given that the protagonists' well-being and dangerousness are at issue in each.

[76] ECtHR (GC) 31 January 2019, 18052/11 (*Rooman/Belgium*), par. 208 (emphasis added).

[77] ECtHR 9 January 2024, 30138/21 (*Miranda Magro/Portugal*), par. 92.

[78] ECtHR 9 January 2024, 30138/21 (*Miranda Magro/Portugal*), par. 92 (emphasis added).

[79] It is possible that the UN Special Rapporteur's explicit connecting of mental health to "healthy non-violent relations between individuals and groups, with mutual trust of, tolerance of and respect for the dignity of every person" in their 2015 annual report on the right to health has some affinities with the ECtHR's comments regarding mental health and dangerousness; see UN Special Rapporteur on the right of everyone to the enjoyment of the highest attainable standard of physical and mental health, 2 April 2015, A/HRC/29/33, par. 77.

6.4 A STATE DUTY TO PROVIDE NEUROREHABILITATION?

In the remainder of this chapter, we assume a positive conceptualisation of mental health akin to that found in human rights law, including the protection of well-being and the reduction of dangerousness. Let us also assume that at least some neurointerventions will contribute to a convicted person's mental health on this positive conceptualisation. Given these assumptions, when might the right to mental health successfully be invoked by a convicted person to support their being provided with safe and effective neurorehabilitation?

There are perhaps two kinds of situations where the right to mental health could successfully be invoked, at least in theory. The first is when access to affordable, accepted and generally available neurointerventions is *necessary* for preserving and/or restoring a reasonable standard of mental health. The second is when access to affordable, accepted and generally available neurointerventions makes preserving a reasonable standard of mental health substantially *easier* than an approach that eschews neurorehabilitation.

Four things to note about our reference to "affordable", "accepted", "generally available" and "reasonable standard". First, for there to be any chance of someone successfully invoking the right to mental health to make a claim to receive neurorehabilitation, it must be the case that neurorehabilitation is not too costly. Recall our earlier highlighting of how the right to health of Article 12 ICESCR, including mental health, is subject to a progressive realisation standard such that the precise healthcare provision required of states depends at least in part on their available resources. Consider, too, that all "positive" rights – that is, rights that require state provision of goods, services etc. – will necessarily be limited by resource considerations, at least to some extent. Regarding the ECHR, Leijten observes that the ECtHR leaves room for making choices, in view of the available recourses, regarding which and to whom care is provided, as long as an adequate standard of care is generally met. When an omission in providing certain health care is not in conflict with domestic procedural rules or requirements, "a complaint about expensive or unauthorized medication seems unlikely to be successful."[80] Neurorehabilitation will thus have to be reasonably affordable if an argument for its provision from the right to mental health is to get off the ground. Whether or not it will be is an empirical matter, and the answer is yet unclear. On the one hand, neurotechnological interventions are currently expensive.[81] However, they may in the future turn out to be more cost-effective than some alternatives – perhaps when compared to the cost of delivering long-term (unsuccessful) psychotherapies within a prison or other detention setting.[82]

80 Leijten 2017, p. 255.
81 See, for example, Bishay et al. 2024.
82 A relatively recent study concluded that DBS for the management of obsessive-compulsive disorder (OCD) was cost-effective when compared to conventional OCD management over the long-term; see

Secondly, the reference to "accepted" denotes "scientifically accepted" or "scientifically proven" interventions. It seems clear that the ECtHR and the CESCR have little appetite for an interpretation of the right to health that includes a right to access "experimental" treatments. The ECtHR ruled in the case of *Hristozov and Others/Bulgaria* that there was no violation of Articles 2, 3 and 8 ECHR in refusing to allow the applicants access to an unauthorised experimental cancer treatment – even though conventional treatments for cancer had been exhausted.[83] Elsewhere, the ECtHR rejected an applicant's claim to access an unproven, experimental therapy for degenerative cerebral illness, declaring the application inadmissible under Articles 8 and 14, at least in part because "the therapeutic value of the [therapy in question] had, to date, not yet been proven scientifically".[84] Similar patterns can be observed at the international level, where Article 12 ICESCR implies that health facilities, goods and services must be "scientifically and medically appropriate and of good quality".[85]

The third thing to note is our reference to "generally available" interventions. It seems that success in invoking the right to mental health to support access to neurorehabilitation can only occur when the relevant neurointerventions are *also* available to the wider populace and when their provision does not conflict with a given jurisdiction's domestic law. Jurisprudence related to the right to health seems to illustrate this. Consider how the ECtHR found a breach of Article 3 ECHR when a given applicant was not provided with reproductive diagnostic services – and hence deprived of the opportunity to make a decision to have a legal abortion (should the results have satisfied the conditions for permissible abortion) – when the "services which she had requested were at all times available and that she was entitled as a matter if domestic law to avail herself of them".[86] Consider, alternatively, how the ECtHR denied a breach of Article 3 ECHR in a different case: when the requested treatment – in this case medicinal cannabis – was not legally permitted in the relevant jurisdiction.[87]

Ooms et al. 2017. Similar conclusions were reached in an assessment of the cost-effectiveness of DBS for Parkinson's disease; see Smilowska et al. 2021.

83 ECtHR 13 November 2012, 47039/11 and 358/12 (*Hristozov and Others/Bulgaria*).

84 ECtHR 6 May 2014, 62804/13 (*Durisotto/Italy*) (text from English press release ECHR 153, 28 May 2014).

85 CESCR General Comment No. 14, par. 12(d). See also Donders 2011.

86 ECtHR 26 May 2011, 27617/04 (*R.R./Poland*), par. 160. Note, that in the partly dissenting opinion of Judge De Gaetano, it was pointed out that "the doctors concerned were perfectly entitled, on grounds of conscientious objection, to refuse to terminate the life of the unborn child by performing an abortion or, indeed, even to refuse to refer the applicant for an abortion". There was a shared consensus, though, that doctors "were not entitled (…) to keep [the applicant] in the dark and increase her stress and anxiety", and the Court observed that Article 8 ECHR obliges states "to organise the health services system in such a way as to ensure that an effective exercise of the freedom of conscience of health professionals in the professional context does not prevent patients from obtaining access to services to which they are entitled under the applicable legislation" (par. 206).

87 ECtHR 22 September 2022, 24547/18 (*Thorn/Sweden*).

The relevance of existing domestic practices for successful invocation of the right to health is also evident in the EU Charter of Fundamental Rights' (CFR) reference to "the right to benefit from medical treatment under the conditions established by national laws and practices" (Article 35 CFR). It is further evident in the ECtHR's observation about incarcerated persons specifically: that they are entitled to health treatment, "at a level *comparable* to that which the State authorities have committed themselves to provide to the population as a whole".[88] Moving to the international context, the CESCR's reference to the necessity of "health facilities, goods and services [being] accessible to everyone without discrimination, within the jurisdiction of the State party", in its discussion of Article 12 ICESCR, suggests a similar line of reasoning.[89] Indeed, the CESCR specifically references "vulnerable or marginalised sections of the population",[90] which plausibly includes those who are incarcerated.[91] The CESCR indicates that vulnerable or marginalised groups should not be deprived of access to health services that are enjoyed by other sections of the population, emphasising that access is "especially" important in situations of vulnerability.[92] For access to neurorehabilitation to come under the remit of the right to mental health, then, it seems that the relevant technology – such as tDCS, TMS or DBS – must be legally available and more generally accessible, within a given jurisdiction. At present, TMS and DBS are FDA-approved and available in health care for the treatment of different mental disorders.[93]

Note, fourthly, that our reference to "reasonable standard" is included so as to take the "progressive realisation" caveat on the right to health into account. Invoking the right to mental health to support a claim to neurorehabilitation is unlikely to be successful unless the affected applicant's mental health is judged to be lower than a minimally adequate standard, notwithstanding that Article 12 ICESCR stresses health optimisation. In practice, if the applicant's mental health *is* deemed minimally adequate (even if still not excellent), the fact that the right is subject to progressive realisation may preclude the possibility of a rights claim successfully being invoked.

88 ECtHR (GC) 31 January 2019, 18052/11 (*Rooman/Belgium*), par. 147 (emphasis added).

89 CESCR General Comment No. 14, par. 12.

90 CESCR General Comment No. 14, par. 12.

91 Cf. ECtHR (GC) 27 June 2000, 21986/93 (*Salman/Turkey*), par. 99.

92 CESCR General Comment No. 25, par. 70.

93 Here, we assume that what is relevant is whether the relevant *technologies* (such as tDCS, DBS or TMS) are available outside of the criminal justice context. However, one might argue that the main question is whether these technologies are available for *the same purpose*. If that is the question, the outcome may be different. The reason is that neurointerventions for rehabilitative purposes are likely to be somewhat specific to the forensic context as they will be used to reduce aggression and violence. Such an effect is particularly relevant to people convicted of violent crimes receiving forensic treatment – less so to people receiving treatment outside of the criminal justice context. So, even though the same *kind* of technology may be available in society (e.g. TMS or tDCS), the *purpose for which it is applied* is likely to differ from how it is used in the wider population.

Returning now to the two kinds of situations where (we think) the right to mental health might support a claim to neurorehabilitation, the first is where affordable, accepted and available neurorehabilitation is *necessary* for realising a reasonable standard of mental health. Clearly, human rights treaties do not provide for a right to *all* and *every* treatment option in cases of poor mental health. Within the context of Article 5(1) ECHR, the ECtHR "affords the authorities a certain latitude with regard both to the form and the content of the therapeutic care or of the medical programme" to be adopted, and hence does not guarantee access to any particular treatment.[94] But when neurorehabilitation is the *only* remaining option for realising mental health – let's say alternative measures have been exhausted and either mental disorder, poor emotional or social well-being, or a risk of dangerousness remains – then a case for access to neurorehabilitation could reasonably be mounted. Denying a person the only remaining treatment that might alleviate their mental distress intuitively seems to be cruel and inhumane. The ECtHR has elsewhere judged that the denial of specific and necessary health care violates Article 3 ECHR on some occasions – for example, denying an incarcerated person dentures when they lack teeth,[95] denying pain-relief for chronic back pain[96] or denying a detainee glasses when their eyesight is defective.[97] Furthermore, in *Murray/the Netherlands*, the Court found a violation of Article 3 ECHR because the absence of psychiatric treatment hampered the person's real opportunity to rehabilitate and, one day, to regain his freedom.[98]

The CESCR likewise emphasises the importance of providing people with "essential" treatment,[99] which surely includes essential treatment for managing mental health, and which may in the future at least sometimes include neurorehabilitation. This observation provides legislators with a moral reason for interpreting the relevant human rights provisions as extending to neurorehabilitation in at least some instances.

What, then, about our second situation? The situation where incorporating neurorehabilitation will make preserving mental health substantially easier for a given person. Here we suggest it may also sometimes be possible to successfully appeal to the right to mental health. Making it such that those who are incarcerated must struggle with their mental health issues – as against having access to more efficacious therapeutic assistance – also appears inhumane, and thus may raise an issue under Article 3 ECHR. Recently, the ECtHR judged that a detainee was treated inhumanely, in violation of Article 3 ECHR, when he was denied

94 ECtHR (GC) 31 January 2019, 18052/11 (*Rooman/Belgium*), par. 209.
95 ECtHR 16 February 2010, 7078/02 (*V.D./Romania*).
96 ECtHR 25 January 2011, 2627/09 (*Kupczak/Poland*).
97 ECtHR 20 April 2010, 60333/00 (*Slyusarev/Russia*).
98 ECtHR (GC) 26 April 2016, 10511/10 (*Murray/the Netherlands*). See Chapter 7.
99 CESCR General Comment No. 25, para 62, 69 and 79; CESCR General Comment No. 14, pars. 22, 39.

opioid-substitution therapy to manage his long-term drug addiction[100] – a therapy often considered to make recovery from addiction more effective and easier.[101] Similar reasoning could be invoked with respect to relevant neurotechnologies in the future, as and when their use helps to make it easier to realise a reasonable standard of mental health.

Also pertinent to this second situation is the right to participate in and enjoy the benefits of scientific progress and its applications, pursuant to Article 15(1) ICESCR.[102] The General Comment to this right emphasises a link with the right to health. Among other things, state parties "have a duty to make available and accessible to all persons, without discrimination, especially to the most vulnerable, all the best available applications of scientific progress necessary to enjoy the highest attainable standard of health".[103] It thus appears that, even when neurorehabilitation is not *strictly necessary* for ameliorating poor mental health, there may be reason to claim that denying persons (more effective) neurorehabilitation means denying them access to these "best available applications".

As a final comment on this second situation, affording persons access to neurorehabilitation that might ease their realisation of mental health, seems especially likely to lend itself to rights claims when persons' *liberty is restricted*. Existing jurisprudence and associated literature pay particular attention to the mental health needs of those who have been detained. As Riedel observes, since the year 2000, the CESCR regularly addresses problems of prison conditions, including access to external specialist treatments, special healthcare provision for persons with disabilities and mental health issues among incarcerated persons.[104] In 2018, the Special Rapporteur on the right to the highest attainable standard of health devoted the entire annual report to the right to health vis-à-vis the deprivation of liberty. There, it was noted that "actual and de facto deprivation of liberty" itself has negative effects on mental health,[105] and consequently, that extra care needs to be taken to ensure adequate access to mental health services, goods and facilities in closed settings.[106]

In the European context, the ECtHR, too, devotes particular attention to the mental health situation of incarcerated persons, who "are in a vulnerable position and the authorities are under a duty to protect".[107] The ECtHR recognises that "detainees with mental disorders are more vulnerable than ordinary detainees, and that certain requirements of prison life pose a greater risk that their health will suffer,

100 ECtHR 1 September 2016, 62303/13 (*Wenner/Germany*). The Court does not state that it was the *only* therapy but that it was the *most effective* (see in particular pars. 69 and 31).
101 Farrell et al. 1994; Gordon et al. 2008; Mattick et al. 2009; Kinlock et al. 2017.
102 Romano & Boggio 2024, p. 615 et seq.
103 CESCR General Comment No. 25, par. 70. See also Donders 2011.
104 Riedel 2020, p. 116.
105 UN Special Rapporteur on the right of everyone to the enjoyment of the highest attainable standard of physical and mental health, 10 April 2018, A/HRC/38/36 (2018), par. 46.
106 UN Special Rapporteur on the right of everyone to the enjoyment of the highest attainable standard of physical and mental health, 10 April 2018, A/HRC/38/36 (2018), pars. 46, 34.
107 ECtHR (GC) 27 June 2000, 21986/93 (*Salman/Turkey*), par. 99.

exacerbating the risk that they suffer from a feeling of inferiority, and are necessarily a source of stress and anxiety".[108] This calls for increased vigilance in assessing whether the detention of mentally ill persons complies with Article 3 ECHR. In that regard, the Grand Chamber finds it insufficient for such detainees to be merely *examined* and *diagnosed*. Rather, "it is essential that proper *treatment* for the problem diagnosed and suitable medical supervision should also be provided".[109]

The fact that the particularly exigent challenges to mental health within closed settings is recognised may thus make the case for affording incarcerated persons access to neurorehabilitation easier to make.[110] And perhaps, for some populations of incarcerated persons – that is, those sentenced to preventive detention – the case may be even stronger. Consider how, at the European level, when reviewing the lawfulness of detention under Article 5(1) ECHR, the ECtHR attaches "increasing weight to the need to provide appropriate treatment to persons who have been deprived of their liberty for the purpose of relieving their illness or reducing their dangerousness".[111] The ECtHR has noted that an individualised and specialised programme should be adopted, taking account of the specific details of the incarcerated persons' mental health with a view to preparing them for possible future reintegration into society.[112] Preventive detention may become unlawful according to Article 5(1) sub e ECHR, when a person

> is detained due to the risk that he or she may reoffend, but at the same time is deprived of the measures – such as appropriate therapy – that are necessary in order to demonstrate that he or she is no longer dangerous.[113]

Article 5 ECHR thus could provide an additional route by which mental health-improving neurorehabilitation could be demanded by some subpopulations of incarcerated persons, alongside Article 3 ECHR.

Having said all this, the prospects for an applicant to successfully invoke the right to mental health (or associated health-related rights) to support a claim to neurorehabilitation are slim for the near future. One big obstacle is that many jurisdictions have not accepted the individual complaints procedure of the Optional Protocol to the ICESCR and do not have a legally established right to health within their domestic law. International treaties on their own have weak enforcement mechanisms. The health provisions of domestic law are also judged to be important and are afforded deference within these very treaties. Recall the EU Charter of Fundamental Rights' qualification that the right to benefit from medical treatment is a right "under the conditions established by national laws and practices" (Article

108 ECtHR (GC) 31 January 2019, 18052/11 (*Rooman/Belgium*), par. 145.

109 ECtHR (GC) 26 April 2016, 10511/10 (*Murray/the Netherlands*), par. 106 (emphasis added).

110 At least when neurorehabilitation promises to ameliorate mental health/well-being more effectively than alternative options on their own.

111 ECtHR (GC) 31 January 2019, 18052/11 (*Rooman/Belgium*), pars. 194, 209.

112 ECtHR (GC) 31 January 2019, 18052/11 (*Rooman/Belgium*), pars. 194, 209, 203, 194.

113 ECtHR (GC) 31 January 2019, 18052/11 (*Rooman/Belgium*), pars. 194, 209, 210.

35 CFR). Recall too how the ECtHR has sometimes judged that refusal of a specific treatment does not violate the right to health when the treatment in question is banned in the relevant jurisdiction.[114]

And even if the prospects for successful invocation are somewhat stronger in the case of incarcerated persons who experience poor mental health, success will still be difficult. Notwithstanding their emphasis on non-discrimination with respect to health treatment, the ECtHR has also emphasised that this "comparable" treatment does "not mean that every detainee must be guaranteed the same level of medical treatment that is available in the best health establishments outside prison facilities".[115] The ECtHR acknowledges and accepts that the resources of medical facilities within the penitentiary system are, in principle, limited compared to those of civil clinics.[116] Furthermore, the ECtHR stresses that "Article 3 cannot be interpreted as requiring a prisoner's every wish and preference regarding medical treatment to be accommodated (...) the practical demands of legitimate detention may impose restrictions a prisoner will have to accept."[117] Against this background, it seems difficult even for incarcerated persons to successfully invoke Article 3 ECHR to demand the provision of a specific neurotechnology that should contribute to their mental health. This, of course, may change in the further future, as and when neurorehabilitation becomes more affordable and more generally available.

The right to mental health may also contribute to the shaping of *general policies* within which context other rights, such as the right to self-determination and rehabilitation (*supra* Chapter 5 resp. *infra* Chapter 7), might provide a more forceful argument in favour of making certain neurointerventions available to some populations of convicted persons.[118]

6.5 CONCLUDING REMARKS

The right to mental health has a solid basis in human rights law and can be supported by different moral justifications. Meanwhile, the right's scope depends, at least in part, on how we understand "mental health" in this context. Both the

114 ECtHR 22 September 2022, 24547/18 (*Thorn/Sweden*); ECtHR 26 November 2019, 58502/11 (*Abdyusheva and Others/Russia*).

115 ECtHR (GC) 31 January 2019, 18052/11 (*Rooman/Belgium*), par. 147.

116 ECtHR 15 November 2007, 30983/02 (*Grishin/Russia*), par. 76.

117 ECtHR 29 September 2005, 24919/03 (*Mathew/the Netherlands*), par. 186.

118 As a caveat, note that, in the UN Special Rapporteur's 2017 annual report on the right to health, Special Rapporteur Dainius Pūras warns against overemphasising a biomedical model of mental health that regards neurobiological aspects and processes as explaining mental conditions, and which considers these processes as legitimate *primary* target of interventions. Instead, according to Pūras, "[f]or any mental health system to be compliant with the right to health, the biomedical and psychosocial models and interventions must be appropriately balanced, avoiding the arbitrary assumption that biomedical interventions are more effective" (UN Special Rapporteur on the right of everyone to the enjoyment of the highest attainable standard of physical and mental health, 28 March 2017, A/HRC/35/21, par. 20).

ICESCR and the ECHR appear to have a broader understanding of mental health than the mere absence of a recognised mental disorder. How much broader remains unclear. Still, it is plausible that, under Article 12 ICESCR, mental health includes "good emotional and social well-being". In addition, the case law of the ECtHR indicates a link between mental health, well-being and medical treatment for reducing a person's dangerousness. Neurotechnology has the potential to contribute to mental health so defined. And the possibilities and potential of neurotechnology vis-à-vis mental health may be particularly important in the case of incarcerated persons, given that the prevailing human rights perspective is that the mental health of those who are incarcerated should receive special attention.

Given this solid basis for a right to mental health, it seems that the right could *theoretically* be invoked to support the provision by the state of neurorehabilitation in certain circumstances. We distinguished between two kinds of situations. The first is when access to safe, affordable, accepted and generally available neurointerventions are *necessary* for preserving and/or restoring a reasonable standard of mental health – that is, when alternative measures on their own are, or would be, insufficient. The second is when access to safe, affordable, accepted and generally available neurointerventions would make preserving a reasonable standard of mental health substantially *easier* than an approach that eschews neurorehabilitation.

Nevertheless, successful appeal to the right to mental health (together with the right to science) in order to be provided with a specific neurointervention seems *practically* unlikely in the near future for various reasons – in particular because of the leeway typically allowed for by socio-economic rights. Meanwhile, the right to mental health (and associated health-related rights) could contribute to establishing general policies that would support making certain neurointerventions available at a population level as well as to some subpopulations of convicted persons.

7

The Right to Rehabilitation

On Penal Degradation and Social Contribution

7.1 INTRODUCTION

States are increasingly thought to have a duty to enable convicted persons' rehabilitation, with some seeing this duty as grounded in convicted persons' *right* to rehabilitation. This rights-based argument for rehabilitation emerged alongside the increase in rights litigation for carceral populations within the United States in the 1970s,[1] and the contemporaneous development of the idea of imprisoned persons as "*Rechtsburgers*" or rights bearers in Europe.[2]

Admittedly, legal recognition of a right to rehabilitation is not universal. Many countries present rehabilitation as a "guiding concept" rather than a right that can be enforced against the state.[3] The United States had also considered it necessary to re-emphasise the importance its criminal justice system attaches to the goals of retribution, deterrence and incapacitation, following their ratification of the International Covenant on Civil and Political Rights (ICCPR) – which highlights the need for rehabilitative treatment within prison settings in Article 10 ICCPR.[4]

Still, even if rehabilitation's status as a legal right is not universally accepted, there is a trend within penal policy and prison law (particularly within Europe) towards a human-rights-based argument for rehabilitation.[5] This behoves us to ask what, if anything, this argument might imply for the use of neurotechnologies in criminal justice – specifically for those technologies that promise to reduce offending persons' risk of recidivism and otherwise facilitate their rehabilitation and reintegration into society.

In this chapter, we take up this question. We examine the existing law and jurisprudence surrounding rehabilitation (section 7.2), present the rationales that have been (or may be) advanced in support of a right to rehabilitation (section 7.3)

1 Rotman 2024, pp. 22–25.

2 Snacken & Van Zyl Smit 2008, pp. 573–584; Van Zyl Smit 2018, p. 11.

3 Ploch 2012, p. 911.

4 U.S. Reservations, Declarations, and Understandings on ICCPR, 138 Cong. Rec. S4781-01 (2 April 1992).

5 Van Zyl Smit 2018, p. 9. See also Meijer 2017; Coppola & Martufi 2024.

and analyse what these judgements and arguments imply for the case of *neuro*rehabilitation (section 7.4). Throughout, we understand the right to rehabilitation as the right to have access to rehabilitative *interventions* that can be expected to facilitate desistance from crime and rehabilitation more generally.[6] We recognise that "rehabilitation" also refers to the psychological process that renders a person no longer disposed to engage in crime. But when speaking of a *right* to rehabilitation, we are not alluding to a right to *become rehabilitated* but rather to a right to (various forms of) means aimed at *enabling* convicted persons to become rehabilitated. This aligns with the European position on state duties with respect to rehabilitation. The ECtHR makes it clear that the obligation to offer rehabilitation is "an obligation of means, not one of result", and that actual rehabilitation is the personal responsibility of convicted persons themselves.[7]

We also understand the right to rehabilitation as a (waivable) claim-right, as opposed to merely a permission or freedom to make use of rehabilitative interventions. We are examining whether and when rehabilitation is something that convicted persons may *claim*, and hence whether and when states have a duty to make rehabilitation – and neurorehabilitation – available to convicted persons.

Rehabilitative interventions, on our understanding (and as indicated in Chapter 1), are also those interventions that better enable persons to desist from future offending, to (re)integrate into the community and to lead fulfilling lives, but which do not produce these effects by making crime physically impossible or by merely disincentivising the potential perpetrator from committing crime.[8] Such an understanding allows that a broad range of interventions fall under the umbrella of rehabilitation – for example, psychotherapeutic, educational, vocational, social and restorative justice interventions that promise to promote the aforementioned outcomes.[9] But it distinguishes rehabilitative interventions from interventions that merely incapacitate or deter. This leaves room for the possibility that some neurotechnologies will not count as rehabilitative interventions.[10] Our analysis of the right

6 Determining whether a given intervention can be expected to facilitate a person's rehabilitation, of course, necessitates some other sorts of interventions as a prerequisite – for example, interventions to assess the particular risks a person poses to the community so that the rehabilitative interventions made available to them can be tailored accordingly. If those who offend have a right to rehabilitation, then exercising this right may also require submission to these kinds of assessment.

7 ECtHR (GC) 26 April 2016, 10511/10 (*Murray/the Netherlands*), par. 104. See also ECtHR (GC) 8 July 2014, 15018/11 and 61199/12 (*Harakchiev and Tolumov/Bulgaria*), par. 264.

8 See Forsberg & Douglas 2022, p. 105, for a similarly broad understanding of rehabilitation.

9 It would, for example, also encompass interventions such as therapeutic gardening; see Timler, Brown & Varcoe 2019; Lee et al. 2021.

10 For example, non-invasive brain stimulation that promises to mitigate a person's tendency to lash out aggressively when provoked might count as a rehabilitative intervention on this understanding. In contrast, brain stimulation that merely causes a person to become nauseous or physically weak whenever they become aggressive instead counts as an incapacitating or deterring intervention, depending on the extent of these effects.

to rehabilitation in this chapter only pertains to those interventions and neurotechnologies that can be classed as rehabilitative.

As in other chapters, our concern is whether the right at hand exists in law or ought to be embraced by the law and, if so, what this might mean for neurorehabilitation in criminal justice. We are thus examining whether there ought to be a *legal* right to rehabilitation, but we appeal to both legal and moral rationales for such a right.[11] We consider both how a right to rehabilitation might be derived from existing legal rights and also how it might be supported by moral rights as yet unrecognised in the law.

7.2 OBLIGATION TO ENABLE REHABILITATION IN HUMAN RIGHTS LAW

Several international and European human rights instruments generate a mandatory requirement on the part of states to provide what has been described as "real opportunity" for rehabilitation.[12] These instruments do not couch this requirement in the language of rights; nor do all relevant instruments converge on the view that this requirement necessarily implies a right to rehabilitative *interventions*. The ICCPR gestures towards a requirement to deliver rehabilitation within prison settings when stating that "the penitentiary system shall comprise *treatment* of prisoners, the essential aim of which shall be their reformation and social rehabilitation" (Article 10(3)).[13] The Human Rights Committee (CCPR) uses similar mandatory language when stating that "penitentiary system[s] (…) should essentially seek the reformation and social rehabilitation of the prisoner".[14] This includes "teaching, (re)education, vocational guidance, work programmes".[15]

Within Europe, some hesitancy to endorse a right to rehabilitative *interventions* is observable.[16] The European Convention on Human Rights (ECHR)

[11] For this distinction between legal and moral rights, see Douglas & Forsberg 2021, pp. 179–201.

[12] ECtHR (GC) 8 July 2014, 15018/11 and 61199/12 *(Harakchiev and Tolumov/Bulgaria)*, par. 264. Here, rehabilitation denotes the (psychological) process of rehabilitation.

[13] Emphasis added.

[14] CCPR General Comment No. 21, par. 10. The United Nations Standard Minimum Rules for the Treatment of Prisoners likewise suggests an imperative to promote imprisoned persons rehabilitation, including through treatment; see, for example, Rules 25, 88, 90, 102 and 107.

[15] CCPR General Comment No. 21, par. 11; Taylor 2020, p. 314. Note that the American Convention on Human Rights (ACHR) does not mention rehabilitative treatment or interventions specifically when referring to state responses to those who offend. Article 5(6) ACHR instead emphasises that "reform and social readaptation of prisoners" is an "essential aim" of liberty-depriving punishments, without specifying whether said aim ought to be fulfilled by affording detained persons access to rehabilitative interventions or treatment.

[16] This hesitancy is evident at the ECtHR though it is not found within the Constitutions and jurisprudence of some European nations. The German Federal Constitutional Court, for instance, insists that a right to rehabilitation or "resocialisation" is an "integral part of the rights guaranteed" by Articles 1 and 2(1) of the country's Constitution or Basic Law, and further maintains that this right is "constitutionally required in any society that has human dignity as its centrepiece"; see German Federal Constitutional Court, 5 June 1973, 35 BVerfGE 202. In Italy, the Constitutional Court of 1974 has

does not explicitly mention rehabilitation, nor guarantee a broad obligation to provide rehabilitative interventions to those who have offended. An imperative to *enable* the (psychological) process of rehabilitation is, however, articulated in a number of (non-binding) legal instruments to which the European Court of Human Rights (ECtHR) attaches importance.[17] For example, Rule 6 of the European Prison Rules stipulates that "all detention shall be managed so as to facilitate the reintegration into free society of persons deprived of their liberty". Rule 33.3 of this same document further states that "all prisoners shall have the benefit of arrangements designed to assist them in returning to free society after release". Rule 102.1 relatedly states that prison regimes "shall be designed to enable [prisoners] to lead a responsible and crime-free life".[18]

The ECtHR also identifies an imperative to *enable* the psychological process of rehabilitation, with reference to Article 3 ECHR. Four key cases are *Vinter and Others/the United Kingdom*,[19] *Harakchiev and Tolumov/Bulgaria*,[20] *Khoroshenko/Russia*,[21] and *Murray/the Netherlands*,[22] each of which focus either primarily or exclusively on the situation of *life-sentenced* persons. In *Vinter*, the Grand Chamber concluded that

> there is (...) now clear support in European and international law for the principle that all prisoners, including those serving life sentences, be offered the possibility of rehabilitation and the prospect of release if that rehabilitation is achieved.[23]

The Grand Chamber in *Harackchiev and Tolumov/Bulgaria*, referencing *Vinter*, reinforced this conclusion, stating:

> Article 3 (...) require[s] the authorities to give life prisoners a chance, however remote, to someday regain their freedom. For that chance to be genuine and tangible, the authorities must also give life prisoners a real opportunity to rehabilitate themselves.[24]

likewise ruled that, on the basis of the Italian Constitution, all incarcerated persons have a right to benefit from rehabilitative opportunities; see Italian Constitutional Court, 27 June 1974, 201/1974.

17 Meijer 2017, p. 147.

18 The 1955 United Nations Standard Minimum Rule for the Treatment of Prisoners – the document from which the European Prison Rules is adapted – is somewhat more specific in stipulating, across rules 59 and 58, that "the institutions should utilise all the remedial, educational, moral, spiritual and other forces and other forms of assistance which are appropriate and available" to enable imprisoned persons "to lead a law-abiding and self-supporting life".

19 ECtHR (GC) 9 July 2013, 66069/09, 130/10 and 2896/10 (*Vinter and Others/UK*).

20 ECtHR (GC) 8 July 2014, 15018/11 and 61199/12 (*Harakchiev and Tolumov/Bulgaria*).

21 ECtHR (GC) 30 June 2015, 41418/04 (*Khoroshenko/Russia*).

22 ECtHR (GC) 26 April 2016, 10511/10 (*Murray/the Netherlands*).

23 ECtHR (GC) 9 July 2013, 66069/09, 130/10 and 2896/10 (*Vinter and Others/UK*), par. 114.

24 ECtHR (GC) 8 July 2014, 15018/11 and 61199/12 (*Harakchiev and Tolumov/Bulgaria*), par. 264.

The "general evolution in European penal policy towards (...) the rehabilitative aim of imprisonment, particularly towards the end of a long prison sentence" was noted in *Khoroshenko/Russia.*[25] The Grand Chamber in this case also emphasised that "rehabilitation and reintegration has become a *mandatory factor* that the member states need to take into account in designing their penal policies".[26] The Grand Chamber case of *Murray/the Netherlands* moved to characterise states' obligations with respect to rehabilitation as *positive* ones, stating that states have "a *positive obligation* to secure prison regimes to life prisoners which are compatible with the aim of rehabilitation".[27]

Precisely which kinds of "positive obligations" are required in order to afford convicted persons a "real opportunity" for rehabilitation is still open for debate. The precise meaning, scope and practical implications of the imperative to enable rehabilitation remain deliberately, and perhaps necessarily, vague. Meijer interprets the *Murray* reference to "positive obligations" as indicating that states are bound to "abide by certain standards" and to ensure "a minimum level of protection" with respect to person's prospects of rehabilitating themselves.[28] More specifically, she argues that, in recognising this positive obligation, the ECtHR "makes the provision of rehabilitative *activities* legally enforceable, which allows courts to intervene in the case of administrative reluctance".[29]

Yet, it is not clear that the ECHR imposes a duty on states to provide rehabilitative *interventions* as against other measures that might enable, or uphold persons' opportunity for, rehabilitation – such as shorter prison sentences, good conditions of detention or regular family visits while imprisoned. More precisely, it is not obvious that the duty to enable rehabilitation guarantees convicted persons a right to demand access to rehabilitation across the board and in all cases. For one thing, and as said, the case law referencing rehabilitation focuses on the situation of imprisoned persons and particularly those serving life sentences. The Grand Chamber in *Harackchiev and Tolumov/Bulgaria*, moreover, effectively denied that the ECHR guarantees a right to rehabilitative interventions in observing that

> the Convention does not guarantee, as such, a right to rehabilitation, and (...) Article 3 cannot be construed as imposing on authorities an absolute duty to provide prisoners with rehabilitation and reintegration programmes and activities, such as courses or counselling.[30]

Perhaps, then, the more accurate conclusion to draw is that the ECHR implicitly recognises imprisoned persons' right to have their rehabilitation enabled by the state,

[25] ECtHR (GC) 30 June 2015, 41418/04 *(Khoroshenko/Russia)*, par. 121. This is similarly noted in ECtHR (GC) 4 December 2007, 44362/04 *(Dickson/the United Kingdom)*, par. 75.

[26] ECtHR (GC) 30 June 2015, 41418/04 *(Khoroshenko/Russia)*, par. 121 (emphasis added).

[27] ECtHR (GC) 26 April 2016, 10511/10 *(Murray/the Netherlands)*, par. 104 (emphasis added).

[28] Meijer 2017, p. 161.

[29] Meijer 2017, p. 161 (emphasis added).

[30] ECtHR (GC) 8 July 2014, 15018/11 and 61199/12 *(Harakchiev and Tolumov/Bulgaria)*, par. 264.

and that this sometimes implies a right to be provided with rehabilitative interventions. The Grand Chamber in *Murray* allows that providing a "real opportunity" for rehabilitation might sometimes require that convicted persons "be enabled to undergo treatments or therapies – be they medical, psychological or psychiatric – adapted to their situation with a view to facilitating their rehabilitation".[31] It also allows that it might require affording convicted persons the opportunity to "take part in occupational or other activities where these may be considered to benefit rehabilitation".[32] But the reluctance of the ECtHR to endorse a right to rehabilitation across the board indicates that the provision of rehabilitative interventions will not always be necessary to preserve real opportunity for rehabilitation, in the Court's eyes. Sometimes, perhaps, simply ensuring that punishment is not excessive, that the conditions of detention are humane and that persons' social and other basic needs are met will be sufficient to preserve opportunity for rehabilitation. Consider a situation where the relevant party is already motivated, and has sufficient individual and familial resources and skills, to effect their own rehabilitation without state assistance.[33]

7.3 RATIONALES FOR A RIGHT TO REHABILITATION

Working on the understanding, then, that the imperative to enable rehabilitation at least sometimes implies a right to rehabilitation (i.e., to rehabilitative interventions), we shall now examine the moral and legal rationales lending support to a right to rehabilitation in certain circumstances. These rationales will bring us closer to elucidating the kinds of situations where a right to "real opportunity" for rehabilitation might imply a right to rehabilitation.

Our analysis focuses on two rationales that have (or which are extensions of arguments that have) been advanced in the philosophical and legal literature. The first (legal) rationale sees persons' right to rehabilitation as deriving from the established human right against cruel, inhuman and/or degrading punishment enshrined in Article 3 ECHR and Article 7 ICCPR (which closely relates to Article 10 ICCPR).[34] The second (moral) rationale is more aspirational, in that it argues that a right to rehabilitation is contained in an (as yet unrecognised) human right to social contribution.[35]

31 ECtHR (GC) 26 April 2016, 10511/10 *(Murray/the Netherlands)*, par. 109. In the case of *James, Wells and Lee/UK*, the Court similarly suggests that real opportunity for rehabilitation might mean having the opportunity to "undertake courses aimed at helping [convicted persons] address their offending behaviour and the risks they pose"; see ECtHR 18 September 2012, 25119/09, 57715/09 and 57877/09 *(James, Wells and Lee/UK)*.

32 ECtHR (GC) 26 April 2016, 10511/10 *(Murray/the Netherlands)*, par. 109.

33 Meijer also acknowledges that the existing legal situation seems to suggest that assessments of what "proper opportunity for rehabilitation" consists in must be made on a case-by-case basis; see Meijer 2017, pp. 161–162.

34 Taylor 2020, p. 285.

35 For the case for persons' right to social contribution, see Brownlee 2020.

There may well be other rationales too. A right to rehabilitation might, for instance, also derive from or be supported by the established human right to liberty (Article 5 ECHR and Article 9 ICCPR), such that imprisoned persons subject to long or indeterminate sentences have a right to rehabilitation.[36] A right to rehabilitation might further derive from persons' putative moral right to reparation for structural injustice, such that convicted persons whose crimes emanate at least in part from institutionally created poverty or concentrated disadvantage have a right to rehabilitation as a means of reparation for these injustices.[37] But for our present analysis, we focus on the two abovementioned rationales.

We focus on these two rationales for a number of reasons. One reason for focusing on the relationship between the right against cruel punishment and rehabilitation is that the jurisprudence invoking this relationship is reasonably extensive, and more extensive than the jurisprudence on the implications of the right to liberty for rehabilitation.[38] The right to liberty also likely generates support for a right to rehabilitation in the *same kinds* of situations as those in which the right against cruel and inhuman punishment provides support.[39] Focusing on just one of these established human rights thus prevents our analysis from being too repetitive, notwithstanding that a forceful argument for a right to rehabilitation could potentially also be made from the right to liberty. One reason for focusing on the implications of the putative human right to social contribution for rehabilitation is that the principal defender of the former right, Kimberley Brownlee, gestures towards this right's implications for criminal justice.[40] A focus on social contribution is also prudent because of the growing emphasis on human sociality, and its relevance for rights, in the philosophical literature on human rights.[41]

7.3.1 *The Right against Cruel, Inhuman and/or Degrading Punishment*

Consider first the idea that a right to rehabilitation is a derivative right of persons' right against cruel, inhuman and/or degrading punishment. As already mentioned

36 This rationale has been invoked in a case of the United Kingdom's Supreme Court, where it was observed that it should be taken "*as implicit in the scheme of Article* 5 [ECHR] that the state is under a duty to provide an opportunity reasonable in all the circumstances for such a prisoner to rehabilitate himself and to demonstrate that he no longer presents an unacceptable danger to the public"; see *R (Haney & Ors)* v. *Secretary of State for Justice* [2014] UKSC 66, par. 36 (emphasis added).

37 By institutionally created poverty, we mean systematic poverty that is generated and perpetuated by various governmental policies, such as policies that give rise to unequal access to education, health care and job opportunities. See Dore-Horgan 2023 for discussion of this right-to-reparation-line of argument as a candidate justification for a right to neurorehabilitation.

38 Though relevant cases discussing the latter relationship include ECtHR 18 September 2012, 25119/09, 57715/09 and 57877/09 (*James, Wells and Lee/UK*), pars. 217–218. See also ECtHR 24 January 2022, 11791/20 (*Sy./Italy*).

39 For example, both the right against cruel punishment and the right to liberty might support the provision of rehabilitation in the case of life sentences.

40 Brownlee 2020, chapter 8.

41 See Liao 2015; Brownlee 2020; Brownlee, Jenkins & Neal 2022; Metz 2024; McTernan 2024.

in this section, this latter right is enshrined in Article 7 ICCPR – closely related to Article 10 ICCPR – and in Article 3 ECHR. It can also be justified at the level of fundamental morality in a myriad of ways: for example, by pointing to the strength and moral urgency of persons' interest in avoiding cruel and inhuman treatment;[42] by pointing to how a rights-based prohibition against cruel punishment produces the best overall consequences for persons;[43] or by suggesting that a group of hypothetical bargainers would agree upon a prohibition against cruel punishment, not knowing their own position in the world.[44] Often in the legal literature, however, the right against cruel, inhuman and/or degrading punishment has given a "dignitarian" justification. That is, persons' dignity, intrinsic value or full moral status is often invoked as justifying persons' right against cruel, inhuman or degrading punishments.[45]

How might the right against cruel and/or inhuman punishment serve as the source for a right to rehabilitation? There are at least two different ways by which it might, but each only serves to establish that *some* subpopulations of convicted persons have a right to rehabilitation. A first way appeals to the effects some forms of punishment might have on those convicted in the absence of rehabilitation. The thought typically advanced is that *carceral* punishment without attendant rehabilitation can have sufficiently degenerative effects as to constitute cruel, inhuman and degrading punishment, particularly when dispensed over a long period of time.[46] Prisons' potential degenerative effects are well-documented. Being imprisoned can lead to a decline in one's ability to interact socially[47] and to make decisions for oneself.[48] It can also be traumatising,[49] brutalising[50] and can incur damage to one's ability to exert inhibitory control or to self-regulate (i.e., to control one's automatic urges and think before one acts),[51] which could in fact frustrate a person's

42 For a prominent interest-based account of rights, see Raz 1986.

43 For a rule-consequentialist approach to justifying rights, see Mill 2014 [1861].

44 For a contractarian or contractualist approach to rights, see Scanlon 2003 and Rawls 1999a.

45 See, for example, ECtHR (GC), 28 September 2015, 23380/09 (*Bouyid* v. *Belgium*) par. 81; and *Laaman* v. *Helgemoe* 437 F. Supp. 269 (District of New Hampshire, 1977) at 307. The ECtHR has also often suggested that dignity is a foundational value for the generation and protection of the Convention's rights more generally: see, for example, ECtHR (GC) 9 July 2013, 66069/09, 130/10 and 2896/10 (*Vinter and Others/UK*), par. 113; ECtHR 31 July 2001, 41340/98, 41342/98, 41343/98 and 41344/98 (*Refah Partisi and Others* v. *Turkey*), par. 43; and Heri 2024. The ECtHR also most frequently references dignity in the case law pertaining to Article 3; see Fikfak & Izvorova 2022, for discussion.

46 Other forms of punishment that involve some form of detention or movement restrictions (e.g., house arrest or probation) may also risk producing some degenerative effects. However, this first justification for a right to rehabilitation typically focuses on the case of imprisoned persons, presumably because imprisonment is home to particularly harsh realities across many jurisdictions.

47 Sapsford 1978; Jose-Kampfner 1990.

48 Haney 2012.

49 DeVeaux 2013; Leidenfrost & Antonius 2020.

50 Levan 2006.

51 Meijers 2018 – this was a pilot study involving a limited number of prisoners. See also Umbach, Raine & Leonard 2018.

achievement of rehabilitation.[52] Imprisonment can also increase the likelihood that a person will recidivate.[53] This increased likelihood risks making persons more susceptible to reconviction and repeat punishment – a created risk that itself could be argued to be cruel.

A second way the right against cruel punishment might serve as a source for a right to rehabilitation appeals to the impact that imprisonment without rehabilitation might have on persons' *prospect of release* when they are subject to life, long or indeterminate sentences. The initial thought here is that carceral punishment can be rendered cruel and inhuman if it is dispensed with little realistic prospect of release and/or societal reintegration. The further thought is that, insofar as the provision of rehabilitation is necessary to sustain hope of release (as might be the case when a person is serving a life, long or indeterminate sentence and their release depends on their demonstrating that they have become rehabilitated),[54] then providing rehabilitation is necessary to avoid subjecting persons to cruel and/or inhuman punishment.

The first way identified above receives greater emphasis in U.S jurisprudence. The case law of the Federal Courts has repeatedly granted that persons are subject to cruel and unusual punishment when punitive conditions make it impossible or highly unlikely for them to make progress toward their rehabilitation.[55] The case of *Laaman* v. *Helgemoe* is an important example in this regard. In *Laaman*, the District Court judged that the right against cruel punishment is violated when "the cumulative impact of the conditions of incarceration threatens the physical, mental and emotional health and well-being of the inmates and/or creates a probability of recidivism and future incarceration".[56] Invoking the concepts of "human dignity" and the "intrinsic worth" of human beings as grounds for the right against cruel and unusual punishment, the District Court suggested that a "debilitating" prison environment that is "counterproductive to the inmates' efforts to rehabilitate themselves" is marked by "needless suffering" and hence is cruel.[57] It is marked by needless suffering, firstly, because debilitating prison environments pose risks to imprisoned persons' "sanity or mental well-being".[58] It is also marked by needless suffering because, in increasing the likelihood of prisoner degeneration, it makes recidivism and reincarceration – and hence further pain and suffering – "probable".[59]

[52] Ligthart et al. 2019; Ligthart et al. 2023b.
[53] Vieraitis, Kovandzic & Marvell 2007; Cid 2009.
[54] See, for example, *James* v. *Wallace*, 382 F. Supp. 1177 (M.D. Ala 1974); *Holt.* v. *Sarver*, 309 F. Supp. 362, 379.
[55] *Dawson* v. *Kendrick*; *Miller* v. *Carson*; *James* v. *Wallace*; *Laaman* v. *Helgemoe*, 437 F. Supp. 269 (D.N. H. 1977).
[56] *Laaman* v. *Helgemoe*, 437 F. Supp. 269 (D.N.H. 1977), 323.
[57] *Laaman* v. *Helgemoe*, 437 F. Supp. 269 (D.N.H. 1977), 323, 316, 315.
[58] *Laaman* v. *Helgemoe*, 437 F. Supp. 269 (D.N.H. 1977), 323, 316.
[59] *Laaman* v. *Helgemoe*, 437 F. Supp. 269 (D.N.H. 1977), 323.

Note, that in *Laaman*, and in all the case law of the U.S. Federal Courts, the legal instrument under analysis is the Eight Amendment of the U.S. Constitution, which proscribes cruel and unusual punishment. However, given the near-identity between the content of this Eight Amendment and both Article 3 ECHR and Article 7 ICCPR, the reasoning here seems also relevant for – and could potentially be applied in the interpretative analysis of – these international human rights documents. Note, too, that U.S. jurisprudence teeters over whether persons' right to serve their sentences in non-debilitating, potentially rehabilitative prison environments requires that they are provided with rehabilitative *interventions*. The judgement in *Laaman* is that punishment *cannot hinder* the rehabilitation of those who offend, not expressly that those incarcerated can demand access to rehabilitative interventions or programmes.

Several outputs from the Federal Courts' jurisprudence, moreover, explicitly state that a broad duty to provide rehabilitation is *not* required. The Supreme Court, in *Rhodes* v. *Chapman*, for instance, claims that "we would have to wrench the Eighth Amendment from its language and history to hold that delay of (. . .) desirable aids to rehabilitation violates the Constitution".[60] The Court in the case of *Holt* v. *Sarver* was similarly unwilling to grant that detention in "an otherwise unexceptional penal institution" violated a person's right against cruel and unusual punishment "simply because the institution does not operate a school, or provide vocational training, or other rehabilitative facilities and services".[61] The Court in *James* v. *Wallace* likewise rejected the claim that those imprisoned have "an absolute entitlement to the provision of rehabilitative services".[62]

Still, many orders set forth by the Federal Courts have insisted that prison authorities provide rehabilitation to those they incarcerate. In *Laaman*, the Court ordered that the relevant prison provide work opportunities and vocational training "in order to minimise degeneration and succour what rehabilitative attempts were being made by inmates".[63] The Court in *Pugh* v. *Locke* similarly ordered that imprisoned persons "be assigned a meaningful job", and be given "the opportunity to participate in basic educational programs", "vocational training programs" and "transition program[s] designed to aid [their] re-entry into society".[64] The Court in *Barnes* v. *Government of the Virgin Islands* also ordered that imprisoned persons have access to "meaningful rehabilitational opportunities which would prepare inmates to return to society".[65] The U.S. position therefore seems to be that a right

60 *Rhodes* v. *Chapman*, 452 U.S. 337 (1981), 348.
61 *Holt.* v. *Sarver*, 309 F. Supp. 362 (E.D.Ark.1970), 379.
62 *James* v. *Wallace*, 382 F. Supp. 1177 (M.D. Ala 1974), 1180.
63 *Laaman* v. *Helgemoe*, 437 F. Supp. 269 (D.N.H. 1977), 318.
64 *Pugh* v. *Locke*, 406 F. Supp. 318 (M.D. Ala. 1976), 335.
65 *Barnes* v. *Government of the Virgin Islands*, 415 F. Supp. 1218 (D.V.I. 1976), 1227.

to rehabilitation can be derived from the right against cruel punishment but only applies in *specific* cases. It does not imply a *broad* right to rehabilitative interventions.

The second way of deriving a right to rehabilitation from persons' right against cruel, inhuman and/or degrading punishment has been invoked (in the jurisprudence of the ECtHR and elsewhere) in relation to life imprisonment cases, and it involves two principal steps. The first step – prominent in the landmark ECtHR case of *Vinter and Others/the United Kingdom*[66] and in the German Constitutional Court's 1977 life imprisonment case[67] – interprets the prohibition against cruel and/or inhuman punishment as requiring real or *de facto* prospect of release for those imprisoned.[68]

In her concurring opinion to the *Vinter* judgement, Judge Power-Forde explicitly connects the lack of real prospect for release with degradation. She maintains that denying imprisoned persons "the right to hope" for atonement and release would deny them "a fundamental aspect of their humanity" and hence "would be degrading".[69] The German Federal Constitutional Court likewise affirms that real prospect of release must exist if life imprisonment is to be tolerable.[70]

Similar thoughts are advanced in the reports of the Council of Europe's Committee for the Prevention of Torture (CPT). For example, in its 2012 report to the Bulgarian government, the CPT asserted that "it is inhuman to imprison a person for life without any realistic hope of release" and expressed its "serious reservations about the very concept according to which life-sentenced prisoners are considered (...) to be a permanent threat to the community and are deprived of any hope of (...) conditional release".[71] The CPT's 25th General Report likewise affirmed that "excluding (...) any hope of rehabilitation and return to the community effectively dehumanises the prisoner".[72]

66 ECtHR (GC) 9 July 2013, 66069/09, 130/10 and 2896/10 (*Vinter and Others/UK*).

67 German Federal Constitutional Court, 21 June 1977, 45 BVerfGE 187.

68 Note, it is not the *imposition* of a life sentence that contravenes the Convention's prohibition against cruel or inhuman punishment, according to the Courts, but rather the *practical irreducibility* that might attend such a sentence. This point is explicitly made in ECtHR (GC) 12 February 2008, 21906/04 (*Kafkaris/Cyprus*), par. 97: "the imposition of a sentence of life imprisonment (...) is not itself (...) incompatible with Article 3" but "the imposition of an *irreducible* life sentence on an adult may raise an issue under Article 3" (emphasis added).

69 Concurring opinion of Judge Power-Forde in ECtHR (GC) 9 July 2013, 66069/09, 130/10 and 2896/10 (*Vinter and Others/UK*). See also ECtHR 23 May 2017 22662/13, 51059/13, 58823/13, 59692/13, 59700/13, 60115/13, 69425/13 and 72824/13 (*Matiosaitis and Others* v. *Lithuania*), 180.

70 German Federal Constitutional Court, 21 June 1977, 45 BVerfGE 187.

71 CPT/Inf (2012) 32, point 32.

72 CPT/Inf(2016)10, point 73. See also Rogan 2024, pp. 154–171.

Now, it is one thing to claim that the *absence of hope* for release renders the dispensed punishment cruel and inhuman. It is a further step to claim that providing rehabilitation is necessary to sustain hope for release. This further step has been taken in the post-*Vinter* jurisprudence of the ECtHR, notably in the case of *Murray/the Netherlands*.[73] In *Murray*, the ECtHR's Grand Chamber ruled that the applicant – a person serving a life sentence in the Dutch Antilles – lacked a de facto prospect of release because he had not been provided with opportunities that could enable him to progress towards the rehabilitation on which his eligibility for release depended. The applicant argued that while his life sentence could, in theory, be reviewed, he could not realistically hope for release because, having never received psychiatric treatment, his recidivism risk would be deemed too high for him to be eligible for release.[74] The Grand Chamber concurred with the assessment of the applicant. It found a violation of Article 3 ECHR because this lack of treatment and assessment of treatment needs meant that any review of the applicant's request for release "was in practice incapable of leading to the conclusion that he had made (...) significant progress towards rehabilitation".[75] The Grand Chamber in this case also acknowledged, as already mentioned, that genuine prospect for rehabilitation may require, in certain circumstances, that imprisoned persons "be enabled to undergo treatments or therapies – be they medical, psychological or psychiatric – adapted to their situation" that can be expected to facilitate their rehabilitation.[76] It further acknowledged that imprisoned persons "should also be allowed to take part in occupational or other activities where these may be considered to benefit rehabilitation".[77]

The conclusion in *Murray* is thus that providing rehabilitation may sometimes be necessary to effect the possibility of release for those serving life, or otherwise indeterminate, sentences – something itself deemed necessary for compliance with Article 3 ECHR.

This echoes the position voiced in *Harakchiev and Tolumov/Bulgaria*.[78] Recall that the ECtHR observed, in this earlier case, that while Article 3 ECHR "cannot be construed as imposing on the authorities an *absolute* duty to provide prisoners with rehabilitation or reintegration programmes and activities (...) it does require the authorities to give life prisoners a chance, however remote, to someday regain their freedom".[79] Note, too, that the Court in this case further observed that "for that chance to be *genuine* and *tangible*, the authorities must also give life prisoners a real

73 ECtHR (GC) 26 April 2016, 10511/10 (*Murray/the Netherlands*).
74 ECtHR (GC) 26 April 2016, 10511/10 (*Murray/the Netherlands*), pars. 4, 87.
75 ECtHR (GC) 26 April 2016, 10511/10 (*Murray/the Netherlands*), par. 125.
76 ECtHR (GC) 26 April 2016, 10511/10 (*Murray/the Netherlands*), par. 109.
77 ECtHR (GC) 26 April 2016, 10511/10 (*Murray/the Netherlands*), par. 109.
78 ECtHR 8 July 2014, 15018/11 and 61199/12 (*Harakchiev and Tolumov/Bulgaria*), pars. 264–266.
79 ECtHR 8 July 2014, 15018/11 and 61199/12 (*Harakchiev and Tolumov/Bulgaria*), par. 264 (emphasis added).

opportunity to rehabilitate themselves".[80] It also insisted that "efforts need to be made by the prison authorities" to promote these individuals' rehabilitation and resocialisation.[81]

Various non-binding human rights instruments likewise suggest a link between the provision of rehabilitation and the avoidance of cruel punishment in cases of life sentences. The Council of Europe holds that those sentenced to life should have the possibility of conditional release and that prison conditions "consistent with the principles of justice, equity and fairness" should afford persons "constructive preparations for release" with opportunities for "work, education, training and other activities".[82] The CPT similarly emphasises that "having a purely formal possibility to apply for release (. . .) is not sufficient" to satisfy this "prospect of release" requirement.[83] Rather, "member states must ensure, notably through the way they treat life-sentenced prisoners, that this possibility is real and effective".[84]

The foregoing discussion demonstrates that there is precedent within human rights law for deriving a right to rehabilitation from the existing human rights prohibition on cruel, inhuman and/or degrading treatment or punishment, at least in certain circumstances. Some scepticism might nonetheless arise about the *value* of linking rehabilitation with the right against cruel punishment, notwithstanding the support that this position receives within the case law. One thought might be that the prohibition on degrading punishment should not imply that convicted persons have a right to interventions that might counteract punishment's degrading effects, but rather that states must not impose punishments that have the potential to be degrading in the first place. Another thought might be that *providing* rehabilitation is unnecessary to preserve genuine hope for release, even in the case of life or long-term sentences, so long as ample opportunity to review sentences and reassess persons' risk of reoffending is preserved. Every imprisoned person *qua* rational agent, after all, has the capacity and potential to rehabilitate *themselves*.[85]

Three comments by way of assuaging this scepticism can be made. First, it goes without saying that the prohibition against degrading punishments would be *better* upheld if our punishment practices did not have the potential to have degenerative

80 ECtHR 8 July 2014, 15018/11 and 61199/12 *(Harakchiev and Tolumov/Bulgaria)*, pars. 264–266.

81 ECtHR 8 July 2014, 15018/11 and 61199/12 *(Harakchiev and Tolumov/Bulgaria)*, pars. 264–266.

82 Committee of Ministers of the Council of Europe, Recommendation Rec(2003)23 of the Committee of Ministers to member states on the Management by Prison Administrations of Life Sentence and Other Long-Term Prisoners (9 October 2003) (available from https://rm.coe.int/09000016805dec7a).

83 CPT/Inf(2016)10, point 82.

84 CPT/Inf(2016)10, point 82.

85 Dore-Horgan 2023, p. 439. Or at least, in order to be held criminally responsible and hence convicted of a crime, a person has to pass some threshold of rationality. There may be some situations where an imprisoned person no longer meets this threshold – for example, due to the development of a severe psychiatric disorder. Also, some detained people judged as legally insane by the court may, depending on the course of their illness, lack the capabilities needed to rehabilitate themselves.

effects. Reform of our carceral practices consequently should be a priority of criminal justice institutions in order to ensure compliance with Article 3 ECHR, Article 7 ICCPR and Article 10 ICCPR, and should take precedence over reform efforts that merely seek to counter penal degradation. That said, it remains the case that many persons *currently are*, or will *inevitably soon be*, subject to potentially degenerative punishments. So long as this is the case – and it is possible that criminal justice systems will always rely on some sort of detention-based (and hence potentially degenerating) sanctions for persons who pose a serious risk to the public[86] – then linking the avoidance of cruel punishment to the provision of rehabilitation makes sense and should be welcomed. We can accept this without diverting our attention away from the need and imperative to reform our punishment practices.

Second, while regular sentence review and regular risk reassessment should be sufficient to preserve genuine prospect for release *in theory* – *in practice*, it is not always sufficient. Sentence review procedures in many jurisdictions often require that long-term- or life-sentenced persons *demonstrate* that they have made progress toward their rehabilitation.[87] One option would, of course, be to change this requirement. But again, so long as this requirement exists, demonstrating that one has made progress towards rehabilitation will likely be easier if there are positive reports from various courses, interventions and/or therapies undertaken to draw upon. And this may be particularly relevant for those serving indefinite sentences based on the presumption that they pose a danger to the public (i.e., preventive detention). Consider how the ECtHR's approach to rehabilitation under Article 5 ECHR, as Martufi summarises below, emphasises the relevance of rehabilitation for this kind of situation:[88]

> even when detention is justified on grounds of public protection, prisoners shall be offered real opportunities to rehabilitate and, as a result, must be entitled to an effective possibility to progress through the prison system and become eligible for parole. In the absence of such offending-behaviour programmes, a deprivation of

86 We say this while acknowledging that there are moral reasons that can be advanced in support of an upper limit on punishment length. Negative retributivists, for instance, maintain that there should be an upper limit on punishment based on considerations of proportionality, such that imprisoned persons should be released when this point is reached regardless of their dangerousness. See Lippke 2014 for discussion of negative retributivism.

87 For example, in Sweden, parole decision-makers are required to make decisions about release on the basis of a number of criteria, including the candidate parolee's "rehabilitative efforts" and their "overall behaviour and development"; see Schartmueller 2013, table 1. Similarly, in Ireland, parole decision-makers must consider whether a parole applicant "has become rehabilitated and would, upon being released, be capable of reintegrating into society"; see Parole Act 2019.

88 ECtHR 18 September 2012, 25119/09, 57715/09 and 57877/09 (*James, Wells and Lee/UK*), pars. 217–218; ECtHR 24 January 2022, 11791/20 (*Sy./Italy*); ECtHR (GC) 31 January 2019, 18052/11 (*Rooman/Belgium*).

liberty based exclusively on the presumed dangerousness of the offenders would amount to "arbitrary detention", within the meaning of Article 5(1)(a) ECHR.[89]

Third, while all persons *qua* rational agents are in principle capable of rehabilitating themselves, it seems overly demanding, and arguably inhuman, to expect people to do so without support. The right to have a genuine "prospect of release" is surely most acceptably understood as a right to this prospect through *realistic* effort – not through gargantuan effort. Achieving rehabilitation and eligibility for release without external support will likely sometimes be a gargantuan task. Consider how it likely would be extremely difficult for a person whose violent crimes stem in part from impulsive aggression to curb their aggressive behaviour without some form of professional support.[90] Consider also how rehabilitation might be very difficult to achieve when one's crimes emanate, at least in part, from economic and educational disadvantage unless one is helped to improve one's employability and job prospects. Given these realities, the mere fact that persons could in principle rehabilitate themselves does not undermine the claim – voiced in *Murray* and elsewhere – that rehabilitative interventions may sometimes be necessary to make rehabilitation and release reasonably achievable.[91] Linking the avoidance of cruel punishment to the provision of rehabilitation is thus a reasonable link to make, at least in certain circumstances.

7.3.2 *The Right to Socially Contribute*

In the previous subsection, we focused on the ways in which a right to rehabilitation might be derived from the established human right against cruel, inhuman and/or degrading punishment. We shall now articulate another route by which a right to rehabilitation might be supported, drawing on the recent scholarship of Kimberley Brownlee.[92] Brownlee defends a human right to *socially contribute*. By this, she means that persons have a moral right to "contribute (. . .) to others' survival and well-being"[93] that applies universally and which ought to be recognised in law.

Contributing to others' survival and well-being, according to Brownlee, includes providing others with material support and security, and also companionship and

89 Martufi 2018, p. 678. See also *R (Haney & Ors)* v. *Secretary of State for Justice* [2014] UKSC 66, par. 36.

90 Professionals tasked with the delivery of rehabilitation, after all, can direct people to helpful rehabilitative tools. These professionals also have the knowledge and experience to help people navigate the challenges that arise on their path to reform, while providing much needed emotional support.

91 ECtHR (GC) 26 April 2016, 10511/10 (*Murray/the Netherlands*), par. 104. Recall, also, the claim voiced in ECtHR (GC) 8 July 2014, 15018/11 and 61199/12 (*Harakchiev and Tolumov/Bulgaria*), par. 264, that life prisoners must have a "genuine and tangible" chance to rehabilitate themselves.

92 Brownlee 2016a, 2016b, 2020, 2022.

93 Brownlee 2016a, p. 328.

closeness.[94] She defends a right to socially contribute by appealing to humans' fundamental *need to belong* – viz., to affiliate with and be accepted by a minimum quantity of others.[95] She emphasises that this need is a "non-contingent, morally urgent need" of ours[96] – something that we must have if we are to "survive and flourish".[97] She then contends that contributing to others' survival and well-being "is a key way to satisfy our need to belong",[98] and argues for a *human right* to social contribution by appealing to the idea that persons have "human right(s) to the conditions necessary to realize a minimally good human life".[99]

Brownlee considers her proposed right to social contribution to have both positive and negative dimensions. It contains both a right *against* having one's opportunities to socially contribute thwarted and a right *to* the material and temporal resources required for social contribution.[100] Brownlee also sees the right as sharing the same moral standing as existing civil and political rights. She acknowledges that social human rights – that is, rights that pertain to interpersonal, as against political or economic, interests – "have long been the poorest of the poor cousins in human rights debates",[101] often considered "desirable goal[s]" or "liberal aspirations" rather than "things to which we can have human rights".[102] Brownlee takes issue with this and maintains that many social rights, including the right to socially contribute, are *as* important to fulfil as those rights classed as "first generation rights".[103] They are important because of the role that social rights play in helping people lead minimally good lives.[104]

We shall not defend the credentials of the proposed human right to socially contribute here. Our interest is in exploring what a right to socially contribute, as defended by Brownlee, could imply for the provision of rehabilitation in criminal justice. Interestingly, Brownlee's defence of this right is partly motivated by her concern for the situation of convicted persons.[105] She points to how convicted persons are one subpopulation often denied a right to socially contribute insofar as they are subjected to exclusionary punishments that "sever their social bonds", or are

94 Brownlee 2020, pp. 78–79. As examples of acts of companionship and closeness, Brownlee points to engaging in "meaningful joint projects" and spending quality time with, and speaking to, others with affection and kindness.

95 Brownlee 2020, pp.17–19. For some of psychological literature documenting and defending this need, see Baumeister & Leary 1995; Seligman 2011; DeWall 2013.

96 Brownlee 2020, p. 26.

97 Brownlee 2020, pp. 26, 24.

98 Brownlee 2020, p. 76.

99 Brownlee 2020, pp. 76, 55. Here, Brownlee is following Nickel 2007 and Shue 1996 in assuming that we have human rights to the conditions necessary for having a minimally good life.

100 Brownlee 2016a, p. 332. See also Calhoun 2023.

101 Brownlee, Jenkins & Neal 2022, p. 4.

102 Brownlee, Jenkins & Neal 2022, pp. 4, 1.

103 Brownlee, Jenkins & Neal 2022, pp. 2–4.

104 Brownlee 2020, p. 8. See Brownlee, Jenkins & Neal 2022 for an anthology that aims to remedy this neglect of social rights in human rights theory and practice.

105 Brownlee 2016a, p. 328; Brownlee 2020, p. 172.

given "criminal records they can never spend".[106] And while Brownlee does not explicitly argue that her proposed human right implies a right to rehabilitation, we think that the right to socially contribute (if it exists) *would imply* this, at least for some subpopulations of convicted persons.[107]

Consider how Brownlee insists that the right to socially contribute places governments under a defeasible duty to help protect and preserve people's *social resources*, to a minimally adequate level.[108] By social resources, Brownlee means a person's social abilities (the set of skills that people need for interacting with others); their social opportunities (occasions at which interaction is possible); and their social connections (enduring links with others that meet a standard of decency). Consider, too, how this putative governmental duty to help protect and preserve people's social resources entails a duty to make rehabilitation available to convicted persons, if and when rehabilitation is *necessary* to help protect and preserve people's social resources to a minimally adequate level.

Whether and when rehabilitation *is* necessary for preserving one's social resources is, of course, an empirical question. However, it is reasonable to suppose that it might sometimes be necessary. Rehabilitative interventions such as family therapy/group counselling could conceivably be necessary for preserving a convicted persons' supportive social connections in cases where their crime(s) are serious in nature and/or when they involve victims from their own social circle.[109] Educational or vocational interventions might likewise be necessary to preserve people's social opportunities in cases where imprisonment forecloses previously relied upon opportunities and networks. Various psychotherapies could further be necessary when persons, due to mental illness or particular personality traits, have difficulty forging and sustaining supportive social connections. As said, we cannot pass judgement on how *commonly* rehabilitation will be necessary to effect these outcomes. Our point is simply that, assuming there will be some occasions when preserving convicted persons' social resources requires rehabilitative interventions, the (defeasible) moral right to social contribution implies a defeasible moral right to have access to them. Defeasible because access and availability will always be subject to resource constraints, and because rights to access various interventions will need to be balanced against other rights' considerations.[110]

[106] Brownlee 2016a, p. 327. Brownlee does not consider that people, in committing crime, forfeit this right; see Brownlee 2020, chapters 3 and 8.

[107] Brownlee may take this to be implicit in her argument. She does, after all, stress the importance of post-prison provisions to mitigate the damage done to a person's social connections during their time in prison and to ease their reintegration into society, see Brownlee 2016a, pp. 348–349; Brownlee 2020, p. 188.

[108] Brownlee 2020, pp. 20–21. This suggests that Brownlee takes the moral right to social contribute to be a defeasible rather than an absolute moral right.

[109] For a discussion of the promise and challenges of rehabilitative interventions that involve family members, see Garofalo 2020.

[110] For example, the rights of other persons who participate in family therapy, educational or psychotherapeutic interventions. Consider how permissible infringement of the putative moral right to

7.4 A STATE DUTY TO PROVIDE NEUROREHABILITATION?

We shall now assess what these two candidate justifications for a right to rehabilitation imply for the specific case of neurorehabilitation. More precisely, we ask whether the right against cruel and degrading punishment and/or the putative right to social contribution imply a right to have access to safe and effective neurorehabilitation, at least in certain circumstances and provided that the intervention in question does not violate (other) human rights.[111]

Consider first the prohibition against cruel and/or degrading punishment. How might this support a right to *neuro*rehabilitation? We suggest that the right against cruel punishment implies a defeasible right to neurorehabilitation when either (a) neurorehabilitation would counter the degenerative effects of punishment more effectively than conventional rehabilitation would do alone; or (b) when neurorehabilitation is necessary to make the achievement of rehabilitation and eligibility for release reasonably achievable.[112] In suggesting this, we assume the prohibition against cruel and/or degrading punishment – insofar as it implies a right to rehabilitation – further implies a right to an *effective* package of interventions for offsetting punishment's degenerative effects or for preserving genuine prospect for release. Such a view seems to be accepted when it comes to offering traditional forms of rehabilitation: while convicted persons do not have a right to all and every rehabilitative intervention, insofar as they *have* a right to rehabilitative interventions, this right is to effective interventions from among the reasonably affordable alternatives.[113]

Whether neurorehabilitation will in the future be part of an effective approach is again an empirical question. However, it is reasonable to postulate that in some cases it might be. For one thing, neurorehabilitation combined with conventional rehabilitative measures might sometimes help counteract imprisonment's potential degenerative effects effectively when conventional rehabilitative measures *alone* do not. Neurorehabilitation might also sometimes provide a means for preserving genuine hope of rehabilitation and release in situations where hope is lost. We cannot defend these thoughts definitively here. Still, we shall provide some motivation for them.

First, consider the potential *anti*-degeneration effects of some existing and emerging neuropharmaceuticals and technologies. At one level, we have the

access social contribution-enabling interventions might reasonably occur when delivering these interventions threatens, for instance, others' physical safety and mental health.

111 For example, the right to bodily integrity.

112 Some of the reasoning advanced here borrows from Dore-Horgan 2023.

113 For example, in *Barnes* v. *Government of the Virgin Islands*, 415 F. Supp. 1218 (D.V.I. 1976), 1232-33, an emphasis is placed on "effective rehabilitation" and on the importance of "determin[ing] the educational, recreational (...) work (...) [and] physical and mental health care" needs of each imprisoned person" if "effective rehabilitation is to take place". Recall also the observation in ECtHR (GC) 26 April 2016, 10511/10 (*Murray/the Netherlands*), par. 109, that imprisoned persons should "be enabled to undergo treatments or therapies (...) adapted to their situation".

neuropharmaceuticals already in use within forensic psychiatry – so, for example, medication that might help to combat the traumatising and brutalising effects that sometimes attend incarceration.[114] These kinds of interventions clearly can be utilised to help counter the potentially degenerative effects of our carceral practices. Providing these interventions might also sometimes be required, not only to protect and fulfil the right to rehabilitation but also to protect and fulfil persons' right to mental health.[115] And in the future, novel developments might further broaden the range of interventions at our disposal for forestalling penal degeneration.[116] Again, the prospect of these anti-degeneration neurointerventions does not obviate the need to reform our carceral practices such that they do not produce degenerative effects in the first place. Indeed, it might be objected that a person is *still* subjected to cruel and degrading punishment if neurointerventions are required for, and harnessed for the purpose of, making prison tolerable.[117] Our point here is thus not that neurorehabilitation might render otherwise unacceptable punishments acceptable but rather that *as and when* persons are subject to punishment-induced degeneration that can be countered more effectively with neurorehabilitation, *refraining* from providing neurorehabilitation may be cruel and in violation of the prohibition on cruel treatment.

Consider next how the offer of neurorehabilitation might sometimes be necessary to preserve hope for release in cases where a person is subject to life, long or indeterminate (preventive) detention and where conventional rehabilitative measures have *failed* to enable rehabilitation. Again, we cannot comment on how *likely* it is that candidate and emerging neurotechnologies will succeed when conventional measures have failed. But as things stand, conventional rehabilitation proves ineffective for some individuals. Some such individuals consequently lack genuine prospect of release when their release depends on their demonstrating that they have become rehabilitated.[118] Offering safe and effective neurorehabilitation in these circumstances – if it exists – would put hope back on the table. The right against cruel, inhuman and degrading punishment would thus support a (defeasible) right to access safe and effective neurotechnologies *if and when* these are necessary to preserve hope for rehabilitation and release.[119]

Looking next to the putative human right to socially contribute and the implications this proposed right might have for neurorehabilitation, one possible implication is a right to have access to neurorehabilitation when one exhibits dispositions

114 Harner et al. 2015; Jakobowitz et al. 2017.

115 See Chapter 6.

116 See Friedman et al. 2016; Tan et al. 2020 for ongoing research on treatments for depressive symptoms.

117 We thank Tom Douglas for pressing us on this point.

118 An example may be some persons scoring highly on measures of psychopathy. Indeed, no specific conventional rehabilitative intervention is consistently efficacious in this population; see Rice and Harris 2013; and Hecht, Latzman & Lilienfeld 2018. Cf. González Moraga et al. 2019.

119 The right to liberty (article 7 ECHR and article 9 ICCPR) would perhaps also support a right to access neurotechnologies here.

and behaviours that hinder one's ability to socially contribute, and when these dispositions and behaviours are amenable to alteration via neurorehabilitation. Clearly, some convicted persons exhibit dispositions and behaviours that may hinder their efforts to socially contribute. Think of people who lash out aggressively or who have significant difficulty experiencing compassion for others.[120] These challenges are not confined to offending populations.[121] Nor do such challenges necessarily impede one's ability to socially contribute – we each vary in our dispositions and most of us still manage to contribute to the survival and well-being of at least some others notwithstanding. Our point is simply that there are some persons who appear unable to successfully forge social connections, and for whom this hampers their rehabilitation. For these persons, we think the putative right to socially contribute implies defeasible governmental duties of assistance to enable social contribution. And as and when neurotechnologies are a necessary component of an effective assistance package, then relevant neurotechnologies may be something to which persons have a right, accepting their right to social contribution.

Only time will tell what these relevant neurotechnologies might be. Research is still at a very early stage, so we can only speculate. One relevant technology might be the use of transcranial magnetic stimulation on regions of the brain involved in inhibitory control and communication to help increase brain activity in these regions.[122] Other examples might be the use of neurofeedback techniques or neuropharmaceuticals to train or stimulate inhibitory control or compassionate responses in their users.[123]

The analysis in this section will likely meet with some reservations. Some may doubt, on the one hand, that the right against cruel punishment implies a right to *neuro*rehabilitation specifically. Others – while accepting that the putative right to socially contribute, insofar as it implies a right to rehabilitation, will also imply a right to neurorehabilitation – may worry about the consequences of recognising this relationship. More precisely, the first objection might be that the right against cruel punishment does not imply a right to *neuro*rehabilitation because rehabilitation ought to be the responsibility of the convicted person themselves – and effective neurorehabilitation essentially *rehabilitates*, rather than leaving the responsibility for rehabilitation to, the relevant party.[124] The second objection might be that

[120] Some such persons may meet the criteria for diagnosis of a personality disorder. They may face enduring difficulties in social interaction and unstable social connections.

[121] As Brownlee points out, it is possible that "no one person could ever realize the full set of social abilities"; see Brownlee 2020, p. 20.

[122] For the protocol for an ongoing trial on the effectiveness of repetitive transcranial magnetic stimulation for promoting social communication in a population with autism spectrum disorder, see Enticott et al. 2021.

[123] For research providing preliminary support for the thought that neurofeedback can be used to build empathy or compassion, see Moll et al. 2014. For some evidence to suggest that the neuropeptide oxytocin promotes emotional empathy, see Le et al. 2020.

[124] Recall how personal responsibility for one's own rehabilitation is emphasised in ECtHR (GC) 8 July 2014, 15018/11 and 61199/12 (*Harakchiev and Tolumov/Bulgaria*), par. 264; and ECtHR (GC) 26 April 2016, 10511/10 (*Murray/the Netherlands*), par. 104.

appealing to a right to social contribution to support a right to neurorehabilitation expresses objectionably disrespectful messages about those who exhibit (neuro) diverse forms of sociality and hence is a line of reasoning that should be resisted.

These objections require more extended discussion than we can afford them here. However, we shall make two brief remarks by way of reply to them. First, neurorehabilitation does not necessarily absolve persons of the responsibility for rehabilitating themselves. On the one hand, a person has to *choose* to undergo neurorehabilitation when exercising their right to it – something that itself is the first step in taking responsibility for one's rehabilitation. Furthermore, candidate dispositional changes elicited by neurorehabilitation – for example, attenuated aggression, enhanced empathy or increased social understanding – probably do not in-and-of-themselves lead to desistance from crime. For desistance to occur, it is likely that those who have offended still have to be *willing*, and *make the decision*, to desist. A parallel can be made here with how the neurostimulant caffeine can enhance, but is not responsible for, a person's productivity. Just as caffeine may help facilitate concentration while leaving decisions about how to direct this newly focused state up to the individual consumer, most candidate neurointerventions may only deliver on their promise of reducing reoffending if the person is, in fact, willing to desist.[125]

The objection that deriving a right to neurorehabilitation from a right to social contribution expresses objectionably disrespectful messages about those who exhibit neurodiverse forms of sociality should give us cause for pause. Clearly, a broad range of interactional styles can and should be recognised as acceptable, and neurorehabilitation should be developed and delivered in an environment that acknowledges this. Yet, *does* acknowledging a relationship between a right to social contribution and a right to neurorehabilitation express such a disrespectful message? We think not necessarily, particularly if (a) the right to neurorehabilitation is understood as a right to have *access to* neurorehabilitation while retaining the prerogative to refuse it (as per our understanding); and (b) neurorehabilitation is not proffered as a tool for changing a person's particular interactional style. The above discussion endeavoured to illustrate that *sometimes*, persons' prerogative to alter their (justice-relevant) dispositions and behaviours might be something they are entitled to claim assistance for, accepting a right to social contribution. But this is not the same as saying that a right to social contribution implies a right to neurotechnological tools that promote neurotypical sociality or that neurotypical sociality is necessary for social contribution. Any movement towards this kind of conclusion should be resisted.[126]

125 Dore-Horgan 2023.

126 We concede that, collectively, convicted persons and their clinicians might tend to choose interventions that promote neurotypical traits, and that this collective tendency might express a negative message about neurodivergent traits. We thus accept that there will be *challenges* in ensuring that any messages expressed in delivering neurorehabilitation remain respectful of those who exhibit neurodivergent sociality. However, we do not believe these challenges are insurmountable, nor do we think they constitute a knock-down reason for resisting the line of argument for

This second objection thus underscores the need for safeguards in making neurorehabilitation available even when there is reason to think persons have a right to it, given the potential unintended sequelae that might follow from introducing neurorehabilitation.

7.5 CONCLUDING REMARKS

To conclude, this chapter has documented existing law and jurisprudence with respect to rehabilitation, raised and interrogated two arguments that seem to support convicted persons' right to rehabilitation under certain conditions and queried what these candidate justifications might imply for the specific case of neurorehabilitation. More specifically, we explored how persons' moral and legal right against cruel, inhuman or degrading punishment, and persons' putative moral right to socially contribute, implies a right to rehabilitation under certain conditions. These conditions are when rehabilitation is necessary to prevent or counter the degrading impact of imprisonment, when it is necessary or important for preserving genuine hope for release in the case of life-sentenced or preventatively detained persons; and when it is necessary for preserving convicted persons' ability to contribute to the survival and well-being of at least some others.

Based on this analysis, we argued that the right to rehabilitation implies a defeasible right to neurorehabilitation, when neurorehabilitation is necessary to effect the above outcomes. In practice, this would of course depend, in the first place, on the availability of neurotechnologies that have been shown to be effective for rehabilitative purposes at least in some subgroups of convicted persons.

a right to neurorehabilitation advanced above. We thank Tom Douglas for drawing our attention to the possibility of this collective tendency.

8

Synthesis and Conclusion

8.1 INTRODUCTION

Can neurotechnologies be used responsibly in the rehabilitation of convicted persons, respecting fundamental freedoms and rights? This is the question we have endeavoured to answer throughout this book. The human rights challenges generated by new and emerging neurotechnologies have been widely noted by scholars, ethics committees and human rights bodies.[1] This has prompted a debate on how and to what extent human rights protect – and should protect – against unsolicited interference with our brains and minds.[2] In a recent report on the impact, opportunities and challenges of neurotechnology in relation to human rights, the Human Rights Council Advisory Committee concluded that neurotechnologies can affect human rights in a "unique manner". Therefore, developing an actionable human rights approach is of the "utmost importance". Some of their concerns relate to the potential use of neurotechnology in the criminal justice system, holding that "most of the applications proposed are extremely problematic from a human rights perspective". For example, they consider that "forceful extraction of information from detainees or offenders through the use of neurotechnology is prohibited".[3]

In this book, we explored the permissibility of the use of neurotechnology for the rehabilitation of convicted persons in view of international and European human rights law. This entailed three central tasks: (A) clarifying the scope of the relevant human rights to identify potential *infringements* of these rights, (B) clarifying these

[1] For overview and discussion of emerging neurotechnologies in different fields, see Farahany 2023. For recent policy initiatives see, inter alia, United Nations Human Rights Council, Neurotechnology and Human Rights, A/HRC/51/L.3 (29 September 2022); UNESCO, First draft of the Recommendation on the Ethics of Neurotechnology (2024). See also Ienca, M., *Common human rights challenges raised by different applications of neurotechnologies in the biomedical field*, Council of Europe, October 2021; Bublitz & Ligthart 2024.

[2] Bublitz & Merkel 2014; Ienca & Andorno 2017; Ligthart et al. 2023a.

[3] Advisory Committee, UNHRC, Impact, opportunities and challenges of neurotechnology with regard to the promotion and protection of all human rights, A/HRC/AC/31/CRP.1 (8 August 2024), pars. 47–48.

rights' permissible limitations to identify potential *violations*, and (C) exploring the scope of *positive obligations* of states that can be derived from these rights. Our analysis has provided us with the first contours of a normative, human rights-based framework for neurorehabilitation in criminal justice. We shall now synthesise our results in this final chapter.

From a human rights perspective, the permissibility of neurotechnological interventions will usually depend on all relevant circumstances of the individual case. Still, with this reservation in mind, based on our analysis we can make a tentative distinction between, roughly, three different types of neurotechnological interventions for the purpose of criminal rehabilitation: (1) plausibly permissible interventions, (2) plausibly impermissible interventions, and (3) interventions of which the permissibility is largely unclear. While acknowledging its oversimplicity and stressing, again, that from a human rights perspective the lawfulness of neurotechnological interventions will normally depend on the facts and circumstance of individual cases, we do think that attempts to clarify different categories of (im)permissible interventions has value. Such endeavours are particularly relevant in relation to ongoing developments in policymaking and the regulation of neurotechnologies through general guidelines, often informed by and grounded in human rights.[4]

Therefore, based on the analyses in the preceding chapters, we will try to tentatively identify at least *some* categories of neurotechnological applications of which their use in criminal justice appears prima facie permissible (8.2) and prima facie impermissible (8.4). We also consider neurotechnological applications whose permissibility is largely unclear (8.3). The three categories are meant to structure our thoughts about the human rights protection of the person in relation to neurotechnology. The candidate examples of the respective categories provided in the next sections are certainly not meant to be exhaustive nor definitive.

8.2 PLAUSIBLY PERMISSIBLE INTERVENTIONS

An instance of neurorehabilitation seems prima facie permissible when (i) valid consent to the intervention is obtained, (ii) the intervention is known to be safe,[5] and (iii) the intervention is expected to be effective in its professed goal (i.e., the goal of facilitating neurorehabilitation or of identifying neural markers that are relevant for assessing recidivism risk).[6]

[4] Such as the projects running at UNESCO and the Human Rights Council Advisory Committee.

[5] And has no degrading or otherwise dehumanising effects.

[6] Exceptions to (ii) and (iii) might arise if an intervention is in the research phase. In this kind of scenario, it seems likely that the permissibility of an intervention will strongly depend on the acquisition of valid consent, with particular attention being paid to disclosure of the risks and uncertainties involved – and, clearly, the permission of an ethics review board.

This category of prima facie permissible neurorehabilitation includes situations in which making safe and effective neurorehabilitation available to a given person – and delivering it when consent to it is obtained – is not only permissible but plausibly *required* from a human rights perspective. We discussed this idea of a *right to* neurorehabilitation in Chapters 5, 6 and 7. In Chapter 5, we suggested that states might have a positive obligation under the right to respect for private life to make mental control-enhancing neurotechnologies available to convicted persons on certain occasions.[7] For instance, when these persons have mental states that significantly limit their ability to live the kind of life that they want. We suggested in Chapter 6 that states might have a positive obligation under the right to mental health to make neurorehabilitation available to some subpopulations of convicted persons: for instance, when it would be necessary for, or would make it substantially easier for these populations to achieve, a reasonable standard of mental health. And in Chapter 7, we suggested that states might have a positive obligation to make neurorehabilitation available, when neurorehabilitation is necessary (i) to counter the degenerative impact of imprisonment, (ii) to preserve genuine hope for release from prison or (iii) to preserve convicted persons' ability to socially contribute.

That neurorehabilitation might sometimes be required from a human rights perspective has yet received little support from the case law, though. The use of neurotechnologies in criminal justice is still largely in the research phase and no cases involving neurorehabilitation have been brought before human rights courts. It is also unlikely that rights-based claims to be provided with neurorehabilitation will be successfully invoked in the near future, given (among other things) the resource constraints with which states operate. Still, the suggestion that neurorehabilitation might sometimes be required (absent defeaters) from a human rights perspective receives support from the case law and literature pertaining to other kinds of interventions – for example, standard medical interventions and traditional rehabilitative interventions – and from some general observations of the courts.[8] We thus posit that the category of plausibly permissible neurotechnological intervention in criminal justice includes some interventions that states also have a defeasible duty to provide.

7 We also noted that while Article 17 ICCPR refers only to persons' right to legal protection from 'arbitrary or unlawful *interference*' with their privacy (emphasis added), positive duties to facilitate people's mental self-determination or mental control may also arise under this right in certain circumstances.

8 For instance, recall that the ECtHR in *Sengtes/The Netherlands* observed that Article 8 ECHR may impose positive obligations on states when a 'direct and immediate link' exists between the measures sought by an applicant and their private life, and when 'the State's failure to adopt [such] measures interferes with that individual's right to personal development', see ECtHR 8 July 2003, 27677/02 (*Sengtes/The Netherlands*), pp. 5–6.

8.3 INTERVENTIONS OF WHICH THE PERMISSIBILITY IS UNCLEAR

As follows from the analyses in Chapters 2, 3 and 4, the question about the permissibility of *non-consensual* use of neurotechnology for rehabilitation is complex.

On first inspection, non-consensual neurorehabilitation might seem like a paradigmatically impermissible interference with the person's body and mind, and as such, something that is clearly impermissible. The Human Rights Council Advisory Committee seems to lean towards such a position. For example, they write that the prohibition of ill-treatment pursuant to Article 7 ICCPR "provides offenders with protection against brain-reading and brain-writing techniques, particularly 'neurocorrectives', which constitute an inherently degrading treatment *in all circumstances*".[9] Furthermore, they hold that "[t]he forceful extraction of information from detainees or offenders through the use of neurotechnologies is prohibited".[10] Similar claims have been made based on the right to freedom of thought.[11]

Our analysis provides reasons for more nuance, however. The human rights protection of personal interests over brains and minds, such as the interest in mental privacy, personal integrity and identity, has both a qualified and absolute dimension.[12] First and foremost, the protection of these interests is covered by qualified rights – in particular, the right to privacy and personal integrity. Furthermore, a limited number of (grave) interferences can engage additional protection within the absolute dimension – particularly from the prohibition of ill-treatment and the right to freedom of thought and, to some extent, by the arguably absolute protection of the core essence of privacy and integrity rights.

As far as non-invasive brain stimulation and neuroprediction is concerned, we found that their non-consensual use is unlikely to infringe either the prohibition of ill-treatment or the right to freedom of thought. Regarding the prohibition of ill-treatment, the bodily and mental effects of non-invasive brain stimulation may often be too subtle to qualify as the infliction of severe physical pain or mental suffering, failing to attain the prohibition's minimum level of severity threshold. Furthermore, when embedded in a larger and diverse rehabilitation programme, complemented by interventions that actively engage the person – as ends in themselves, not only as

[9] Advisory Committee, UNHRC, Impact, opportunities and challenges of neurotechnology with regard to the promotion and protection of all human rights, A/HRC/AC/31/CRP.1 (8 August 2024), par. 34 (emphasis added).

[10] Advisory Committee, UNHRC, Impact, opportunities and challenges of neurotechnology with regard to the promotion and protection of all human rights, A/HRC/AC/31/CRP.1 (8 August 2024), par. 34 (emphasis added), par. 48.

[11] Bublitz 2014; Bublitz 2018. Cf. UN Special Rapporteur on the Freedom of religion or belief, 5 October 2021, A/76/380.

[12] Cf. Bublitz 2024, speaking of the 'multi-layered protection of the person' in established human rights law.

means – the risk of disrespecting human dignity by objectification will reasonably be reduced.

Regarding the right to freedom of thought, we argued that at least part of the mental phenomena relevant to the neurotechnological assessment and/or reduction of a person's recidivism risk – such as certain tendencies, behavioural control, empathic abilities and emotional responses – do not qualify as "thoughts" in the meaning of this right. Hence, when such mental phenomena are the targets of non-consensual neurorehabilitation, the right to freedom of thought is unlikely to be infringed.

Still, in most cases, non-consensual neurorehabilitation will infringe one or more qualified rights and are therefore prima facie prohibited. In particular, they may infringe the right to (mental) privacy, bodily and mental integrity, and, in some cases, the right to personal identity. These are all inherent in the umbrella rights to privacy and to private life pursuant to Article 17 ICCPR and 8 ECHR. Whether an infringement of these qualified rights will constitute a rights *violation* – rendering a neurotechnological interference impermissible – depends on an ultimate *balancing* of competing interests, which, in turn, depends on the facts and circumstances of the individual case.

This is no neutral balancing act. Specific restrictions and requirements apply. To be justified, an infringement of the qualified rights to mental privacy and personal integrity should have a non-arbitrary basis in the law and must be proportionate to a legitimate aim, such as crime prevention. Consequently, the permissibility of neurotechnological interventions that infringe these qualified human rights is largely unclear, as it strongly depends on the circumstances of the individual case. Still, some general aspects of the balancing act can be considered.

First, as discussed, the more *severe* a rights infringement, the more substantial the reasons must be for its justification. Applying this rule to preventive measures in the context of criminal justice often implies that severe rights infringements can only be justified to prevent serious crimes. Assuming that both neuroprediction and neurointerventions aim to contribute to preventing future crime, this means that, to be justified, the interference with a convicted person's privacy, personal integrity and/or identity should be proportionate to the severity of the harm the authorities aim to protect against.

For example, we argued that the *bodily* interference of non-invasive brain stimulation will often be minor. Such minor bodily interference could reasonably be considered proportionate to the prevention of a variety of non-trivial criminal offences. Meanwhile, we also argued that the *mental* effects of these interventions may be significant, which could lead to a severe infringement of the right to mental integrity. If such infringements can be justified at all, their justification would require weighty reasons, such as the prevention of severe crimes like murder, rape or abuse.

However, since the right to mental integrity is currently underdeveloped, it is unclear how exactly the severity of infringements of this right should be assessed. We suggested the potential relevance of the directness of a mental interference and the level of mental harm that it causes. If the primary aim of a right to mental integrity is to protect *autonomy* over mental states and processes, then it is plausible that the less mental *control* an intervention leaves to the affected person, the more severe the infringement of the right to mental integrity can be considered to be. If we assume that, generally, direct interventions leave less control over mental states than indirect interventions, this would imply that, in general, stronger reasons are needed to justify infringements through direct interventions compared to indirect interventions. And when an infringement of the right to mental integrity entails additional mental harm, such as anxiety, stress or discomfort as a side effect of medication or brain stimulation, this likely adds to the severity of the rights infringement, therefore requiring more substantial reasons for justification.

The tools we considered in the context of neurorehabilitation – such as tDCS, TMS and psychopharmaceutical interventions – are of a direct nature as they target brain processes. The mental changes they induce leave little (if any) room for mental control to the person. Therefore, on the proposed account, these interventions could be considered to interfere with the person's mental autonomy to a significant degree, requiring weighty and very important reasons to be justified, such as reducing recidivism risks related to manslaughter or sexual abuse. Clearly, the need for such substantial reasons may further increase when the intervention entails harmful psychological side effects. Hence, whether such interferences can be permissible in some cases is an open question and the answer to it may strongly depend on the circumstances of each individual case.

Another consideration that could be relevant to the permissibility of neurorehabilitative tools that infringe qualified human rights is whether they interfere with the "core" or "essence" of those rights. The essence of rights doctrine has been employed for the interpretation and adjudication of human rights under both the ICCPR and the ECHR.[13] Respect for the essence of international human rights arguably follows from Article 5(1) ICCPR.[14] Furthermore, according to the Siracusa Principles on the Limitation and Derogation of Provisions in the International Covenant on Civil and Political Rights, permissible limitations of Covenant rights "shall not be interpreted so as to jeopardize the essence of the right concerned".[15] Likewise, considering Article 2(1) ICCPR, the Human Rights Committee states that, when restricting Covenant rights, "[s]tates must demonstrate their necessity and only take such measures as are proportionate to the pursuance of legitimate aims in order to ensure continuous and effective protection of Covenant rights. In no case may the

[13] Leijten 2017; Thielbörger 2019; Van Drooghenbroeck & Rizcallah 2019.

[14] Thielbörger 2019.

[15] E/CN.4/1985/4, Annex (1985) at A.2.

restrictions be applied or invoked in a manner that would *impair the essence* of a Covenant right".[16]

In the same vein, the ECtHR has stressed, on various occasions, that restrictions on human rights may not impair the "very essence" of those rights.[17] As Gerards observes, in some cases, it seems that the essence of the right constitutes an "inviolable and absolute core" that cannot be balanced away, operating as a real limit of limits.[18]

Meanwhile, in other cases, the ECtHR appears to favour a rather relative approach to the essence of rights, holding that, in principle, the margin of appreciation of states will be narrowed if the essence of a Convention right is affected. In Chapter 3 we saw that such core rights reasoning generally implies that the closer a certain aspect of a right relates to the central values underlying the ECHR – democracy and the rule of law, pluralism, human dignity and personal autonomy – the more important it can be considered to be. Meanwhile, the more a certain aspect is in the periphery of the right, the less weighty it can be taken to be. Because restrictions of core rights might threaten the realisation of the ECHR's central objectives, the ECtHR considers it justified to apply strict scrutiny.[19] For example, under the right to respect for private life pursuant to Article 8 ECHR, the ECtHR holds that when "a particularly important facet of an *individual's existence* or *identity* is at stake, the margin of appreciation allowed to the State will be restricted".[20]

Hence, when the non-consensual stimulation of a convicted person's brain interferes with behavioural traits or mental states that must be considered an essential aspect of the person's identity,[21] the state's margin of appreciation is plausibly narrow. In such cases, the national authorities have limited discretion in balancing the convicted person's private interests against the public interest of crime prevention.

Note, however, that in human rights law, the essence of rights doctrine has not yet come to full development. Its application by different courts and treaty bodies is often considered vague, unreliable and inconsistent.[22] Therefore, the implications of this doctrine for neurorehabilitation under both the ECHR and ICCPR are yet unclear.

[16] CCPR General Comment No. 31, par. at 6 (emphasis added).

[17] ECtHR 22 December 2020, 14305/17 (*Selahattin Demirtaş/Turkey (no. 2)*), par. 387; ECtHR 11 July 2002 (Christine Goodwin/UK), par. 99. See also Gerards 2023, pp. 365–366.

[18] Gerards 2023, pp. 366–367.

[19] Gerards 2023, pp. 272–273.

[20] ECtHR (GC) 10 April 2007, 6339/05 (*Evans/UK*), par. 77 (emphasis added); ECtHR (GC) 4 December 2007, 44362/04 (*Dickson/UK*), par. 78.

[21] For example, due to severe side effects of brain stimulation.

[22] See, for example, Van der Schyff 2008; Leijten 2017; Van Drooghenbroeck & Rizcallah 2019; Tridimas & Gentile 2020; Thielbörger 2019.

8.4 PLAUSIBLY IMPERMISSIBLE INTERVENTIONS

Based on our analysis, we can identify two general circumstances where non-consensual neurorehabilitation is impermissible under established human rights law – that is, when the interference (i) infringes and therefore violates an absolute human right or (ii) infringes a qualified right in a way that cannot reasonably be justified, therefore constituting a rights violation.

Non-consensual or mandatory employment of neurotechnology will be impermissible if it infringes the prohibition of ill-treatment or the right to freedom of thought – two rights that are generally considered to be absolute.[23] Although we concluded that the relevance of these rights and freedoms appear limited regarding the case of neurorehabilitation in criminal justice, they do set some clear and absolute boundaries. First, the involuntary employment of neurotechnology is impermissible if the effects (or side effects) are severe, for example, because it is very painful, dehumanizing, has dreadful impact on the person's health or severely affects the person's agency or autonomy, which all plausibly qualify as inhuman or at least degrading treatment, prohibited by Article 7 ICCPR and 3 ECHR.

Furthermore, non-consensual neurorehabilitation is impermissible when it changes or reveals the person's religious beliefs, conscientious convictions or their unexpressed thoughts. Although the precise interpretation of "thought" in human rights law is yet unsettled, some mental features clearly qualify, such as political and philosophical beliefs. Other candidates that might qualify include a person's deepest wishes and sexual desires. Non-consensual interference with such mental properties will infringe the right to freedom of thought and is therefore prohibited.

Finally, supposing the use of neurorehabilitation is safe and effective, has a non-arbitrary legal basis and pursues a legitimate interest,[24] its non-consensual use will be impermissible if it constitutes an *unnecessary* or *disproportionate* infringement of one of the considered qualified rights. Although considerations of necessity and proportionality usually require a balancing of interests in view of all relevant circumstances of the individual case, some clear instances of impermissible interference can be identified.

For example, when the targeted person is willing to submit to traditional forms of rehabilitation and these interventions promise to be equally effective, the non-consensual administration of neuropharmaceuticals or mandatory employment of brain stimulation is unnecessary and would, therefore, constitute an impermissible infringement of the relevant right, like the right to personal integrity. Furthermore, compulsory neurointerventions will likely be disproportionate when applied to persons who are not a severe threat to public safety. Likewise, interferences with

[23] Here we assume that these rights are absolute, while acknowledging that this has been contested. See, for example, Greer 2015; Ligthart 2025c.

[24] Such as preventing crime and disorder.

the person's mental privacy during neuroprediction can be excessive and unnecessary, for example, when targeting non-crime-relevant mental properties.

8.5 CLOSING REMARKS

Neurotechnological developments have led to a lively debate among scholars and policymakers regarding the protection of our minds. The freedom of our minds and the rights that protect them are of the utmost importance to humans and humanity.

One possible area of future application is of particular concern. This area is criminal justice and it is one of concern because it is a domain where non-consensual use of neurotechnology might be considered, where some limitations of rights and freedoms are legally permissible and where the stakes are typically high, both for convicted persons, victims and society at large.

Our analysis has focused on the application of neurotechnologies in this domain. More specifically, we considered neurorehabilitation in relation to human rights that protect the person – their body and mind. We set out to identify whether – and if so, how – neurorehabilitation might be used responsibly from a human rights perspective. As the key components of this analysis – the neurotechnologies and the legal frameworks – are evolving, our conclusions are only provisional.

Still, we conclude that current human rights protection of our bodies and minds is robust. At the same time, with the exception of certain areas, it is not absolute, meaning it will often require a balancing of competing interests. For instance, as we argued that neurointerventions for rehabilitative purposes may usually not target "thoughts" in a strict sense, but rather inclinations and preferences, it appears that absolute protection by the right to freedom of thought, although not impossible, is less likely. That means that the ultimate decision about the admissibility of such interventions would strongly rely on the applicable qualified rights, like the right to privacy and personal integrity. This means that the admissibility of these interventions will ultimately depend on the type of balancing discussed above. This may be reason to seek further protection, for instance in the form of reshaped human rights or by other means.

Emerging neurotechnologies do not only pose threats and create risks and, therefore, require legal protection. They also open up opportunities for people's health, rehabilitation and the enhancement of mental capabilities. Accordingly, we explored the existence and possible implications of *rights to* the application of neurotechnologies, at least to some forms of use.

Based on our analysis in Chapters 5, 6, and 7, we suggested that there may be situations where making safe and effective neurorehabilitation available to a given person – and delivering it when voluntary and competent consent to it is obtained – is not only plausibly permissible but perhaps even *required* from a human rights perspective. Meanwhile, that neurorehabilitation may be required from a human rights perspective receives little support from the case law so far. We suggested that states might have a positive obligation to offer neurorehabilitation when it is necessary (i) to counter the degenerative impact of imprisonment, (ii) to preserve genuine hope for release from prison or (iii) to preserve convicted persons' ability to socially contribute. Meanwhile, practical considerations may be relevant here: the likelihood of successful rights-based claims to neurorehabilitation is also influenced by resource constraints within which states operate.

Still, we feel it is highly important that positive rights receive attention in future debates about responsible use of neurotechnologies in criminal justice, together with the negative rights that protect us from unsolicited interference by others with our brains and minds.

References

Addo, K. & Grief, N., 'Does Article 3 of the European Convention on Human Rights Enshrine Absolute Rights?' *European Journal of International Law* 1998, 9, pp. 510–524.

Aharoni, E. et al., 'Predictive Accuracy in the Neuroprediction of Rearrest', *Society for Neuroscience* 2014, 9(4), pp. 332–336.

Aharoni, E. et al., 'Neuroprediction of Future Rearrest', *The Proceeding of the National Academy of Sciences* 2013, 110(15), pp. 6223–6228.

Ahmed, T. & de Jesús Butler, I., 'The European Union and Human Rights: An International Law Perspective', *European Journal of International Law* 2006, 17(4), pp. 771–801.

Akhlaghi, F., 'Transformative Experience and the Right to Revelatory Autonomy', *Analysis* 2023, 83(1), pp. 3–12.

Alegre, S., *Freedom to Think*, London: Atlantic Books 2022.

Alegre, S., 'Rethinking Freedom of Thought for the 21st Century', *European Human Rights Law Review* 2017, 3, pp. 221–233.

Alfino, M. & Mayes, G. R., 'Reconstructing the Right to Privacy', *Social Theory and Practice* 2003, 29(1), pp. 1–18.

Allen, A. L., 'Privacy-as-Data Control: Conceptual, Practical, and Moral Limits of the Paradigm', *Connecticut Law Review* 2000, 32, pp. 861–875.

Allen, C. H. et al., 'Hemodynamic Activity in the Limbic System Predicts Reoffending in Women', *Neuroimage: Clinical* 2022, 36, 103238.

Alper, M., Update on Prisoner Recidivism: A 9-Year Follow-Up Period (2005–2014), U.S. Department of Justice Office of Justice Programs Bureau of Justice Statistic, May 2018.

American Psychiatric Association, *Diagnostic and Statistical Manual of Mental Disorders: DSM-5* (5th ed.), 2013.

Andreasen, N. C., *Brave New Brain: Conquering Mental Illness in the Era of the Genome*, New York: Oxford University Press 2001.

Andrews, D. A. & Bonta, J., *The Psychology of Criminal Conduct* (4th ed.), Cincinnati: Anderson 2006.

Andrews, D. A., Bonta, J. & Hoge, R. D., 'Classification for Effective Rehabilitation: Rediscovering Psychology', *Criminal Justice and Behavior* 1990, 17(1), pp. 19–52.

Antón, C. B., 'Coercive Persuasion as a Specific Type of Violence in Criminal Law', *International Journal of Coercion Abuse & Manipulation* 2020, 1(1), pp. 61–72.

Archard, D., 'Informed Consent: Autonomy and Self-Ownership', *Journal of Applied Philosophy* 2008, 25(1), pp. 19–34.

Arenella, P., 'Schmerber and the Privilege against Self-incrimination: Reappraisal', *American Criminal Law Review* 1982, 20(1), pp. 31–62.

Ashworth, A. & Zedner, L., *Preventive Justice*, Oxford: Oxford University Press 2014.

Assary, E. et al., 'Gene-environment Interaction and Psychiatric Disorders: Review and Future Directions', *Seminars in Cell & Developmental Biology* 2018, 77, pp. 133–143.

Atherton, M., 'Locke's Theory of Personal Identity', *Midwest Studies in Philosophy* 1983, 8, pp. 273–294.

Ballesteros J. A. et al., 'Facial Emotion Recognition through Artificial Intelligence', *Frontiers in Computer Science* 2024, 6.

Bates, A. P., 'Privacy – A Useful Concept?' *Social Forces* 1964, 42(4), pp. 429–434.

Batterson, J. R. et al., 'A Refresher on Tourette Syndrome', *Missouri Medicine* 2014, 111(3), pp. 202–206.

Baumeister, R. F. & Leary, M. R., 'The Need to Belong: Desire for Interpersonal Attachments as a Fundamental Human Motivation', *Psychological Bulletin* 1995, 117(3), pp. 497–529.

Baylis, F., '"I Am Who I Am": On the Perceived Threats to Personal Identity from Deep Brain Stimulation', *Neuroethics* 2013, 6, pp. 513–526.

Bedard, H. L., 'The Potential for Bioprediction in Criminal Law', *The Colombia Science & Technology Law Review* 2017, 18(2), pp. 268–325.

Behan, D., 'Locke on Persons and Personal Identity', *Canadian Journal of Philosophy* 1979, 9, pp. 53–75.

Bellier, L. et al., 'Music Can Be Reconstructed from Human Auditory Cortex Activity Using Nonlinear Decoding Models', *PLOS Biology* 2023, 21(8), e3002176, pp. 1–27.

Benedetti-Isaac, J. C. et al., 'Deep Brain Stimulation in the Posteromedial Hypothalamic Nuclei in Refractory Aggressiveness: Post-Surgical Results of 19 Cases', *The International Journal of Neuropsychopharmacology* 2021, 24(12), pp. 977–978.

Benn, S. I., 'Privacy, Freedom, and Respect for Persons', in Schoeman, F. D. (ed.), *Philosophical Dimensions of Privacy: An Anthology*, Cambridge: Cambridge University Press 1984, p. 223–244.

Bentham, J., *The Principles of Morals and Legislation*, Prometheus Books 1988 [1780].

Biber, S. E. & Capasso, M., 'The Right to Mental Integrity in the Age of Artificial Intelligence: Cognitive Human Enhancement Technologies', in Custers, B. & Fosch-Villaronga, E. (eds.), *Law and Artificial Intelligence*, Berlin: TMC Asser Press 2022, pp. 503–520.

Bijlsma, J. et al., 'Legal Insanity and Risk: An International Perspective on the Justification of Indeterminate Preventive Commitment', *International Journal of Law and Psychiatry* 2019, Sep–Oct;66:101462.

Birgden, A., 'Therapeutic Jurisprudence and "Good Lives": A Rehabilitation Framework for Corrections', *Australian Psychologist* 2002, 37(3), pp. 180–186.

Birks, D., 'Can Neurointerventions Communicate Censure? (And So What If They Can't?)', in Birks, D. & Douglas, T. (eds.), *Treatment for Crime: Philosophical Essays on Neurointerventions in Criminal Justice*, Oxford: Oxford University Press 2018, pp. 351–368.

Birks, D. & Buyx, A., 'Punishing Intentions and Neurointerventions', The *American Journal of Bioethics Neuroscience* 2018, 9(3), pp. 133–143.

Birks, D. & Douglas, T. (eds.), *Treatment for Crime: Philosophical Essays on Neurointerventions in Criminal Justice*, Oxford: Oxford University Press 2018.

Bishay, A. E. et al., 'Global Economic Evaluation of the Reported Costs of Deep Brain Stimulation', *Stereotactic and Functional Neurosurgery* 2024, 102(4), pp. 257–274.

Blitz, M. J., *Searching Minds by Scanning Brains*, Palgrave Macmillan: Cham 2017.

Bloustein, E., 'Privacy as an Aspect of Human Dignity: An Answer to Dean Prosser', in Schoeman, F. D. (ed.), *Philosophical Dimensions of Privacy: An Anthology*, Cambridge: Cambridge University Press 1984, pp. 156–202.

Blumenthal-Barby, J. & Ubel, P., 'Neurorights in Question: Rethinking the Concept of Mental Integrity', *Journal of Medical Ethics* 2024, 50(10), pp. 670–675.

Boire, R. G., 'On Cognitive Liberty Part I', *Journal of Cognitive Liberties* 2000, 1(1), pp. 7–13.

Bolton, D., *What Is Mental Disorder? An Essay in Philosophy, Science, and Values*, Oxford: Oxford University Press 2008.

Bomann-Larsen, L., 'Voluntary Rehabilitation? On Neurotechnological Behavioural Treatment, Valid Consent and (In)appropriate Offers', *Neuroethics* 2013, 6(1), pp. 65–77. https://doi.org/10.1007/s12152-011-9105-9.

Bonta, J., 'The Risk-Need-Responsivity Model: 1990 to the Present' (Academic Insights 2023/06, pp. 1–13), Manchester: HM Inspectorate of Probation 2023.

Boonin, D., *The Problem of Punishment*, New York: Cambridge University Press 2008.

Boorse, C., 'What a Theory of Mental Health Should Be', *Journal for the Theory of Social Behaviour* 1976, 6(1), pp. 61–84.

Bou-Sfia, S., 'The Right to Identity in the European Convention on Human Rights', in Boone, I. & Vonk, M. (eds.), *The Right to Identity and Access to Information on Genetic Origin and Parentage*, Cambridge: Intersentia 2024, pp. 7–31.

Brownlee, K., *Being Sure of Each Other: An Essay on Social rights and Freedoms*, Oxford: Oxford University Press 2020.

Brownlee, K., 'Acting Defensively for the Sake of Our Attacker', *Journal of Moral Philosophy* 2019, 2, pp. 105–130.

Brownlee, K., 'Don't Call People "Rapists": On the Social Contribution Injustice of Punishment', *Current Legal Problems* 2016a, 69(1), pp. 327–352.

Brownlee, K., 'The Lonely Heart Breaks: On the Right to Be a Social Contributor', *Supplementary Volume – Aristotelian Society* 2016b, 90(1), pp. 27–48.

Brownlee, K., Jenkins, D. & Neal, A. (eds.), *Being Social: The Philosophy of Social Human Rights*, Oxford: Oxford University Press 2022.

Brownsword, B., 'Regulating Brain Imaging: Questions of Privacy, Informed Consent, and Human Dignity', in Richmond, S., Rees, G. & Edwards, S. J. L. (eds.), *I Know What You're Thinking*, Croydon: Oxford University Press 2012.

Brugman, D. & Bink, M. D., 'Effects of the EQUIP Peer Intervention Program on Self-serving Cognitive Distortions and Recidivism among Delinquent Male Adolescents', *Psychology, Crime & Law* 2011, 17(4), pp. 345–358.

Bublitz, J. C., 'What Is Thought? Interpreting and Constructing Article 18 ICCPR in Light of the Vienna Convention', in Blitz, M. & Bublitz, J. C. (eds.), *The Law and Ethics of Freedom of Thought Vol. 2: Cognitive Liberty and Privacy*, Cham: Palgrave Macmillan 2025 (in press).

Bublitz, J. C., 'Neurotechnologies and Human Rights: Restating and Reaffirming the Multi-layered Protection of the Person', *The International Journal of Human Rights* 2024, 28(5), pp. 782–807.

Bublitz, J. C., 'Novel Neurorights: From Nonsense to Substance', *Neuroethics* 2022, 15(7), pp. 1–15.

Bublitz, J. C., 'Freedom of Thought as an International Human Right: Elements of a Theory of a Living Right', in Blitz, M. J. & Bublitz, J. C. (eds.), *The Law and Ethics of Freedom of Thought, Vol. 1*, Cham: Palgrave Macmillan 2021, pp. 49–101.

Bublitz, J. C., 'The Nascent Right to Psychological Integrity and Mental Self-Determination', in Von Arnauld, A., Von der Decken, K. & Susi, M. (eds.), *The Cambridge Handbook of New Human Rights: Recognition, Novelty, Rhetoric*, Padstow: Cambridge University Press 2020a, pp. 387–403.

Bublitz, J. C., 'Why Means Matter', in Vincent, N. A., Nadelhoffer, T. & McCay, A. (eds.), *Neurointerventions and the Law: Regulating Human Mental Capacity*, New York: Oxford University Press 2020b, pp. 49–88.

Bublitz, J. C., '"The Soul Is in the Prison of the Body" – Mandatory Moral Enhancement, Punishment & Rights against Neuro-rehabilitation', in Birks, D. & Douglas, T. (eds.), *Treatment for Crime: Philosophical Essays on Neurointerventions in Criminal Justice*, New York: Oxford University Press 2018, pp. 289–320.

Bublitz, J. C., 'Cognitive Liberty or the International Human Right to Freedom of Thought', in Clausen, J. & Levy, N. (eds.), *Handbook of Neuroethics*, Dordrecht: Springer Netherlands 2015, pp. 1309–1333.

Bublitz, J. C., 'Freedom of Thought in the Age of Neuroscience', *Archiv Für Rechts- Und Sozialphilosophie* 2014, 100, pp. 1–25.

Bublitz, J. C., 'My Mind Is Mine!? Cognitive Liberty as a Legal Concept', in Hildt, E. & Francke, A. (eds.), *Cognitive Enhancement*, Dordrecht: Springer Netherlands 2013, pp. 233–264.

Bublitz, J. C. & Ligthart, S., 'The New Regulation of Non-Medical Neurotechnologies in the European Union: Overview and Reflection', *Journal of Law and the Biosciences* 2024, 11(2), lsae021.

Bublitz, J. C. & Merkel, R., 'Crimes against Minds: On Mental Manipulations, Harms and a Human Right to Mental Self-Determination', *Criminal Law and Philosophy* 2014, 8(1), pp. 51–71. https://doi.org/10.1007/s11572-012-9172-y.

Buchanan, A., *The Heart of Human Rights*, Oxford: Oxford University Press 2013.

Buchanan, A. E., 'The Right to a Decent Minimum of Health Care', *Philosophy & Public Affairs* 1984, 13(1), pp. 55–78.

Buchanan, J. M., *Liberty, Market, and State: Political Economy in the 1980s*, New York: New York University Press 1986.

Buelens, W., Herijgers, C. & Illegems, S., 'The View of the European Court of Human Rights on Competent Patients' Right of Informed Consent: Research in the Light of Article 3 and 8 of the European Convention on Human Rights', *European Journal of Health Law* 2016, 23(5), pp. 481–509.

Bychawska-Siniarska, D., *Protecting the Right to Freedom of Expression under the European Convention on Human Rights: A Handbook for Legal Practitioners*, Strasbourg: Council of Europe 2017.

Cabrera, L. Y., Evans, E. L. & Hamilton, R. H., 'Ethics of the Electrified Mind: Defining Issues and Perspectives on the Principled Use of Brain Stimulation in Medical Research and Clinical Care', *Brain Topography* 2014, 27, pp. 33–45.

Calhoun, C., 'Social Connections, Social Contributions, and Why They Matter: Comments on Being Sure of Each Other', *Criminal Law and Philosophy* 2023, 17(2), pp. 453–462.

Campbell, T., 'Moral Dimensions of Human Rights', in Campbell, T. & Miller, S. (eds.), *Human Rights and the Moral Responsibilities of Corporate and Public Sector Organisations*, Springer: Dordrecht 2004, pp. 11–30.

Card, A. J., 'Moving beyond the WHO Definition of Health: A New Perspective for an Aging World and the Emerging Era of Value-Based Care', *World Medical & Health Policy* 2017, 9, pp. 127–137.

Caruso, D. G., *Rejecting Retributivism: Free Will, Punishment and Criminal Justice*, New York: Cambridge University Press 2021.

Carvalho, H., *The Preventive Turn in Criminal Law*, Oxford: Oxford University Press 2017.

Cassinadri, C., 'The Right to Mental Integrity: Multidimensional, Multilayered and Extended', *Neuroethics* 2025, 18, pp. 1–21.

Caulfield, K. A. et al., 'A Transdiagnostic Review of Safety, Efficacy, and Parameter Space in Accelerated Transcranial Magnetic Stimulation', *Journal of Psychiatric Research* 2022, 152, pp. 384–396.

Chail, A., 'Transcranial Magnetic Stimulation: A Review of Its Evolution and Current Applications', *Industrial Psychiatry Journal* 2018, 27(2).

Chamberlain, C., 'What Am I? Descartes's Various Ways of Considering the Self', *Journal of Modern Philosophy* 2020, 2(1), pp. 1–30.

Chang, E. F., Englot, D. J. & Vadera, S., 'Minimally Invasive Surgical Approaches for Temporal Lobe Epilepsy', *Epilepsy & Behavior* 2015, 47, pp. 24–33.

Chang, Z. et al., 'Association between Prescription of Major Psychotropic Medications and Violent Reoffending after Prison Release', *The Journal of American Medical Association* 2016, 316(17), pp. 1798–1807.

Chase, H. W. et al., 'Transcranial Direct Current Stimulation: A Roadmap for Research, from Mechanism of Action to Clinical Implementation', *Molecular Psychiatry* 2020, 25(2), pp. 397–407.

Chatham, A. N., Shafi, H. & Hermida, A. P., 'The Use of ECT in the Elderly-Looking Beyond Depression', *Current Psychiatry Reports* 2022, 24(9), pp. 451–461.

Chesak, J., 'What Psychedelics Legalisation and Decriminalisation Looks Like around the World', www.bbc.com, 21 March 2024.

Chew, C. et al., 'Biological Interventions for Crime Prevention', in Birks, D. & Douglas, T. (eds.), *Treatment for Crime: Philosophical Essays on Neurointerventions in Criminal Justice*, New York: Oxford University Press 2018, pp. 11–43.

Choy, O., Focquaert, F. & Raine, A., 'Benign Biological Interventions to Reduce Offending', *Neuroethics* 2020, 13(1), pp. 29–41.

Christoffersen, J., *Fair Balance: Proportionality, Subsidiarity and Primarity in the European Convention on Human Rights*, Leiden: Martinus Nijhoff 2009.

Churchland, P., 'The Brain and Its Self', *Proceedings of the American Philosophical Society* 2011, 155(1), pp. 41–50.

Cid, J., 'Is Imprisonment Criminogenic? A Comparative Study of Recidivism Rates between Prison and Suspended Prison Sanctions', *European Journal of Criminology* 2009, 6(6), pp. 459–480.

Coppola, F., 'The Brain in Solitude: An(other) Eighth Amendment Challenge to Solitary Confinement', *Journal of Law and the Biosciences* 2019, 6(1), pp. 184–225.

Coppola, F. & Martufi, A. (eds.), *Social Rehabilitation and Criminal Justice*, New York: Routledge 2024.

Corlett, J. A., 'The Nature and Value of the Moral Right to Privacy', *Public Affairs Quarterly* 2002, 16(4), pp. 329–350.

Cotrena, C. et al., 'Executive Functions and Memory in Bipolar Disorders I and II: New Insights from Meta-Analytic Results', *Acta Psychiatrica Scandinavica* 2020, 141(2), pp. 110–130.

Craig, J. N., 'Incarceration, Direct Brain Intervention, and the Right to Mental Integrity – a Reply to Thomas Douglas', *Neuroethics* 2016, 9(2), pp. 107–118.

Crewe, B. & Ievins, A., 'The Prison as a Reinventive Institution', *Theoretical Criminology* 2020, 24(4), pp. 568–589.

Crisp, R., 'Hedonism Reconsidered', *Philosophy and Phenomenological Research* 2006, 73(3), pp. 619–645.

Cunha, O. et al., 'The Impact of Imprisonment on Individuals' Mental Health and Society Reintegration: Study Protocol', *BMC Psychology* 2023, 11(215), pp. 1–6.

Daniels, N., *Just Health: Meeting Health Needs Fairly*, Cambridge: Cambridge University Press 2008.

Dann, B. M., 'The Fifth Amendment Privilege against Self-Incrimination: Extorting Physical Evidence from a Suspect', *Southern California Law Review* 1970, 43, pp. 597–630.

Davis, A. Y., *Are Prisons Obsolete?* New York: Seven Stories Press 2003.

Day, A., Tucker, K. & Howells, K., 'Coerced Offender Rehabilitation – a Defensible Practice?' *Psychology, Crime & Law* 2004, 10(3), pp. 259–269.

De Groot, N. F., Tesink, V. & Meynen, G., 'Nissenbaum and Neurorights: The Jury Is Still Out', *The American Journal of Bioethics Neuroscience* 2024, 15(2), pp. 136–138.

De Jesus, L. M., '*Artavia Murillo v. Costa Rica*: The Inter-American Court on Human Rights' Promotion of Non-Existent Human Rights Obligations to Authorize Artificial Reproductive Technologies', *UCLA Journal of International Law and Foreign Affairs* 2014, 18(2), pp. 275–302.

De Jong, C. D., *The Freedom of Thought, Conscience and Religion or belief in the United Nations (1946–1992)*, Antwerp: Intersentia 2000.

De Vries, K., 'Right to Respect for Private and Family Life', in van Dijk, P. et al. (eds.), *Theory and Practice of the European Convention on Human Rights*, Cambridge: Intersentia 2018, pp. 667–734.

DeGrazia, D., 'Enhancement Technologies and Human Identity, *Journal of Medicine and Philosophy* 2005, 30, pp. 261–283.

DeGrazia, D., *Human Identity and Bioethics*, Cambridge: Cambridge University Press 2005.

Delfin, C. et al., 'Prediction of Recidivism in a Long-Term Follow-Up of Forensic Psychiatric Patients: Incremental Effects of Neuroimaging Data', *PLoS ONE* 2019, 14(5).

Delisi, M., 'Revisiting Lombroso', in Cullen, F. T. & Wilcox, P. (eds.), *The Oxford Handbook of Criminological Theory*, Oxford: Oxford University Press 2015, pp. 5–21.

Denson, T. F. et al., 'A Meta-Analysis of the Effects of Transcranial Direct Current Stimulation on Anger and Aggression', *Aggressive Behavior* 2025, 51(4), pp. 1–16.

Denson, T. F., Griffiths M. & Smith, L., 'Attitudes toward Incarceration, Neuronormalization and Psychological Treatment for Violent Offenders', *Psychology, Crime & Law* 2024, pp. 1–20.

DeVeaux, M., 'The Trauma of the Incarceration Experience', *Harvard Civil Rights – Civil Liberties Law Review* 2013, 48(1), pp. 257–277.

DeWall, C. N., *The Oxford Handbook of Social Exclusion*, Oxford: Oxford University Press 2013.

Donders, Y., 'The Right to Enjoy the Benefits of Scientific Progress: In Search of State Obligations in Relation to Health', *Medicine Health Care and Philosophy* 2011, 14, pp. 371–381.

Dore-Horgan, E., 'Do Criminal Offenders Have a Right to Neurorehabilitation?' *Criminal Law and Philosophy* 2023, 17, pp. 429–451.

Dore-Horgan, E. & Douglas, T., 'Thinking What We Want: A Moral Right to Acquire Control over Our Thoughts', in Blitz, M. & Bublitz, J. C. (eds.), *The Law and Ethics of Freedom of Thought Vol. 2: Cognitive Liberty and Privacy*, Cham: Palgrave Macmillan 2025 (in press).

Douglas, T., 'An Intuitive, Abductive Argument for a Right against Mental Interference', *The Journal of Ethics* 2024, 29, pp. 133–115.

Douglas, T., 'If Nudges Treat Their Targets as Rational Agents, Nonconsensual Neurointerventions Can Too', *Ethic Theory Moral Prac* 2022, 25, pp. 36–384.

Douglas, T., 'Neural and Environmental Modulation of Motivation: What's the Moral Difference?' in Birks, D. & Douglas, T. (eds.), *Treatment for Crime*, New York: Oxford University Press 2018, pp. 208–223.

Douglas, T. & Forsberg, L., 'Three Rationales for a Legal Right to Mental Integrity', in Ligthart, S. et al. (eds.), *Neurolaw: Advances in Neuroscience, Justice, and Security*, Cham: Palgrave Macmillan 2021, pp. 179–201.

Douglas, T. et al., 'Risk Assessment Tools in Criminal Justice and Forensic Psychiatry', *European Psychiatry* 2017, 42, pp. 134–137.
Dressler, J., Michaels, A. C. & Simmons, R., *Understanding Criminal Procedure. Volume 1: Investigation*, Durham: Carolina Academic Press 2021.
Duff, A., *Punishment, Communication and Community*, Oxford: Oxford University Press 2001.
Duffy, P. J., 'Article 3 of the European Convention on Human Rights', *International and Comparative Law Quarterly* 1983, 32, pp. 316–346.
Dworkin, R., 'Autonomy and the Demented Self', *The Milbank Quarterly* 1986, 64(Suppl. 2), pp. 4–16.
Ebrahimi, C. et al., 'Augmenting Extinction Learning with D-Cycloserine Reduces Return of Fear: A Randomized, Placebo-Controlled fMRI Study', *Neuropsychopharmacology* 2020, 45(3), pp. 499–506.
Ellis, A., *The Philosophy of Punishment*, Exeter: Imprint Academic 2012.
Ellis, A., 'A Deterrence Theory of Punishment', *The Philosophical Quarterly* 2003, 53(212), pp. 337–351.
Enticott, P. G. et al., 'Repetitive Transcranial Magnetic Stimulation (rTMS) in Autism Spectrum Disorder: Protocol for a Multicentre Randomised Controlled Clinical Trial', *BMJ Open* 2021, 11(7), e046830.
Escobar Vidarte, O. A. et al., 'Deep Brain Stimulation for Severe and Intractable Aggressive Behavior', *Stereotactic Functional Neurosurgery* 2022, 100(4), pp. 210–213.
Esmaili, M. et al., 'Executive Functions and Public Health: A Narrative Review', *Iranian Journal of Public Health* 2023, 52(8), pp. 1589–1599.
Evans, C., *Freedom of Religion under the European Convention on Human Rights*, New York: Oxford University Press 2001.
Evans, M. D., *Religious Liberty and International Law in Europe*, Cambridge: Cambridge University Press 1997.
Ewing, A., *The Morality of Punishment* (Routledge Revivals), Oxon: Routledge 2013.
Fallin, M., Whooley, O. & Barker, K. K., 'Criminalizing the Brain: Neurocriminology and the Production of Strategic Ignorance', *BioSocieties* 2019, 14, pp. 438–462.
Farah, M. J., 'Emerging Ethical Issues in Neuroscience', *Nature Neuroscience* 2002, 5(11), pp. 1123–1129.
Farahany, N. A., *The Battle for Your Brain: Defending the Right to Think Freely in the Age of Neurotechnology*, New York: St. Martin's Press 2023.
Farahany, N. A., 'The Costs of Changing Our Minds', *Emory Law Journal* 2019, 69(1), pp. 75–110.
Farahany, N. A., 'Searching Secrets', *University of Pennsylvania Law Review* 2012a, 160, pp. 1239–1307.
Farahany, N. A., 'Incriminating Thoughts', *Stanford Law Review* 2012b, 64, pp. 351–408.
Faria, M., 'Violence, Mental Illness, and the Brain – a Brief History of Psychosurgery: Part 1 – From Trephination to Lobotomy', *Surgical Neurology International* 2013, 4(49).
Farrell, M. et al., 'Methadone Maintenance Treatment in Opiate Dependence: A Review', *British Medical Journal* 1994, 309, pp. 997–1001.
Favril, L., Shaw, J. & Fazel, S., 'Prevalence and Risk factors for Suicide Attempts in Prison', *Clinical Psychology Review* 2022, 97.
Fazel, S. et al., 'Mental Health of Prisoners: Prevalence, Adverse Outcomes, and Interventions', *Lancet Psychiatry* 2016, 3(9), pp. 871–881.
Fazel, S. et al., 'Use of Risk Assessment Instruments to Predict Violence and Antisocial Behaviour in 73 Samples Involving 24 827 People: Systematic Review and Meta-Analysis', *British Medical Journal* 2012, 345, pp. 1–12.

Feinberg, J., *The Moral Limits of the Criminal Law Volume 3: Harm to Self*, New York: Oxford University Press 1989.

Feinberg, J., *Doing and Deserving: Essays in the Theory of Responsibility*, Princeton: Princeton University Press 1970.

Feldman, D., 'The Developing Scope of Article 8 of the European Convention on Human Rights', *European Human Rights Law Review* 1997, 3, pp. 265–274.

Felthous, A. R. et al., 'Pharmacotherapy of Primary Impulsive Aggression in Violent Criminal Offenders', *Frontiers in Psychology* 2021, 12.

Fernandes, B., Wright, M. & Essau, C. A., 'The Role of Emotion Regulation and Executive Functioning in the Intervention Outcome of Children with Emotional and Behavioural Problems', *Children* 2023, 10(1), pp. 139–151.

Fikfak, V. & Izvorova, L., 'Language and Persuasion: Human Dignity at the European Court of Human Rights', *Human Rights Law Review* 2022, 22(3), ngac018, pp. 1–24.

Fineman, M. A., 'The Vulnerable Subject: Anchoring Equality in the Human Condition', *Yale Journal of Law & Feminism* 2008, 20(1), pp. 1–23.

First, M. B. et al., 'DSM-5-TR: Overview of What's New and What's Changed', *World Psychiatry* 2022, 21(2), pp. 218–219.

Flanagan, T. J., 'Dealing with Long-Term Confinement: Adaptive Strategies and Perspectives among Long-Term Prisoners', *Criminal Justice and Behavior* 1981, 8(2), pp. 201–222.

Fletcher, G., 'A Fresh Start for the Objective-List Theory of Well-Being', *Utilitas* 2013, 25(2), pp. 206–220.

Focquaert, F. & Schermer, M., 'Moral Enhancement: Do Means Matter Morally?' *Neuroethics* 2015, 8, pp. 139–151.

Focquaert, F., Van Assche, K. & Sterckx, S., 'Offering Neurointerventions to Offenders with Cognitive-Emotional Impairments: Ethical and Criminal Justice Aspects', in Vincent N. A., Nadelhoffer, T. & McCay, A. (eds.), *Neurointerventions and the Law*, New York: Oxford University Press 2020, pp. 127–148.

Foltynie, T. et al., 'Medical, Surgical, and Physical Treatments for Parkinson's Disease', *Lancet* 2024, 403(10423), pp. 305–324.

Forsberg, L., 'Anti-libidinal Interventions and Human Rights', *Human Rights Law Review* 2021, 21(2), pp. 384–408.

Forsberg, L. & Douglas, T., 'What Is Criminal Rehabilitation?' *Criminal Law and Philosophy* 2022, 16, pp. 103–126.

Forstmann, M. et al., 'Transformative Experience and Social Connectedness Mediate the Mood-Enhancing Effects of Psychedelic Use in Naturalistic Settings', *Proceedings of the National Academy of Sciences* 2020, 117(5), pp. 2338–2346.

Fortune, C. A. & Ward, T., 'The Rehabilitation of Offenders: Striving for Good Lives, Desistance, and Risk Reduction', in Helfgott, J. (ed.), *Criminal Psychology*, New York: Praeger 2013.

Foucault, M., *Discipline and Punish: The Birth of the Prison* (1975), translated and republished by Penguin Classics 2020.

Fourie, C., 'Sufficiency of Capabilities, Social Equality, and Two-Tiered Health Care Systems', in Fourie, C. & Rid, A. (eds.), *What Is Enough?: Sufficiency, Justice, and Health*, New York: Oxford University Press 2016, pp. 185–204.

Francis, D. L. et al., 'Why Should We Invest in Health? Evidence from the Lens of Second-Order Benefits of Health', *Journal of Global Health Reports* 2023, 7, e2023059.

Frank, M. J. et al., 'Hold Your Horses: Impulsivity, Deep Brain Stimulation, and Medication in Parkinsonism', *Science* 2007, 318, pp. 1309–1312.

Franzini, A. et al., 'Deep-Brain Stimulation for Aggressive and Disruptive Behavior', *World Neurosurgery* 2013, 80(3–4).
Frase, R. S. et al., 'Proportionality of Punishment in Common Law Jurisdictions and in Germany', in Ambos, K. et al. (eds.), *Core Concepts in Criminal Law and Criminal Justice*, Cambridge: Cambridge University Press 2020, pp. 213–260.
Freeman, S., 'Problems with Some Consequentialist Arguments for Basic Rights', in Ernst, G. & Heilinger, J. C. (eds), *The Philosophy if Human Rights: Contemporary Controversies*, Berlin: De Gruyter 2012, pp. 107–128.
Fried, C., 'Privacy', *The Yale Law Journal*, 1968, 77, pp. 475–492.
Friedman, A. K. et al., 'KCNQ Channel Openers Reverse Depressive Symptoms via an Active Resilience Mechanism', *Nature Communications* 2016, 7(1), pp. 1–7.
Fuss, J. et al., 'Deep Brain Stimulation to Reduce Sexual Drive', *Journal of Psychiatry and Neuroscience* 2015, 40, pp. 429–431.
Gable, L. & Gostin, L. O., 'Mental Health as a Human Right', *Wayne State University Law School Legal Studies Research Paper Series* 2009, 9(15), pp. 252–253.
Galderisi, S. et al., 'Toward a New Definition of Mental Health', *World Psychiatry* 2015, 14, pp. 231–233.
Galligan, D. J., 'The Right to Silence Reconsidered', *Current Legal Problems* 1988, 41(1), pp. 69–92.
Garofalo, M., 'Family Therapy in Corrections: Implications for Reentry into the Community', *Journal of Correctional Health Care* 2020, 26(3), pp. 240–248.
Gerards, J., *General Principles of the European Convention on Human Rights*, Cambridge: Cambridge University Press 2023.
Gerards, J., 'The Scope of ECHR Rights and Institutional Concerns', in Brems, E. & Gerards, J. (eds.), *Shaping Rights in the ECHR: The Role of the European Court of Human Rights in Determining the Scope of Human Rights*, Cambridge: Cambridge University Press 2013, pp. 84–106.
Gerety, T., 'Redefining Privacy', *Harvard Civil Rights-Civil Liberties Law Review* 1977, 12(2), pp. 233–296.
Gerstein, R. S., 'Privacy and Self-incrimination', *Ethics* 1970, 80(2), pp. 87–101.
Gilbert, F., Ienca, M. & Cook, M., 'How I Became Myself after Merging with a Computer: Does Human-Machine Symbiosis Raise Human Rights Issues?' *Brain Stimulation* 2023, 16, pp. 783–789.
Gilbert, F., Viaña, J. N. M. & Ineichen, C., 'Deflating the "DBS Causes Personality Changes" Bubble' *Neuroethics* 2021, 14, pp. 1–17.
Gilbert, F. et al., 'I Miss Being Me: Phenomenological Effects of Deep Brain Stimulation', *The American Journal of Bioethics Neuroscience* 2017, 8(2), pp. 96–109.
Giustino, T. F., Fitzgerald, P. J. & Maren, S., 'Revisiting Propranolol and PTSD: Memory Erasure or Extinction Enhancement?' *Neurobiology of Learning and Memory* 2016, 130, pp. 26–33.
Glannon, W., 'Stimulating Brains, Altering Minds', *Journal of Medical Ethics* 2009, 35, pp. 282–292.
Glenn, A. L. & Raine, S., 'Neurocriminology: Implications for the Punishment, Prediction and Prevention of Criminal Behaviour', *Nature Reviews Neuroscience* 2014, 15(1), pp. 54–63.
Glover, J. et al., *Fertility & the Family. The Glover Report on Reproductive Technologies to the European Commission*, London: Fourth Estate 1989.
Goddard, E., 'Deep Brain Stimulation through the "Lens of Agency": Clarifying Threats to Personal Identity from Neurological Intervention', *Neuroethics* 2017, 10, pp. 325–335.

Godien, D., *Short Guide to the European Convention on Human Rights*, Strasbourg: Council of Europe 2005.
Goering, S. et al., 'Recommendations for Responsible Development and Application of Neurotechnologies', *Neuroethics* 2021, 14, pp. 365–386.
Goethals, I. et al., 'Brain Activation Associated with Deep Brain Stimulation Causing Dissociation in a Patient with Tourette's Syndrome', *Journal of Trauma & Dissociation* 2008, 9(4), pp. 543–549.
Goffman, E., *Asylums: Essays on the Social Situation of Mental Patients and Other Inmates*, New York: Anchor Books 1961.
Golash, D., *The Case against Punishment: Retribution, Crime Prevention, and the Law*, New York: New York University Press 2005.
González Moraga, F. R. et al., 'Facets of Psychopathy, Intelligence, and Aggressive Antisocial Behaviors in Young Violent Offenders', *Frontiers in Psychology* 2019, 10, pp. 984–984.
Goodin, R. E., *Protecting the Vulnerable*, Chicago: University of Chicago Press 1985.
Gordon, M. S. et al., 'A Randomized Clinical Trial of Methadone Maintenance for Prisoners: Findings at 6 Months Post-Release', *Addiction* 2008, 103, pp. 1333–1342.
Gottfredson, M. R. & Hirschi, T., *A General Theory of Crime*, Stanford: Stanford University Press 1990.
Green, S. A., 'An Ethical Argument for a Right to Mental Health Care', *General Hospital Psychiatry* 2000, 22(1), pp. 17–26.
Greer, S., 'Is the Prohibition against Torture, Cruel, Inhuman and Degrading Treatment Really "Absolute" in International Human Rights Law?' *Human Rights Law Review* 2015, 15, pp. 101–137.
Green, W., 'Depo-provera, Castration, and the Probation of Rape Offenders: Statutory and Constitutional Issues', *University of Dayton Law Review* 1986, 12(1), pp. 1–26.
Griffin, J., *On Human Rights*, Oxford: Oxford University Press 2008.
Griffin, J., *Well-Being: Its Meaning, Measurement and Moral Importance*, Oxford: Clarendon Press 1986.
Griffin, S. A., Lynam D. R. & Samuel D. B., 'Dimensional Conceptualizations of Impulsivity', *Personality Disorders: Theory, Research, and Treatment* 2018, 9(4), pp. 333–345.
Gross, H., 'Privacy and Autonomy', in Pennock, R. & Chapman, J. W. (eds.), *Privacy: Nomos XIII*, New York: Atherton Press 1971, pp. 169–181.
Gross, J. J. & Muñoz, R. F., 'Emotion Regulation and Mental Health', *Clinical Psychology: Science and Practice* 1995, 2(2), pp. 151–164.
Halse, M. et al., 'Longitudinal Relations between Impaired Executive Function and Symptoms of Psychiatric Disorders in Childhood', *Journal of Child Psychology and Psychiatry, and Allied Disciplines* 2022, 63(12), pp. 1574–1582.
Hampson, M., Ruiz, S. & Ushiba, J., 'Neurofeedback', *Neuroimage* 2020, 218.
Hampton, J., 'The Moral Education Theory of Punishment', *Philosophy & Public Affairs* 1984, 13(3), pp. 208–238.
Haney, C., 'Prison Effects in the Era of Mass Incarceration', *The Prison Journal (Philadelphia, Pa.)* 2012, pp. 1–24.
Harat, M. et al., 'Treating Aggression and Self-destructive Behaviors by Stimulating the Nucleus Accumbens: A Case Series', *Frontiers in Neurology* 2021, 12.
Harcourt, B. E., *Against Prediction: Profiling, Policing, and Punishing in an Actuarial Age*, Chicago: University of Chicago Press 2007.
Hardie-Bick, J., 'Identity Imprisonment, and Narrative Configuration', *New Criminal Law Review* 2018, 21(4), pp. 567–590.

Harner, H. M. et al., 'Posttraumatic Stress Disorder in Incarcerated Women: A Call for Evidence-Based Treatment', *Psychological Trauma: Theory, Research, Practice, and Policy* 2015, 7(1), pp. 58–66.

Harris, D. J. et al., *Harris, O'Boyle, and Warbrick: Law of the European Convention on Human Rights*, New York: Oxford University Press 2023.

Haybron, D. M., 'Mental State Approaches to Well-Being', in Adler, M. D. & Fleurbaey, M. (eds.), *The Oxford Handbook of Well-Being and Public Policy*, Oxford: Oxford University Press 2016, pp. 347–378.

Heathwood, C., 'Desire-Fulfillment Theory', in Fletcher, G. (ed.), *The Routledge Handbook of Philosophy of Well-Being*, Oxon: Routledge 2016, pp. 135–147.

Hecht, L. K., Latzman, R. D. & Lilienfeld, S. O., 'The Psychological Treatment of Psychopathy: Theory and Research', in David, D., Lynn, S. J. & Montgomery, G. H. (eds.), *Evidence-Based Psychotherapy: The State of the Science and Practice*, Hoboken: Wiley Blackwell, 2018, pp. 271–298.

Helmond, P., Overbeek, G. & Brugman, D., 'An Examination of Program Intensity Recidivism of a Cognitive-behavioural Program for Incarcerated Youth in The Netherlands', *Psychology, Crime & Law* 2015, 21(4), pp. 330–346.

Heri, C., 'Deference, Dignity and "Theoretical Crisis": Justifying ECtHR Rights between Prudence and Protection', *Human Rights Law Review* 2024, 24(1), ngad032.

Hertz, N., 'The Human Right to Freedom of Thought—Operationalising a Disputed Right in the Context of Neurotechnologies', *Human Rights Law Review* 2025, 25(3), pp. 1–22.

Hertz, N., 'Neurorights – Do We Need New Human Rights? A Reconsideration of the Right to Freedom of Thought', *Neuroethics* 2023, 16(5).

Hildt, E., 'A Conceptual Approach to the Right to Mental Integrity', in López-Silva, P. & Valera, L. (eds.), *Protecting the Mind*, Series on Ethics of Science and Technology, Cham: Springer 2022, pp. 87–98.

Holbrook, C. et al., 'Neuromodulation of Group Prejudice and Religious Belief', *Social Cognitive and Affective Neuroscience* 2016, 11, pp. 387–394.

Holmen, S. J., 'A Note on Psychological Continuity Theories of Identity and Neurointerventions', *Journal of Medical Ethics* 2022, 48, pp. 742–745.

Hoogsteder, L. et al., 'Response Aggression Regulation Therapy (Re-ART): An Evaluation Study in a Dutch Juvenile Justice Institution in Terms of Recidivism', *International Journal of Offender Therapy and Comparative Criminology* 2018, 62(14), pp. 4403–4424.

Houeto, J. et al., 'Behavioural Disorders, Parkinson's Disease and Subthalamic Stimulation', *Journal of Neurology, Neurosurgery, and Psychiatry* 2002, 72(6), pp. 701–707.

Hulley, S., Crewe, B. & Wright, S., 'Re-examining the Problems of Long-term Imprisonment', *The British Journal of Criminology* 2016, 56(4), pp. 769–792.

Ienca, M., Common Human Rights Challenges Raised by Different Applications of Neurotechnologies in the Biomedical Field, Strasburg: Council of Europe, October 2021.

Ienca, M. & Malgieri, G., 'Mental Data Protection and the GDPR', *Journal of Law and the Biosciences* 2022, 9(1), pp. 1–19.

Ienca, M. & Andorno, R., 'Towards New Human Rights in the Age of Neuroscience and Neurotechnology', *Life Sciences, Society and Policy* 2017, 13(5), pp. 1–27.

Ienca, M. & Haselager, P., 'Hacking the Brain', *Ethics and Information Technology* 2016, 18, pp. 117–129.

Inness, J. C., *Privacy, Intimacy, and Isolation*, New York: Oxford University Press 1992.

Istace, T., 'Human Rights Law: An Incomplete but Flexible Framework to Protect the Human Mind against Neurotechnological Instructions', *Law Innovation and Technology* 2024, 16, pp. 309–334.

Istace, T., 'Protecting the Mental Realm: What Does Human Rights Law Bring to the Table?' *Netherlands Quarterly of Human Rights* 2023, 41(4), pp. 214–234.

Jakobowitz, S. et al., 'Assessing Needs for Psychiatric Treatment in Prisoners: 2. Met and Unmet Need', *Social Psychiatry and Psychiatric Epidemiology* 2017, 52, pp. 231–240.

Janicak, P. et al., 'Transcranial Magnetic Stimulation in the Treatment of Major Depressive Disorder: A Comprehensive Summary of Safety Experience from Acute Exposure, Extended Exposure, and during Reintroduction Treatment', *The Journal of Clinical Psychiatry* 2008, 69, pp. 222–232.

Jolliffe, D. & Hedderman, C., 'Investigating the Impact of Custody on Reoffending Using Propensity Score Matching', *Crime & Delinquency* 2015, 61(8), pp. 1051–1077.

Jolliffe, D., Farrington, D. & Howard, P., 'How Long Did It Last? A 10-Year Reconviction Follow-Up Study of High Intensity Training for Young Offenders', *Journal of Experimental Criminology* 2013, 9(4), pp. 515–531.

Jose-Kampfner, C., 'Coming to Terms with Existential Death: An Analysis of Women's Adaptation to Life in Prison', *Social Justice* 1990, 17(2), pp. 110–125.

Jotterand, F. & Giordano, J., 'Transcranial Magnetic Stimulation, Deep Brain Stimulation and Personal Identity: Ethical Questions, and Neuroethical Approaches for Medical Practice', *International Review of Psychiatry* 2011, 23(5), pp. 476–485.

Jovanovic, M., 'The Essence of Slavery: Exploitation in Human Rights Law', *Human Rights Law Review* 2020, 20, pp. 674–703.

Kagan, S., *The Limits of Morality*, Oxford: Oxford University Press 1991.

Kateb, G., 'On Being Watched and Known', *Social Research* 2001, 68(1), pp. 269–295.

Keese, N. & Leiser, M., 'Online Manipulation as a Potential Interference with the Right to Freedom of Thought', in O'Callaghan, P. & Shiner, B. (eds.), *The Cambridge Handbook on the Right to Freedom of Thought*, Cambridge: Cambridge University Press 2025, pp. 321–334.

Kellmeyer, P. et al., 'The Effects of Closed-Loop Medical Devices on the Autonomy and Accountability of Persons and Systems', *Cambridge Quarterly of Healthcare Ethics* 2016, 25(4), pp. 623–633.

Kelly, E., *The Limits of Blame: Rethinking Punishment and Responsibility*, Harvard: Harvard University Press 2018.

Kiehl, K. A. et al., 'Age of Gray Matters: Neuroprediction of Recidivism', *NeuroImage: Clinical* 2018, 19, pp. 813–823.

Kinlock, T. W. et al., 'A Study of Methadone Maintenance for Male Prisoners: 3-Month Postrelease Outcomes', *Criminal Justice and Behavior* 2008, 35, pp. 34–47.

Kirchmair, L., 'Objections to Coercive Neurocorrectives for Criminal Offenders –Why Offenders' Human Rights Should Fundamentally Come First', *Criminal Justice Ethics* 2019, 38(1), pp. 19–40.

Kivimäki, M., & Steptoe, A., 'Effects of Stress on the Development and Progression of Cardiovascular Disease', *Nature Reviews Cardiology* 2018, 15, pp. 215–229.

Klaming, L. & Haselager, P., 'Did My Brain Implant Make Me Do It? Questions Raised by DBS Regarding Psychological Continuity, Responsibility for Action and Mental Competence', *Neuroethics* 2013, 6.

Knehans, R. et al., 'Modulating Behavioural and Self-Reported Aggression with Non-Invasive Brain Stimulation: A Literature Review', *Brain Sciences* 2022, 12, pp. 1–22.

Kober, H. et al., 'Brain Activity during Cocaine Craving and Gambling Urges: An fMRI Study', *Neuropsychopharmacology* 2016, 41(2), pp. 628–637.

Koops, B.-J., 'Privacy Spaces', *West Verginia Law Review* 2018, 121, pp. 611–665.

Kosta, E. & Boehm, F. (eds.), *The EU Law Enforcement Directive (LED): A Commentary*, Oxford: Oxford University Press 2024.

Kraemer, F., 'Me, Myself and My Brain Implant: Deep Brain Stimulation Raises Questions of Personal Authenticity and Alimentation', *Neuroethics* 2013, 6, pp. 483–497.

Kraiss, J. et al., 'The Relationship between Emotion Regulation and Well-Being in Patients with Mental Disorders: A Meta-Analysis', *Comprehensive Psychiatry* 2020, 102.

Kuhn, L. et al., 'Prefrontal tDCS Modulates Risk-Taking in Male Violent Offenders', *Scientific Reports* 2024, 14.

Laborde, C., *Liberalism's Religion*, Harvard: Harvard University Press 2017.

Larden, M. et al., 'Effectiveness of Aggression Replacement Training in Reducing Criminal Recidivism among Convicted Adult Offenders', *Criminal Behaviour and Mental Health* 2018, 28(6) pp. 476–491.

Lavazza, A., 'Freedom of Thought and Mental Integrity: The Moral Requirements for Any Neural Prosthesis', *Frontiers in Neuroscience* 2018, 12(82), pp. 1–10.

Lavazza, A. & Giorgi, R., 'Philosophical Foundations of the Right to Mental Integrity', *Neuroethics* 2023, 16(10).

Lavrysen, L., 'System of Restrictions', in Van Dijk, P. et al. (eds.), *Theory and Practice of the European Convention on Human Rights*, Cambridge: Intersentia 2018, pp. 307–330.

Le, J. et al., 'Oxytocin Facilitation of Emotional Empathy Is Associated with Increased Eye Gaze toward the Faces of Individuals in Emotional Contexts', *Frontiers in Neuroscience* 2020, 14.

Le Moli, G., *Human Dignity in International Law*, Cambridge: Cambridge University Press 2021.

Lee, A. Y. K., 'Arguing against the Expressive Function of Punishment: Is the Standard Account That Insufficient?' *Law and Philosophy* 2019, 38(4), pp. 359–386.

Lee, S. Y. & Pearce, E. N., 'Hyperthyroidism: A Review', *The Journal of American Medical Association* 2023, 330(15), pp.1472–1483.

Lee, A. et al., 'Horticultural Therapy Program for Mental Health of Prisoners: Case Report', *Integrative Medicine Research* 2021, 10(2).

Leidenfrost, C. M. & Antonius, D., 'Incarceration and Trauma: A Challenge for the Mental Health Care Delivery System', in Javier, R. A., Owen, E. A. & Maddux, J. A. (eds.), *Assessing Trauma in Forensic Contexts*, Cham: Springer International, 2020, pp. 85–110.

Leijten, I., *Core Socio-Economic Rights and the European Court of Human Rights*, Cambridge: Cambridge University Press 2017.

Levan, K., *Prison Violence: Causes, Consequences, and Solutions, Solving Social Problems*, London: Routledge, 2016.

Levenson, J. S. et al., 'Learning from Consumers of Mandated Sex-Offending Programs: "It's Not Treatment, I Wish It Was"', *Sexual Abuse* 2024, 36(2), pp. 203–232.

Levy, N., 'Cognitive Enhancement, in Neurointerventions and the Law', in Vincent, N. A., Nadelhoffer, T. & McCay, A. (eds.), *Neurointerventions and the Law*, New York: Oxford University Press 2020, pp. 33–48.

Levy, N., *Neuroethics: Challenges for the 21st Century*, Cambridge: Cambridge University Press 2007.

Lewis, C., 'Risk-Based Sentencing and the Principles of Punishment', *Journal of Criminal Law and Criminology* 2022, 112(2), pp. 213–264.

Lewis, D., 'Survival and Identity', in Rorty, A. Oksenberg (ed.), *The Identities of Persons*, Berkely: University of California Press 1976, pp. 17–40.

Liao, S. M., *The Right to Be Loved*, New York: Oxford University Press 2015.

Ligthart, S., 'Mental Privacy as Part of the Human Right to Freedom of Thought?' in Blitz, M. & Bublitz, J. C. (eds.), *The Law and Ethics of Freedom of Thought Vol. 2: Cognitive Liberty and Privacy*, Cham: Palgrave Macmillan 2025a (in press).

Ligthart, S., 'What Is Thought, or What Should It Be? – Reply to Bublitz', in Blitz, M. & Bublitz, J. C. (eds.), *The Law and Ethics of Freedom of Thought Vol. 2: Cognitive Liberty and Privacy*, Cham: Palgrave Macmillan 2025b (in press).

Ligthart, S., 'Reconsidering the Absolute Nature of the Right to Freedom of Thought', *Human Rights Law Review* 2025c, 25(3), pp. 1–27.

Ligthart, S., 'The Right to Mental Integrity in the Age of Neurotechnology: Constructing Scope and Exploring Permissible Limitations', *Journal of Law and the Biosciences* 2025d, 12 (1), pp. 1–23.

Ligthart, S., 'Towards a Human Right to Psychological Continuity? Reflections on the Rights to Personal Identity, Self-Determination, and Personal Integrity', *European Convention on Human Rights Law Review* 2024, 5, pp. 199–229.

Ligthart, S., *Coercive Brain-Reading in Criminal Justice*, Cambridge: Cambridge University Press 2022.

Ligthart, S., 'Freedom of Thought in Europe: Do Advances in "Brain-Reading" Technology Call for Revision?' *Journal of Law and the Biosciences* 2020, 7(1), pp. 1–27.

Ligthart, S. et al., 'Minding Rights: Mapping Ethical and Legal Foundations of "Neurorights"', *Cambridge Quarterly of Healthcare Ethics* 2023a, 32(4), pp. 461–481.

Ligthart, S. et al., 'The Relevance of Neuropsychology for Social Rehabilitation: A Human Rights Perspective', in Coppola, F. & Martufi, A. (eds.), *Social Rehabilitation and Criminal Justice*, London: Routledge 2023b, pp. 319–334.

Ligthart, S. et al., 'Rethinking the Right to Freedom of Thought: A Multidisciplinary Analysis', *Human Rights Law Review* 2022, 22(4), pp. 1–14.

Ligthart, S. et al., 'Forensic Brain-Reading and Mental Privacy in European Human Rights Law: Foundations and Challenges', *Neuroethics* 2021, 14, pp. 191–203.

Ligthart, S. et al., 'Prison and the Brain: Neuropsychological Research in the Light of the European Convention on Human Rights', *New Journal of European Criminal Law*, 2019, 10(3), pp. 287–300.

Ligthart, S., Dore-Horgan, E. & Meynen, G., 'The Various Faces of Vulnerability: Offering Neurointerventions to Criminal Offenders', *Journal of Law and the Biosciences* 2023, 10(1), pp. 1–18.

Ligthart, S. & Van de Pol, N., 'Freedom of Thought: Absolute Protection of Mental Privacy and Mental Integrity? Considering the Case of Neurotechnology in Criminal Justice', in O'Callaghan, P. & Shiner, B., *The Cambridge Handbook for Freedom of Thought*, Cambridge: Cambridge University Press 2025, pp. 350–362.

Limanté, A., 'Vulnerable Groups in the Case Law of the European Court of Human Rights', in Limanté, A. & Pūraitė-Andrikienė, D. (eds.), *Legal Protection of Vulnerable Groups in Lithuania, Latvia, Estonia and Poland*, Cham: Springer International 2022, pp. 29–54.

Lippke, R., 'Some Surprising Implications of Negative Retributivism', *Journal of Applied Philosophy* 2014, 31(1), pp. 49–62.

Lipsman, N. & Glannon, W., 'Brain, Mind and Machine: What Are the Implications of Deep Brain Stimulation for Perceptions of Personal Identity, Agency and Free Will?' *Bioethics* 2013, 27(9), pp. 465–470.

Locke, J., 'Of Identity and Diversity', in Nidditch, P. H. (ed.), *An Essay Concerning Human Understanding*, Oxford: Clarendon Press 1975.

Lösel, F. et al., 'On the Effectiveness of Sexual Offender Treatment in Prisons: A Comparison of Two Different Evaluation Designs in Routine Practice', *Sexual Abuse* 2020, 32(4), pp. 452–475.

Loucaides, L. G., 'The Right to Freedom of Thought as Protected by the European Convention on Human Rights', *Cyprus Human Rights Law Review* 2012, 1(1), pp. 79–87.

Luna, F., 'Elucidating the Concept of Vulnerability: Layers Not Labels', *The International Journal of Feminist Approaches to Bioethics* 2009, 2, pp. 121–139.

Lwoff, L., 'New Technologies, New Challenges for Human Rights? The Work of the Council of Europe', *European Journal of Health Law* 2020, 27, pp. 335–344.

Mackenzie, C. & Walker, M., Neurotechnologies, Personal Identity and the Ethics of Authenticity', in Clausen, J. & Levy, N. (eds.), *Handbook of Neuroethics*, Dordrecht: Springer 2015, pp. 373–392.

Maier, K. & Ricciardelli, R., '"Prison Didn't Change Me, I Have Changed": Narratives of Change, Self, and Prison Time', *Criminology & Criminal Justice* 2022, 22(5), pp. 774–789.

Marmor, A., 'What Is the Right to Privacy?' *Philosophy and Public Affairs* 2015, 43, pp. 3–26.

Marshall, J. (ed.), *Personal Identity and the European Court of Human Rights*, New York: Routledge 2022.

Marshall, J., *Human Rights Law and Personal Identity*, New York: Routledge 2016.

Marshall, J., *Personal Freedom through Human Rights Law? Autonomy, Identity and Integrity under the European Convention on Human Rights*, Leiden: Brill 2009.

Martini, S., 'Strong New Branches to the Trunk – Realizing the Right to Health Decentrally', in Von Arnauld, A., Von der Decken, K. & Susi, M. (eds.), *The Cambridge Handbook of New Human Rights: Recognition, Novelty, Rhetoric*, Padstow: Cambridge University Press 2020, pp. 124–133.

Martufi, A., 'The Paths of Offender Rehabilitation and the European Dimension of Punishment: New Challenges for an Old Ideal? *Maastricht Journal of European and Comparative Law* 2018, 25(6), pp. 672–688.

Mater, R. & Murray, D., 'Re-thinking International Human Rights Law's Approach to Identity in Light of Surveillance and AI', *Human Rights Law Review* 2025, 25(3), pp. 1–21.

Mathews, D. J. H., 'Deep Brain Stimulation, Personal Identity and Policy', *International Review of Psychiatry* 2011, 23(5), pp. 486–492.

Mattick, R. P. et al., 'Methadone Maintenance Therapy versus No Opioid Replacement Therapy for Opioid Dependence', *Cochrane Database of Systematic Reviews* 2009 (2).

Mavronicola, M., *Torture, Inhumanity and Degradation under Article 3 of the ECHR: Absolute Rights and Absolute Wrongs*, New York: Hart 2021.

Mayerfield, J., 'In Defense of the Absolute Prohibition of Torture', *Public Affairs Quarterly*, 2008, 22(2), pp. 109–128.

McCarthy-Jones, S., 'The Autonomous Mind: The Right to Freedom of Thought in the Twenty-First Century', *Frontiers in Artificial Intelligence* 2019, 2(19), pp. 1–17.

McMillan, J., 'The Kindest Cut? Surgical Castration, Sex Offenders and Coercive Offers', *Journal of Medical Ethics* 2014, 40(9), pp. 583–590. https://doi.org/10.1136/medethics-2012-101030.

McNeill, F., 'Four Forms of "Offender" Rehabilitation: Towards an Interdisciplinary Perspective', *Legal and Criminological Psychology* 2012, 17, pp. 18–36.

McTernan, E., 'Freedom, Spontaneity, and Our Encounters', *Political Philosophy* 2024, 1(2), 321–343.

McTernan, R., 'Those Who Forget the Past: An Ethical Challenge from the History of Treating Deviance', in Birks, D. & Douglas, T. (eds.), *Treatment for Crime*, New York: Oxford University Press 2018, pp. 273–288.

Meijer, S., 'Rehabilitation as a Positive Obligation', *European Journal of Crime, Criminal Law, and Criminal Justice* 2017, 25(2), pp. 145–162.

Meijers, J., 'Reduced Self-Control after 3 Months of Imprisonment; A Pilot Study', *Frontiers in Psychology* 2018, 9.

Meijers, J., Harte, J. M. & Scherder, J. A., 'Prison and the Brain', in Swaab, H. & Meynen, G. (eds.), *Brain and Crime, Handbook of Clinical Neurology*, Volume 197, Amsterdam: Elsevier 2023, pp. 55–64.

Mendlow, G., 'Why Is It Wrong To Punish Thought?' *The Yale Law Journal* 2018, 127(8), pp. 2342–2486.

Menefee, D. S. et al., 'The Importance of Emotional Regulation in Mental Health', *American Journal of Lifestyle Medicine* 2022, 16(1), pp. 28–31.

Metz, T., 'A Relational Theory of Dignity and Human Rights: An Alternative to Autonomy', *The Monist* 2024, 107(3), pp. 211–224.

Mews, A., Di Bella, L. & Purver, M., 'Impact Evaluation of the Prison-Based Core Sex Offender Treatment Programme', Ministry of Justice Analytical Series London 2017.

Meynen, G., 'Brain-Based Mind Reading: Conceptual Clarifications and Legal Applications', *Journal of Law and the Biosciences* 2018, 5(1), pp. 212–216.

Meynen, G. et al., 'Neurotechnology to Reduce Recidivism: Ethical and Legal Challenges', in H. Swaab & G. Meynen (eds.), *Brain and Crime, Series: Handbook of Clinical Neurology*, Amsterdam: Elsevier 2023, pp. 265–276.

Michalowski, S., 'Critical Reflections on the Need for a Right to Mental Self-Determination', in Von Arnauld, A., Von der Decken, K. & Susi, M. (eds.), *The Cambridge Handbook of New Human Rights: Recognition, Novelty, Rhetoric*, Padstow: Cambridge University Press 2020, pp. 404–412.

Mill, J. S., *Utilitarianism*, Cambridge: Cambridge University Press, 2014 [1861].

Molero, Y. et al., 'Selective Serotonin Reuptake Inhibitors and Violent Crime: A Cohort Study', *PLoS Medicine* 2015, 12(9), e1001875.

Molero-Chamizo, A. et al., 'Bilateral Prefrontal Cortex Anodal tDCS Effects on Self-reported Aggressiveness in Imprisoned Violent Offenders', *Neuroscience* 2019, 15, pp. 31–40.

Moll, J. et al. 'Voluntary Enhancement of Neural Signatures of Affiliative Emotion Using fMRI Neurofeedback', *PLoS ONE* 2014, 9(5), e97343.

Möller, K., *The Global Model of Constitutional Rights*, Oxford: Oxford University Press 2012.

Moore, A. D., *Privacy Rights: Moral and Legal Foundations*, University Park: Penn State University Press 2010.

Morris, H., 'A Paternalistic Theory of Punishment', *American Philosophical Quarterly (Oxford)* 1981, 18(4), pp. 263–271.

Moschella, M., 'Contextualizing, Clarifying, and Defending the Doctrine of Double Effect', *Journal of ethics & social philosophy* 2023, 26(2), pp. 297–324.

Mowbray, A., 'Between the Will of the Contracting Parties and the Needs of Today', in Brems, E. & Gerards, J. (eds.), *Shaping Rights in the ECHR: The Role of the European Court of Human Rights in Determining the Scope of Human Rights*, Cambridge: Cambridge University Press 2013, pp. 17–37.

Murdoch, J., *Protecting the Right to Freedom of Thought, Conscience and Religion under the European Convention on Human Rights*, Strasbourg: Council of Europe 2012.

Nadelhoffer, T. et al., 'Neuroprediction, Violence, and the Law: Setting the Stage', *Neuroethics* 2012, 5(1), pp. 67–99.

Nickel, J., *Making Sense of Human Rights*, 2nd ed., Malden: Blackwell 2007.

Nissenbaum, H., *Privacy in Context: Technology, Policy, and the Integrity of Social Life*, California: Stanford Law Books 2010.

Novisky, M. A. & Peralta, R. L., 'Gladiator School: Returning Citizens' Experiences with Secondary Violence Exposure in Prison', *Victims & Offenders* 2020, 15(5), pp. 1–25.

Nowak, M., 'Article 3 CFR', in EU Network of Independent Experts on Fundamental Rights (ed). Commentary of the Charter of Fundamental Rights of the European Union, Brussels: European Commission 2006.

Nowak, M., 'Social Rights in International Law: Categorization versus Indivisibility', in Binder, C. et al. (eds.), *Research Handbook on International Law and Social Rights*, Northampton: Edward Elgar 2020, pp. 2–18.

Nowak, M., 'What's in a Name? The Prohibitions on Torture and Ill Treatment Today', in Gearty, C. & Douzinas, C. (eds.), *The Cambridge Companion to Human Rights Law*, Cambridge: Cambridge University Press 2012, pp. 307–328.

Nowak, M. & Schabas, W., *U.N. International Covenant on Civil and Political Rights: Nowak's CCPR Commentary*, 3rd revised ed., N.P. Engel: Kehl 2019.

Nussbaum, M. C., *Women and Human Development: The Capabilities Approach*, Cambridge: Cambridge University Press 2000.

O'Callaghan, P. et al., 'The Right to Freedom of Thought: An Interdisciplinary Analysis of the UN Special Rapporteur's Report on Freedom of Thought', *The International Journal of Human Rights* 2024, 28(1), pp. 1–23.

O'Callaghan, P. & Shiner, B., 'The Right to Freedom of Thought in the European Convention of Human Rights', *European Journal of Comparative Law and Governance* 2021, 8(2–3), pp. 112–145.

O'Callaghan, P. & Shiner, B., 'Introduction', in O'Callaghan, P. & Shiner, B. (eds.), *The Cambridge Handbook for Freedom of Thought*, Cambridge: Cambridge University Press 2025, pp. 3–14.

Ooms, P. et al., 'Cost-effectiveness of Deep Brain Stimulation versus Treatment as Usual for Obsessive-Compulsive Disorder', *Brain Stimulation* 2017, 10(4), pp. 836–842.

Pardo, S. & Patterson, D., *Minds, Brains, and Law. The Conceptual Foundations of Law and Neuroscience*, New York: Oxford University Press 2015.

Parfit, D., *Reasons and Persons*, Oxford: Oxford University Press 1984.

Parfit, D., 'Personal Identity', *The Philosophical Review* 1971, 80(1), pp. 3–27.

Parola, A. et al., 'Pragmatics, Theory of Mind and Executive Functions in Schizophrenia: Disentangling the Puzzle Using Machine Learning', *PloS One* 2020, 15(3), e0229603.

Partsch, K. J., 'Freedom of Conscience and Expression, and Political Freedoms', in Henkin, L. (ed.), *The International Bill of Rights*, New York: Columbia University Press 1981.

Paszkiel, S., *Applications of Brain-Computer Interfaces in Intelligent Technologies*, Cham: Springer 2022.

Peroni, L. & Timmer, A., 'Vulnerable Groups', *International Journal of Constitutional Law* 2013, 11(4), pp. 1056–1085.

Perry, J. (ed.), *Personal Identity*, 2nd Ed., London: University of California Press 2008.

Piper, A. & Berle, D., 'The Association between Trauma Experienced during Incarceration and PTSD Outcomes: A Systematic Review and Meta-Analysis', *The Journal of Forensic Psychiatry & Psychology* 2019, 30(5), pp. 854–875.

Ploch, A., 'Why Dignity Matters: Dignity and the Right (or Not) to Rehabilitation from International and National Perspectives', *New York University Journal of International Law and Politics* 2012, 44(3), pp. 887–950.

Poldrack, R. A. et al., 'Predicting Violent Behavior: What Can Neuroscience Add?' *Trends in Cognitive Science* 2018, 22(2), pp. 111–123.

Powers, M. & Faden, R., *Social Justice: The Moral Foundations of Public Health and Health Policy*, New York: Oxford University Press 2006.

Pratt, T. C. & Cullen, F. T., 'The Empirical Status of Gottfredson and Hirschi's General Theory of Crime: A Meta-Analysis', *Criminology* 2000, 38(3), pp. 931–964.

Privitera, A. J. & Du, H., 'Educational Neurotechnology: Where Do We Go from Here?' *Trends in Neuroscience and Education* 2022, 29.

Pugh, J., 'Clarifying the Normative Significance of "Personality Changes" Following Deep Brain Stimulation', *Science and Engineering Ethics* 2020, 26.

Pugh, J., 'Coercion and the Neurocorrective Offer', in Birks, D. & Douglas, T. (eds.), *Treatment for Crime: Philosophical Essays on Neurointerventions in criminal Justice*, New York: Oxford University Press 2018, pp. 94–115.

Pugh, J. et al., 'Brainjacking in Deep Brain Stimulation and Autonomy', *Ethics and Information Technology* 2018, 20, pp. 219–232.

Pycroft, L. et al., 'Brainjacking: Implant Security Issues in Invasive Neuromodulation', *World Neurosurgery* 2016, 92, pp. 454–462.

Radden, J., 'Entry: Mental Disorder (Illness)', Stanford Encyclopedia of Philosophy (online). First published Wed Feb 20, 2019; substantive revision Wed Sep 4, 2024 (accessed May 28, 2025).

Rainey, B., McCormick, P. & Ovey, C., *The European Convention on Human Rights*, New York: Oxford University Press 2021.

Rainey, S. et al., 'Is the European Data Protection Regulation Sufficient to Deal with Emerging Data Concerns Relating to Neurotechnology?' *Journal of Law and the Biosciences* 2020, 7(1), pp. 1–19.

Ratoff, W., 'The Right to Mental Autonomy: It's Nature and Scope', *Journal of Ethics and Social Philosophy* 2024, 27(1), pp. 257–286.

Rawls, J., *The Law of Peoples: With, 'the Idea of Public Reason Revisited'*, Harvard: Harvard University Press 1999a.

Rawls, J., *A Theory of Justice*, Revised ed., Harvard: The Belknap Press of Harvard University Press 1999b.

Raz, J., *The Morality of Freedom*, Oxford: Clarendon Press 1986.

Reich, W., 'Psychiatric Diagnosis as an Ethical Problem', in Bloch, S., Chodoff, P. & Green, S. (eds.), *Psychiatric Ethics*, 3rd ed., Oxford: Oxford University Press 2005.

Reinecke, A. et al., 'Cognitive-Behavioural Therapy Reduces Unwanted Thought Intrusions in Generalized Anxiety Disorder', *Journal of Behavior Therapy and Experimental Psychiatry* 2013, 44(1), pp. 1–6.

Reti, I. M., & Chang, A. D., 'Introduction to Brain Stimulation', in I. Reti (ed.), *Brain Stimulation: Methodologies and Interventions*, Hoboken, NJ: Wiley Blackwell 2015, pp. 1–12. https://doi.org/10.1002/9781118568323.ch1.

Rice, M. E. & Harris, G. T., 'Psychopathy and Violent Recidivism', in Kiehl, K. A. & Sinnott-Armstrong, W. P. (eds.), *Handbook on Psychopathy and Law*, Oxford: Oxford University Press 2013, pp. 231–249.

Richmond, S., Rees, G. & Edwards, S. J. L. (eds.), *I Know What You're Thinking: Brain Imaging and Mental Privacy*, Croydon: Oxford University Press 2012.

Rickli, J. M. & Ienca, M., 'The Security and Military Implications of Neurotechnology and Artificial Intelligence', in Friedrich, O. et al. (eds.), *Clinical Neurotechnology Meets Artificial Intelligence: Advances in Neuroethics*, Cham: Springer 2021, 197–214.

Riedel, E., 'The Right to Health under the ICESCR: Existing Scope, New Challenges and How to Deal with It', in Von Arnauld, A., Von der Decken, K. & Susi, M. (eds.), *The Cambridge Handbook of New Human Rights: Recognition, Novelty, Rhetoric*, Padstow: Cambridge University Press 2020, pp. 107–123.

Ripstein, A., 'Beyond the Harm Principle', *Philosophy & Public Affairs* 2006, 34(3), pp. 215–245.

Roberts, C. K., Reconceptualising the Place of the Forum Internum and Forum Externum in Article 9 of the European Convention on Human Rights (diss. University of Bristol), Bristol 2020.

Roehr, B., 'American Psychiatric Association explains DSM-5', *British Medical Journal* 2013, 346, f3591.

Rogan, M., 'Social Rehabilitation and Torture Prevention Bodies in International Human Rights Law: Remits and Roles', in Coppola F., Martufi A. (eds.), *Social Rehabilitation and Criminal Justice*, London: Routledge 2024, pp. 155–171.

Rogers, W., Mackenzie, C. & Dodds, S., 'Why Bioethics Needs a Concept Vulnerability', *The International Journal of Feminist Approaches to Bioethics* 2012, 5, pp. 11–38.

Romano, C. P. R. & Boggio, A., *The Human Right to Science: History, Development, and Normative Content*, Oxford: Oxford University Press 2024.

Rosell, D. R. & Siever, J. L., 'The Neurobiology of Aggression and Violence', *CNS Spectrums* 2015, 20, pp. 254–279.

Rosenfeld, J. P. (ed.), *Detecting Concealed Information and Deception*, London: Academic Press 2018.

Ross, A., 'Ethics of CIA and Military Contracting by Psychiatrists and Psychologists', *Ethical Human Psychology and Psychiatry* 2007, 9(1), pp. 25–34.

Rotman, E., 'The History of Rehabilitation as a Penological Principle', in Coppola, F., Martufi, A. (eds.), *Social Rehabilitation and Criminal Justice*, London: Routledge 2024, pp. 13–26.

Rubenfeld, J., 'The Right of Privacy', *Harvard Law Review* 1989, 102(4), pp. 737–807.

Ruger, P. J., 'Toward a Theory of a Right to Health: Capability and Incompletely Theorized Agreements', *Yale Journal of Law and Humanities* 2006, 18, pp. 273–326.

Ryan, R. M. & Deci, E. L., *Self-Determination Theory: Basic Psychological Needs in Motivation, Development, and Wellness*, New York: Guilford Press 2017.

Ryberg, J., 'Retributivism and the (Lack of) Justification of Proportionality', *Criminal Law and Philosophy* 2021, 15, pp. 447–462.

Ryberg, J., *Neurointerventions, Crime, and Punishment*, New York: Oxford University Press 2020.

Ryberg, J., 'Neuroscientific Treatment of Criminals and Penal Theory', in Birks, D. & Douglas, T. (eds.), *Treatment for Crime: Philosophical Essays on Neurointerventions in Criminal Justice*, Oxford: Oxford University Press 2018, pp. 177–195.

Ryberg, J., 'Punishment, Pharmacological Treatment, and Early Release', *International Journey of Applied Philosophy* 2012, 26, pp. 231–244.

Safron, A. et al., 'Neural Correlates of Sexual Orientation in Heterosexual, Bisexual, and Homosexual Men', *Scientific Reports* 2017, 7, pp. 1–15.

Salama, H. et al., 'The Role of Neuromodulation in the Management of Drug-Resistant Epilepsy', *Neurological Sciences* 2024, 45(9), pp. 4243–426.

Sapsford, R. J., 'Life-Sentence Prisoners: Psychological Changes during Sentence', *British Journal of Criminology* 1978, 18(2), pp. 128–145.

Scanlon, T., *The Difficulty of Tolerance: Essays in Political Philosophy*, Cambridge University Press, 2003.

Schartmueller, D., 'Too Dangerous to Get Out? The Use of Individualized Release Mechanisms for Lifetime Incarcerated Offenders in Sweden', *Criminal Justice Policy Review* 2014, 25(4), pp. 407–431.

Schechtman, M., *Staying Alive: Personal Identity, Practical Concerns, and the Unity of a Life*, Oxford: Oxford University Press 2014.

Schechtman, M., 'The Narrative Self', in Gallagher, S. (ed.), *The Oxford Handbook of the Self*, Oxford: Oxford University Press 2011, pp. 394–416.

Schechtman, M., 'Philosophical Reflections on Narrative and Deep Brain Stimulation', *The Journal of Clinical Ethics* 2010, 21, pp. 133–139.

Schechtman, M., 'Getting Our Stories Straight: Self-narrative and Personal Identity', in Mathews, D. J. H., Bok, H. & Rabins, P. V. (eds.), *Personal Identity and Fractured Selves*, Baltimore: John Hopkins University Press 2009, pp. 65–94.

Schechtman, M., *The Constitution of Selves*, New York: Cornell University Press 1996.

Schermer, M., 'Changes in the Self: The Need for Conceptual Research Next to Empirical Research', *The American Journal of Bioethics Neuroscience* 2009, 9(5), pp. 45–47.

Schnittker, J., 'The Psychological Dimensions and the Social Consequences of Incarceration', *Annals of the American Academy of Political and Social Science* 2014, 651, pp. 122–138.

Schüpbach, M. et al., 'Neurosurgery in Parkinson Disease a Distressed Mind in a Repaired Body?' *Neurology* 2006, 66(12), pp. 1811–1816.

Schwartz, P. M., 'Internet Privacy and the State', *Connecticut Law Review* 2000, 32, pp. 815–875.

Scott, C. & Macklem P., 'Constitutional Ropes of Sand or Justiciable Guarantees? Social Rights in a New South African Constitution', *University of Pennsylvania Law Review* 1992, 141(1), pp. 1–148.

Seligman, M., *Flourish : A New Understanding of Happiness and Wellbeing: The Practical Guide to Using Positive Psychology to Make You Happier and Healthier*, London: Nicholas Brealey, 2011.

Sensi, M., Eleopra, R., Cavallo, M., et al., 'Explosive-Aggressive Behavior Related to Bilateral Subthalamic Stimulation', *Parkinsonism Related Disorders* 2004, 10(4), pp. 247–51.

Sententia, W., 'Neuroethical Considerations: Cognitive Liberty and Converging Technologies for Improving Human Cognition', *Annals of the New York Academy of Sciences* 2004, 1013(1), pp. 221–228.

Sergiou, C. et al., 'Transcranial Direct Current Stimulation Targeting the Ventromedial Prefrontal Cortex Reduces Reactive Aggression and Modulates Electrophysiological Responses in a Forensic Population', *Biological Psychiatry: CNNI* 2022, 7(1), pp. 95–107.

Sharma, A. & Weintraub, A., 'Neuroimaging', in Kreutzer, J., DeLuca, J. & Caplan, B. (eds.), *Encyclopedia of Clinical Neuropsychology*, Cham: Springer 2016, pp. 1–5.

Shaw, E., 'Neuroscience, Criminal Sentencing, and Human Rights', *William & Mary Law Review* 2022, 63(4), pp. 1409–1443.

Shen, F. X., 'Neuroscience, Mental Privacy and the Law', *Harvard Journal of Law & Public Policy* 2013, 36, pp. 653–713.

Sher, G., *A Wild West of the Mind*, New York: Oxford University Press 2021.

Shih, J. J., Krusienski, D. J. & Wolpaw, J. R., 'Brain-Computer Interfaces in Medicine', *Mayo Clinic Proceedings* 2012, 87(3), pp. 268–279.

Shoemaker, D., 'Personal Identity and Ethics', in Zalta, E. N. (ed.), *The Stanford Encyclopedia of Philosophy* 2021.

Shoemaker, D., 'Persons and Their Pasts', *American Philosophy Quarterly* 1970, 7, pp. 269–285.

Shue, H., *Basic Rights: Subsistence, Affluence, and US Foreign Policy*, Princeton: Princeton University Press, 1996.

Sifferd, K. L., 'Chemical Castration as Punishment', in Vincent, N. A., Nadelhoffer, T. & McCay, A. (eds.), *Neurointerventions and the Law: Regulating Human Mental Capacity*, New York: Oxford University Press 2020, pp. 293–318.

Skogly, S., 'The Requirement of Using the "Maximum of Available Resources" for Human Rights Realisation: A Question of Quality as Well as Quantity?' *Human Rights Law Review* 2012, 12(3), pp. 393–420.

Slobogin, C., 'Principles of Risk Assessment: Sentencing and Policing', *Ohio State Journal of Criminal Law*, 2018, 15, pp. 583–596.

Smilowska, K. et al., 'Cost-Effectiveness of Device-Aided Therapies in Parkinson's Disease: A Structured Review', *Journal of Parkinson's Disease* 2021, 11(2), pp. 475–489.

Smith, R., 'The End of Disease and the Beginning of Health', *BMJ Group Blogs*, 2008, accessed November 15, 2023.

Snacken, S. & van Zyl Smit, D., 'The Prisoner as Rechtsburger: A European Perspective', in Franken, A. A., de Langen, M. & Moerings, M. (eds.), *Constante waarden. Liber Amicorum Prof. mr. Constantijn Kelk*, Den Haag: Boom Juridische Uitgevers, Pompe reeks 2008, pp. 573–584.

Solove, D. J., 'Conceptualizing Privacy', *California Law Review* 2002, 90(4), pp. 1087–1155.

Starcevic, V., 'Benzodiazepines for Anxiety Disorders: Maximising the Benefits and Minimising the Risks', *Advances in Psychiatric Treatment* 2012, 18(4), pp. 250–258.

Starfield, B., 'Basic Concepts in Population Health and Health Care', *Journal of Epidemiology and Community Health* 2001, 55(7), pp. 452–454.

Stevens, A., 'I Am the Person Now I Was Always Meant to Be: Identity Reconstruction and Narrative Reframing in Therapeutic Community Prisons', *Criminology & Criminal Justice* 2012, 12(5), pp. 527–547.

Stoyanova, V., 'Framing Positive Obligations under the European Convention on Human Rights Law: Mediating between the Abstract and the Concrete', *Human Rights Law Review* 2023, 23(3), ngad010.

Susser, D. & Cabrera, L. Y., 'Brain Data in Context: Are New Rights the Way to Mental and Brain Privacy?' *The American Journal of Bioethics Neuroscience* 2023, 15(2), pp. 122–133.

Swaab, H. & Meynen, G., 'Preface', in Swaab, H. & Meynen, G. (eds.), *Brain and Crime, Handbook of Clinical Neurology*, Volume 197, Amsterdam: Elsevier 2023, pp. 3–9.

Swaine, L., 'Freedom of Thought as a Basic Liberty', *Political Theory* 2018, 46(3), pp. 405–425.

Talbott, W. J., 'The Consequentialist Project for Human Rights', in Talbott, W. J. (ed.), *Human Rights and Human Well-Being Oxford*, Oxford: Oxford University Press 2010, pp. 3–27.

Tamimi, Y. Al, 'Human Rights and the Excess of Identity: A Legal and Theoretical Inquiry into the Notion of Identity in Strasbourg Case Law', *Social & Legal Studies* 2018, 27(3), pp. 283–298.

Tan, A. et al., 'Effects of the KCNQ Channel Opener Ezogabine on Functional Connectivity of the Ventral Striatum and Clinical Symptoms in Patients with Major Depressive Disorder', *Molecular Psychiatry* 2020, 25(6), pp. 1323–1333.

Tang, J. et al., 'Semantic Reconstruction of Continuous Language from Non-invasive Brain Recordings', *Nature Neuroscience* 2023, 26, pp. 858–866.

Tarrant, J., 'Neuromeditation: The Science and Practice of Combining Neurofeedback and Meditation for Improved Mental Health', in E. Da-Yin Liao (ed.), *Smart Biofeedback – Perspectives and Applications*, London: IntechOpen 2020, pp. 1–16.

Taylor, P. M., *A Commentary on the International Covenant on Civil and Political Rights*, Cambridge: Cambridge University Press 2020.

Teo, S. A., 'How to Think about Freedom of Thought (and Opinion) in the Age of AI', *Computer Law & Security Review* 2024, 53, 105969.

Tesink, V. et al., 'Right to Mental Integrity and Neurotechnologies: Implications of the Extended Mind Thesis', *Journal of Medical Ethics* 2024, 50, pp. 656–663.

Tesink, V. et al., 'Neurointerventions in Criminal Justice: On the Scope of the Moral Right to Bodily Integrity', *Neuroethics* 2023, 6(3), pp. 16–26.

Thaler, R. H. & Sunstein, C. R., *Nudge: Improving Decisions about Health, Wealth and Happiness* (1st ed.), New York: Penguin 2009.

Thibaut, F. et al., 'The World Federation of Societies of Biological Psychiatry (WFSBP) Guidelines for the Biological Treatment of Paraphilias', *The World Journal of Biological Psychiatry* 2010, 11(4), pp. 604–655.

Thielbörger, P., 'The "Essence" of International Human Rights', *German Law Journal* 2019, 20, pp. 924–939.

Thomson, J. J., 'The Right to Privacy', *Philosophy & Public Affairs* 1975, 4(4), pp. 295–314.

Tiedemann, T. (ed.), Right to Identity: Proceedings of the Special Workshop "Right to Identity" Held at the 27th World Congress of the International Association for Philosophy of Law and Social Philosophy in Washington DC, Franz Steiner Verlag 2015.

Timler, K., Brown, H. & Varcoe, C., 'Growing Connection beyond Prison Walls: How a Prison Garden Fosters Rehabilitation and Healing for Incarcerated Men', *Journal of Offender Rehabilitation* 2019, 58, pp. 1–20.

Timmer, A., 'A Quiet Revolution: Vulnerability in the European Court of Human Rights', in Fineman, M. A. & Grear, A. (eds.), *Vulnerability: Reflections on a New Ethical Foundation for Law and Politics*, Surray: Ashgate 2013, pp. 147–170.

Tonry, M., 'Predictions of Dangerousness in Sentencing: Déjà Vu All Over Again', *Crime and Justice (Chicago, Ill.)* 2019, 48(1), pp. 439–482.

Torres, C. V. et al., 'Long-Term Results of Posteromedial Hypothalamic Deep Brain Stimulation for Patients with Resistant Aggressiveness', *Journal of Neurosurger* 2013, 119(2), pp. 277–287.

Tortora, L. et al., 'Neuroprediction and A.I. in Forensic Psychiatry and Criminal Justice: A Neurolaw Perspective', *Frontiers in Psychology* 2020, 11(222), pp. 1–9.

Travers, R. et al., 'Reconviction Following a Cognitive Skills Intervention: An Alternative Quasi-Experimental Methodology', *Legal and Criminological Psychology* 2013, 18(1), pp. 48–65.

Tridimas, T. & Gentile, G., 'The Essence of Rights: An Unreliable Boundary?' *German Law Journal* 2020, 20(6), pp. 794–816.

Trotter, S., 'Narratives of Absence: On the Construction and Limits of the Category of Personal Identity in European Human Rights Law', in Marshall, J. (ed.), *Personal Identity and the European Court of Human Rights*, New York: Routledge 2022, pp. 27–48.

Tversky, A. & Kahneman, D., 'Judgment under Uncertainty: Heuristics and Biases', *Science* 1974, 185, pp. 1124–113.

Ugwudike, P. et al. (eds.), *The Routledge Companion to Rehabilitative Work in Criminal Justice*, Oxon: Routledge 2020.

Umbach, R., Raine A. & Leonard, N. R., 'Cognitive Decline as a Result of Incarceration and the Effects of a CBT/MT Intervention: A Cluster-Randomized Controlled Trial', *Criminal Justice and Behavior* 2018, 45(1), pp. 31–55.

Vallentyne, P., 'Neurointerventions, Self-Ownership, and Enforcement Rights', in Birks, D. & Douglas, T. (eds.), *Treatment for Crime*, New York: Oxford University Press 2018, pp. 124–139.

Van de Pol, N., 'Neuro-Interventions in Criminal Justice: An Analysis of Article 3 ECHR', *European Human Rights Law Review* 2023 (5), pp. 459–476.

Van der Linden, R. & Schermer, M., 'Health and Disease as Practical Concepts: Exploring Function in Context-Specific Definitions', *Medicine Health Care and Philosophy* 2022, 25(1), pp. 131–140.

Van der Schyff, G., 'Cutting to the Core of Conflicting Rights: The Question of Inalienable Cores in Comparative Perspective', in Brems, E. (ed.), *Conflicts between Fundamental Rights*, Antwerp: Intersentia 2008, pp. 131–147.

Van Drooghenbroeck, S. & Rizcallah, C., 'The ECHR and the Essence of Fundamental Rights: Searching for Sugar in Hot Milk?' *German Law Journal* 2019, 20(6), pp. 904–923.

Van Inwagen, P., 'Materialism and the Psychological-Continuity Account of Personal Identity', *Philosophical Perspectives* 1997, 11, pp. 305–319.

Van Rijn, A., 'Freedom of Expression', in Van Dijk, P. et al. (eds.), *Theory and Practice of the European Convention on Human Rights*, Cambridge: Intersentia 2018, pp. 765–812.

Van Voren, R., 'Ending Political Abuse of Psychiatry: Where We Are at and What Needs to Be Done', *British Journal of Psychiatry Bulletin* 2016, 40(1), pp. 30–33.

Van Zyl Smit, D., 'Rehabilitation as a Dominant Idea in European Prison Law: Problems and Prospect', *Romanian Journal of Sociological Studies* 2018, 1, pp. 9–18.

Vermeulen, B. & Battjes, H., 'Prohibition of Torture and Other Inhuman or Degrading Treatment or Punishment', in Van Dijk, P. et al. (eds.), *Theory and Practice of the European Convention on Human Rights*, Cambridge: Intersentia 2018, pp. 381–423.

Vermeulen, B. & Roosmalen, M., 'Freedom of Thought, Conscience and Religion', in Van Dijk, P. et al. (eds.), *Theory and Practice of the European Convention on Human Rights*, Cambridge: Intersentia 2018, pp. 735–763.

Vieraitis, L. M., Kovandzic, T. V. & Marvell, T. B., 'The Criminogenic Effects of Imprisonment: Evidence from State Panel Data, 1974–2002', *Criminology & Public Policy* 2007, 6(3), pp. 589–622.

Vincent, N., 'Restoring Responsibility: Promoting Justice, Therapy and Reform through Direct Brain Interventions', *Criminal Law and Philosophy* 2014, 8, pp. 21–42.

Vincent, N. A., Nadelhoffer, T. & McCay, A. (eds.), *Neurointerventions and the Law: Regulating Human Mental Capacity*, New York: Oxford University Press 2020.

Wajnerman Paz, S., 'Is Mental Privacy a Component of Personal Identity?' *Frontiers in Human Neuroscience* 2021, 15.

Waldron, J., 'Moral Autonomy and Personal Autonomy', in Christman, J. & Anderson, J. (eds.), *Autonomy and the Challenges to Liberalism: New Essays*, Cambridge: Cambridge University Press 2005, pp. 307–329.

Wang, E. & Diamond, P., 'Empirically Identifying Factors Related to Violence Risk in Corrections', *Behavioral Sciences and the Law* 1999, 17, pp. 377–389.

Ward, T., 'Ethical Issues in the Treatment of Offenders', in Davies, J. & Nagi, C. (eds.), *Individual Psychological Therapies in Forensic Settings*, New York: Routledge 2017, pp. 213–227.

Ward, T., 'Human Rights and Dignity in Offender Rehabilitation', *Journal of Forensic Psychology Practice* 2011, 11(2–3), pp. 103–123.

Ward, T., 'The Management of Risk and the Design of Good Lives', *Australian Psychologist* 2002, 37, pp. 172–179.

Ward, T. & Brown, M., 'The Good Lives Model and Conceptual Issues in Offender Rehabilitation', *Psychology, Crime, & Law* 2004, 10, pp. 243–257.

Warren, S. D. & Brandeis, L.D., 'The Right to Privacy', *Harvard Law Review* 1890, 4, pp. 193–220.

Wendel, B. E., Rocque, M. & Posick, C., 'Rethinking Self-control and Crime: Are All Forms of Impulsivity Criminogenic?' *European Journal of Criminology* 2022, 19(4), pp. 523–541.

Werb, D. et al., 'The Effectiveness of Compulsory Drug Treatment: A Systematic Review', *International Journal of Drug Policy* 2016, 28, pp. 1–9.

Wermink, H. et al., 'ShortTerm Effects of Imprisonment Length on Recidivism in the Netherlands', *Crime & Delinquency* 2018, 64(8), pp. 1057–1010.

Willis, G. M. & Ward, T., 'Risk Management versus the Good Lives Model: The Construction of Better Lives and the Reduction of Harm', in Dréan-Rivette, M. & Evans, M. (eds.), *Transnational Criminology Manual*, Netherlands: Wolf Legal Publishing 2010, pp. 763–781.

Wilson, D., Feder, L. & Olaghere, A., 'Court-Mandated Interventions for Individuals Convicted of Domestic Violence: An Updated Campbell Systematic Review', *Campbell Systematic Reviews* 2021, 17, pp. 1–23.

Winkler, K., 'Locke on Personal Identity', *Journal of the History of Philosophy* 1991, 29(2), pp. 201–226.
Witt, K. et al., 'Deep Brain Stimulation and the Search for Identity', *Neuroethics* 2013, 6, pp. 499–511.
Witzel, J., 'Implications of Neuroimaging for Dangerousness Assessment', in Simpson, J. R. (ed.), *Neuroimaging in Forensic Psychiatry. From Clinic to the Courtroom*, Chichester: Wiley-Blackwell 2012, pp. 195–200.
Witzleb, N. & Paterson, M., 'Micro-targeting in Political Campaigns: Political Promise and Democratic Risk', in Kohl, U. & Eisler, J. (eds.), *Data-Driven Personalisation in Markets, Politics and Law*, Cambridge: Cambridge University Press 2021, pp. 223–240.
Wolff, T., 'Cogency, Seriousness, Cohesion and Importance', *Oxford Journal of Law and Religion* 2023, 11, pp. 177–196.
Wolpe, P. R., 'Is My Mind Mine? Neuroethics and Brain Imaging', in Ravitsky, V., Fiester, A. & Caplan, A. (eds.), *The Penn Center Guide to Bioethics*, New York: Springer 2009, pp. 86–93.
Wren-Lewis, S. & Alexandrova, A., 'Mental Health without Well-Being', *Journal of Medicine & Philosophy* 2021, 46(6), pp. 684–703.
Woolf, V., *A Room of One's Own*. Ontario, ON: Broadview Press 2001.
Yang, S. E. et al., 'Functional Connectivity Signatures of Political Ideology', *Proceedings of the National Academy of Sciences Nexus* 2022, 1(3), pp. 1–11.
Yukhnenko, D., Sridhar, S. & Fazel, S., 'A systematic review of criminal recidivism rates worldwide: 3-year update', Wellcome Open Research 2020.
Yuste, R., Genser, J. & Herrmann, S., 'It's Time for Neuro-Rights', *Horizons* 2021, 18, pp. 154–164.
Zainal, N. H. & Newman, M. G., 'Depression and Executive Functioning Bidirectionally Impair One Another across 9 Years: Evidence from within-Person Latent Change and Cross-Lagged Models', *European Psychiatry* 2021, 64(1), e43, pp. 1–14.
Zawadzki, P., 'Dimensions of the Threat to the Self Posed by Deep Brain Stimulation: Personal Identity, Authenticity, and Autonomy', *Diametros* 2021, 18, pp. 71–98.
Zijlmans, J. et al., 'The Predictive Value of Neurobiological Measures for Recidivism in Delinquent Male Young Adults', *Journal of Psychiatry and Neuroscience* 2021, 46(2), E272.
Zohny, H. et al., 'The Mystery of Mental Integrity: Clarifying Its Relevance to Neurotechnologies', *Neuroethics* 2023, 16: 20, pp. 1–12.
Zuk, P., 'Mental Integrity, Autonomy, and Fundamental Interests', *Journal of Medical Ethics* 2024, 50, pp. 676–683.
Zwolinski, M., Ferguson, B. & Wertheimer, A., 'Exploitation', in Zalta, E. N. & Nodelman, U. (eds.), *The Stanford Encyclopedia of Philosophy*, Winter 2022 Ed.

Index

Printed by Integrated Books International,
United States of America